Persistent Pilgrim
The Life of Mary Baker Eddy

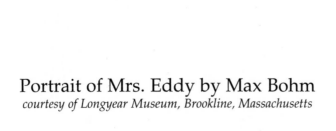

Portrait of Mrs. Eddy by Max Bohm

courtesy of Longyear Museum, Brookline, Massachusetts

PERSISTENT PILGRIM
The Life of Mary Baker Eddy

By Richard A. Nenneman

Nebbadoon Press
Etna, New Hampshire
1997

 Published by Nebbadoon Press,
P.O. Box 333, Etna, New Hampshire 03750
For orders (800) 500-9086

For permission to reprint copyrighted material, acknowledgment is made to the following: The First Church of Christ, Scientist, in Boston, Massachusetts, for quotations from Mrs. Eddy's published and unpublished works; The Christian Science Publishing Society for quotations from works owned by it; Longyear Museum and Historical Society, Brookline, Massachusetts, for excerpts from unpublished letters and essays in its collection.

Library of Congress Cataloging-in-Publication Data

Nenneman, Richard A.
Persistent pilgrim: the life of Mary Baker Eddy/
Richard A. Nenneman.
p. cm.
ISBN 1-891331-02-7
1. Eddy, Mary Baker, 1821-1910. 2. Christian Scientists – United States – Biography. I. Title.
BX6995.N46 1997
289.5'092
[B] – DC21

97-38216
CIP

Only by persistent, unremitting, straightforward toil; by turning neither to the right nor to the left, seeking no other pursuit or pleasure than that which cometh from God, can you win and wear the crown of the faithful.

– Miscellaneous Writings
Mary Baker Eddy

Whoever opens the way in Christian Science is a pilgrim and stranger, marking out the path for generations yet unborn.

– Science and Health with Key to the Scriptures
Mary Baker Eddy

CONTENTS

Preface

Several biographies of Mrs. Eddy have been written over the years since her passing in 1910 – some friendly, some hostile in intent, and some that are essentially inspirational views of her life. When one sets out to describe the life of someone from another century, there is no opportunity to talk to the people who knew her or the events surrounding her life. Yet biography continues to be written about those who have long since passed from the scene. Each generation brings a new perspective to bear on the significance of past events; to some extent, it even recasts them to give them meaning in the context of today's world.

What I have tried to present here is a story from the perspective of the concerns of the 1990s of one of the most remarkable religious figures in history. I have made extensive use of the archives of The First Church of Christ, Scientist (The Mother Church), in Boston. When a historical figure has slipped beyond the personal memory of anyone now living, the biographer can go only to the written record. Fortunately this includes, in Mrs. Eddy's case, several thousand letters that she wrote, as well as the reminiscences of most of the people who were closest to her during the last decade of her life. I have, as far as I know, read all of her letters that are extant. These letters, in fact, have provided the structural skeleton for much of the story as told here, particularly the last thirty years of her life. From about 1890 until her death in 1910, there is a copy of virtually everything she wrote. It is a voluminous correspondence, comprising upwards of ten thousand letters, and from the portion that has been saved, one quickly grasps the continuing strands of thought underlying her actions over the years, as well as what particular events formed the substance of her activity in any given year. In fact, a pattern swiftly emerges of an intellect that proceeded in orderly fashion from one step to the next – be it teaching, writing, organizing her church, or dealing with specific problems confronting her at a particular time.

The story of Mary Baker Eddy is inextricably linked to the development of the Christian Science movement. Much of her life can be understood only to the extent that one has some acquaintance with the teachings of Christian Science. As much as feasible, however, I have refrained from using long quotations from the Christian Science textbook or her other published writings. I have also reminded myself of Mrs. Eddy's desire that one should not dwell on the details of her life. She went so far as to write in her book, *Retrospection and Introspection,* some twenty years before her death, "Mere historic incidents and personal events are frivolous and of no moment, unless they illustrate the ethics of Truth. . .The human history needs to be revised, and the material record expunged." [1]

If this comment were to be taken literally, little room for any biographical detail would remain. What needs to be understood is that in Mrs. Eddy's lifetime there was a tendency either to vilify her or, on the part of some of her early followers and even more harmful in her own opinion, to virtually idolize her. She knew that Christian Science would stand or fall on its own merits, and she did not want the growth of the Christian Science movement during her lifetime to be a phenomenon connected with her personality. Thus she struggled to keep her personality out of the way, although at the same time, she required of her followers an honest recognition of what she, and they, identified as a unique role in religious history. That same need for a proper balance exists today.

Above all else, the story of Mrs. Eddy is the story of how Christian Science changed the life of the woman who discovered it. In looking at her letters, one finds the record of her individual state of mind, the personal weaknesses and disappointments she had to overcome, as well as her utter reliance on what she considered divine guidance in all the steps she took. As the nineteenth-century American writer Donald Grant Mitchell wrote of letter writing, a habit now almost extinct in this era of instant telecommunications, "they are the monitors, they are also the comforters, and they are the only true heart-talkers." In trying to keep the text to a manageable length, I have frequently excerpted sentences or paragraphs from longer letters. To check myself, I have had the assistance of the Church History staff of The First Church of Christ, Scientist, in Boston, to determine that I was maintaining a rigorous standard for contextual honesty.

One cannot write acceptable biography without becoming involved in the life of one's subject. In the case of a religious figure, this means that one takes a sympathetic view toward the religion itself, or quite the opposite. Having grown up within an evangelical tradition and then begun the study and practice of Christian Science in my early adult years, it should be clear at the outset that I write as a Christian Scientist. I will add that I have, however, tried to be as objective as I know how in portraying Mrs. Eddy's character. What I do take as a given is the motivation of Mrs. Eddy. What motivated her from the days when she could scarcely put food on the table until she died in her stone mansion in Chestnut Hill was her consciousness of being answerable to God for all her actions. There were no side issues in Mrs. Eddy's life, and I believe that, in the years to come, any open-minded biographer reading all her letters will be reassured that this singleness of thought and purpose underlay all that she did. As for the rest, history will decide.

I have also presumed, even in this era of psychobiography, that there are readers who have a concept of God strong enough, or clear enough, for them to be able to empathize with a life story told from this point of view. Since I was raised in a household where much of everyday life was questioned in terms of whether one's actions were right in God's sight, I still do not find it difficult to describe a life in terms of its orientation to God rather than in psychological terms. To say this is not to ask the reader to agree with all of Mrs. Eddy's discovery – only with the orientation of her thought toward what she considered the bedrock of her being.

Mrs. Eddy considered her contribution to the continuing narrative of the Christian Church to be in the nature of a discovery –

that is, she never claimed that she was initiating something new, but was merely discovering the method Jesus had used in healing, and explaining the metaphysics that must have been its foundation. Nevertheless, in spite of this claim of discovery, she took many years to articulate fully what she meant by Christian Science. In following her steps both before and after the year 1866, which she considered the turning point, I have shown how even a process that can claim divine guidance had long years of preparation and various episodes that moved her along her path. Though there is necessarily a good deal in the book about the development of Christian Science, since that was her life's work, the book is not intended primarily to explain the religion. Rather, this is the story of the development of Mary Baker Eddy.

Looking at a diamond, each viewer sees its shape, sparkle, and color from a different angle and comes away with a slightly different description of what he has seen. Similarly, no biography, particularly one of this length, of a multi-faceted figure, could hope to encompass all the aspects of her character. Her letters reveal her moments of loneliness – the inevitable loneliness of the pioneer – her longing for the normal family ties she never had after childhood and adolescence, even her occasional sadness. All of these characteristics were part of the same woman who, through a growing sense of spiritual dominion, was able to lead a global religious movement. They only demonstrate that she was a fully human being.

I am indebted to The Christian Science Board of Directors for allowing me free access to the archival material in the Church History Department. I have also had valuable assistance from Frank Smith in that department over a period of several years and have appreciated his readiness to answer innumerable questions. Early in this project, I enjoyed the research assistance of Frances Langum and Suzanne MacLachlan. Numerous friends and associates have read the manuscript and made helpful criticisms of earlier drafts. I am particularly grateful to Margaret Powell for the attention she gave to it and for her critique. Finally, the presentation of the material has been immeasurably improved by the diligent work of Jane Spitzer and my wife, Katherine, who as joint "copy and composition" editors made me think at times I needed to return to school.

Lincoln, Massachusetts
September 1997

PERSISTENT PILGRIM
The Life of Mary Baker Eddy

Prologue

She held her first formal class in August, when the heavy, hot summer air still filled the small room on the second floor of 71 South Common Street, Lynn, Massachusetts. Half a dozen students, most of whom had jobs by day, came to the room in the evening to sit under a single lamp and hear her expound her healing method.

By December, the air had turned cold, and in the dark early winter evenings the scene was repeated: for twelve nights over a three-week period, six students, some of whom had paid the full price of $300, came to learn how they could heal with what she called "moral science."[1]

Mary Baker Glover, as she was known at the time, had run a small advertisement in the Lynn newspaper, for those "who wish to learn how to heal the sick without medicine, and with a success unequaled by any known method of the present day..." Mrs. Glover was in her fiftieth year. She had been a semi-invalid for most of her adult life until 1862, when she had been helped by a "doctor" with a background in mesmerism. For eight years Mrs. Glover had worked to understand how he had healed. But during that time she had experienced a major healing of her own and had also gone back to her biblical roots to search for her answers.

Lynn, like many other small American cities of 1870, had its share of healers, ranging from doctors with the limited academic training of that day all the way to quacks operating from a myriad of theories. The practice of medicine itself was still largely unregulated. Those few students whom Mrs. Glover attracted in 1870 had seen something of her healing ability in Lynn, but none of them had more than a glimpse of what she was convinced she was seeing. The best record of one of those first classes was left by Samuel Putney Bancroft, who wrote of it some 50 years later:

> We who were associated with her at that time could not see with her prophetic vision. To us her predictions seemed incredible. When she told us that the Truth she taught was the "little leaven that would leaven the whole lump," we considered it as the work of ages, not dreaming that in less than fifty years, thousands, probably millions, would accept it wholly or in part, for there is hardly a person of learning who does not quote her and endorse her, to some extent, in teaching or preaching.[2]

Bancroft wrote that "she had the gift of the true orator, the ability to make her listeners forget the speaker in what she was saying."

Given the plain, country New England background of Mrs. Glover and the austere years through which she had lived, her venture into teaching others a new science of healing she claimed to have discovered might appear at first glance highly unlikely to succeed. One can argue that there are always gullible people who can be fooled, or one may conclude that Mrs. Glover had indeed discovered a science that unlocked the Scriptures, and that what she had discovered had been responsible within just a few years for her own remarkable transformation. Throughout her career as the world's first Christian Scientist, she seems, through what she taught, either to have repelled people who came into contact with her or to have had a remarkable ability to attract them to her teaching.

One of the earliest biographies of Mrs. Eddy, written first as a series of magazine articles meant to discredit her in her old age, contains this tribute from some of her early students who did not stay with her in thought:

> [They] still declare that what they got from her was beyond equivalent in gold or silver. They speak of a certain spiritual or emotional exaltation which she was able to impart in her classroom; a feeling so strong that it was like the birth of a new under-

> standing and seemed to open to them a new heaven and a new earth.[3]

Bancroft writes about her presence as "the face of motherhood." Describing a picture of her at the time, he writes that "she had recently given birth to a great idea, brought forth in poverty and among strangers, for friends had deserted her. With her deep-set eyes she is gazing into the future of *this child of her intellect,* to whom the remaining years of her life were devoted."

Elsewhere Bancroft tries to give a word picture of her face and figure:

> Was she attractive? Was she beautiful? Attractive: yes, very. Beautiful: not in an ordinary sense... Her features were regular and finely moulded. The most noticeable were the eyes, large and deep-set, dark blue and piercing, sad, very sad, at times, yet kind and tender. Her figure was a trifle above the average height, and she carried herself very erect. While this gave the appearance of slimness, she was well-rounded. Although her resources were meager, she was always neatly and carefully dressed.[4]

He says that she always remained "ladylike and self-possessed." As for her manner in the classroom, she was animated. This obviously added to her appeal, but, he notes, "It was the animation of conviction, not of excitement or agitation." Teaching by the Socratic method of questions and answers, he says she exemplified Socrates' own rule: "First convince yourself and then you can convince others." He says that she showed no self-consciousness – "rather, self-forgetfulness."

The classes lasted for only three weeks, but the teaching never really ended. She was available between classes to answer questions, and she formed an association of her early students, which met weekly to discuss their progress. "Every meeting with her was a lesson; every letter received from her."

❖ ❖ ❖ ❖

Mrs. Glover never taught large classes. As her reputation grew, the classes, of course, became larger, and she sometimes gave several in one year. She eventually settled on thirty as the maximum number that could be taught at once. This was because she was there not merely as a lecturer, but as one who was dissecting the thought of her students in order to uncover whatever might hold back their healing abilities. She wrote twenty years later of her method of teaching:

> Only a very limited number of students can advantageously enter a class, grapple with this subject, and well assimilate what has been taught them. It is impossible to teach thorough Christian Science to promiscuous and large assemblies, or to persons *who cannot be addressed individually,* so that the mind of the pupil may be dissected more critically than the body of a subject laid bare for anatomical examination.[5] [italics added]

A century later the main method developed by Mrs. Eddy for instruction in Christian Science (other than self-instruction through reading the Christian Science textbook) remains class instruction from authorized teachers of Christian Science. Those who have taken seriously the two-week course in class instruction today know somewhat of both the exhilarating view of a new world, of a different way of looking at reality, and the discomfort that can arise in a small classroom when the very bases of human existence are being examined and challenged. Even during Mrs. Glover's 1870 experience with her first two classes, she found it necessary to dismiss a student who seemed to have come to argue with her more than to learn what she had to teach.

The year 1870 advances the story you are about to read by fifty years. Why, then, begin with the story of these small classes in the small industrial city of Lynn? Because they illustrate the long way that the teacher, Mary Baker Glover, had come from the small-town beginning and unhappy years that fill the first few chapters of this book. And because they are the first substantial pieces of evidence that point to the fulfillment that was to mark the remaining forty years of her life after these very modest beginnings of "moral science," to be renamed Christian Science some five years later.

Chapter 1

New Hampshire Childhood

Baker Family Heritage

Between the years 1815 and 1821 four female infants were born in the relatively settled northeastern corner of the young United States who were destined to be the lifeblood of the women's rights movement, the woman suffragist cause in particular, emergency humanitarian aid, and a revitalized, spiritual Christianity that included physical healing as its energizing thrust.

Although the career paths of these women did not all cross each other, their lifework had more than coincidental similarities. Each lived an extraordinarily long life, even when considered in terms of late twentieth-century longevity, but especially when considered in relation to the earlier mortality of the nineteenth century. Each labored in her field, without thought of retirement, until close to the time she passed on. And the fact that each lived until past the age of eighty-five had a special significance in that it allowed these women to put their individual stamp on the creations of their lives more than if their labors had ended earlier. Finally, each bore in her own fashion the mark of individual independence that reflected the ethos of a vital new civilization.

Elizabeth Cady Stanton, born in Johnstown, in upstate New York, in 1815, became the originator of the women's rights movement. As a relatively young wife and mother, having moved from Boston with her lawyer and abolitionist husband to Seneca Falls, New York, she rebelled against the confines of a woman's expected role – at least in a small New York town – and convened the Seneca Falls Women's Rights Convention in 1848. Although Mrs. Stanton's main work for women's rights came after the Civil War, when she had finished raising her seven children, the orientation of her entire life after 1848 was toward gaining recognition for the complete slate of women's issues that has only gradually been realized 150 years later.

Susan B. Anthony, born in western Massachusetts five years later, in 1820, became Stanton's twin in the women's rights movement. Anthony, who never married, was free earlier in life to promote the emancipation of women. She was raised a Quaker, although she eventually shed even this highly individual approach to religion and said that she found God in the work she did and the cause she supported. Her moral incisiveness and even the impression that some women had of her as a superior person for never having married made her the lightning rod of the women's movement in the late nineteenth century.

Clara Barton, founder of the American Red Cross, was born in 1821 in North Oxford, a small town in central Massachusetts. Barton did not find her own lifework as a professional humanitarian until the Civil War, when she was already forty years old. Prior to that time, she had taught school in several locations and been a clerk in the US Patent Office in Washington. She had exhibited a strong interest in helping people in need and was also looking for something to give her life a fullness that it lacked when the Civil War began. From that moment on, she became a legend for her personal heroism close to the battlefield and, later, for her discernment of the difference between charity and the kind of humanitarian aid most appropriate in emergencies. Barton and Anthony were household heroines by the end of the nineteenth century, but Barton was also almost constantly surrounded by criticism of her alleged egotism. Her weakness lay in her apparent inability to delegate successfully and in making several poor choices for the aides closest to her. She, like the others, worked until the end, once taking a train to Chicago alone at the age of eighty-eight.

The stories of the women's rights movement and of the Red Cross would read somewhat differently but for the lives of Stanton, Anthony, and Barton. Each woman's individual background brought a unique element to her lifework. Each one's biography also tells of struggles that were common to all three because they did their work in what was still a man's world. That was a world of both custom and law that is difficult to appreciate or even comprehend for anyone who has lived only in the melange that constitutes the mental and social environment of late twentieth-century America. Yet there would have been a women's rights movement without Stanton and Anthony, for the development of human thought made it inevitable that some women, somewhere, would eventually lead their sisters out of the system of custom and laws that denied them their rights one hundred fifty years ago (to say nothing of innumerable generations before then). And without Barton, there would have been some similar development of private, but channeled, humanitarian aid in times of emergency. In fact, many of Barton's battles later in life were either with competing organizations or competing individuals. And her work in the Civil War itself was mainly the work of a single heroic individual, which later in the war was partially supplanted by better organized emergency care in the Union army itself.

It cannot be said, however, that the history of religious thought and practice would have been the same without the life of Mary Baker Eddy. The fourth woman in this group, she was born, like Barton, in the year 1821 in the small New Hampshire town of Bow (near the state capital of Concord). Halfway through her life of almost ninety years, Mrs. Eddy claimed to have "discovered" Christian Science. She used the word discovery to indicate that she had no intention of beginning a new religion. Rather, she believed she had discovered the science ("science" here meaning a method or dependable set of rules) that lay behind Jesus' ability to heal and perform other works contrary to normal human expectations. Mrs. Eddy's discovery came at a time when the physical sciences were enjoying a new preeminence in human thought in general and traditional Christian beliefs were under intellectual attack. Through linking the Bible and Jesus' Christianity with the concept of science, albeit a science not dependent on the testimony of the physical senses, and by demonstrating through practice that this science could heal physical ills, through resort to a spiritual law as reliable and everpresent as the laws of physics, Mrs. Eddy believed she had restored Christianity to the firm footing that had accounted for much of its early growth.

Although she was a lifelong student of the Bible, her new approach to Christianity did not come from a cloistered, academic study of theology. It came, rather, from a personal search for health that lasted nearly half her lifetime and had made her familiar with every brand of medicine available to people at that time. Her particular articulation of Christian metaphysics preserved the theological concepts of traditional Christianity while giving new interpretation to most of them. Coming during the years when Christianity was waning as a serious intellectual force in thinking people's lives and when the new fields of psychology and psychiatry were just beginning to have some public familiarity, she developed a metaphysical language that gives precision to a Christian's prayer and practice. This was a precision that the twentieth-century mind would be demanding. At the same time the language she used was based on an explanation of theological concepts that Christians had been dealing with for two thousand years. This remarkable combination of factors could probably not have occurred at any time much earlier or later than it did. Earlier, the precision and need to speak in terms of science and law would have been lacking; there would, in fact, have been little acceptance of a religion that spoke in such terms. Later, the strong tie to and familiarity with biblical characters and with the religious idiom that drew many to Christian Science would have been lacking.

❖ ❖ ❖ ❖

The early years of Mrs. Eddy, born Mary Baker, did not carry with them any visible signal of what would become one of the most notable lives of the nineteenth century. Yet the background of these years did provide some of the elements that were to figure so large in Mary's later life – most notably, some hint of her physical fragility as a child, which later developed into a semi-invalidism; and at the same time an everyday life remarkably centered around the religious impulse in general and the tenets of Calvinism in particular. The stern doctrines of Calvin had begun to be diluted or, in the case of Unitarianism in New England, to be actually rejected by the early nineteenth century. But small communities such as Bow, New Hampshire, were not at the forefront of such changes.

New Hampshire Childhood

Mary Baker was the youngest of six children. Her precociousness was probably due at least in part to her position in the family. The youngest child has the advantage of learning quickly from its older siblings, and, if he or she remains the last child, continues to get somewhat more attention for a period of several years as the baby in the family. At her birth, three brothers, Samuel, Albert, and George, and two sisters, Abigail and Martha, were already members of the family. They had appeared at two-to-three-year intervals beginning with Samuel's birth in 1808. Mary's mother was thirty-eight years old when Mary was born in 1821, and she regarded Mary's appearance as something more significant than merely the appearing on the scene of child number six. In her later years, Mrs. Eddy reminisced that during her pregnancy her mother had confided to a close friend that she felt that this child was destined for something special. "I know these are sinful thoughts for me to entertain," she said, "but I cannot shake them off."[1] Just how this story came down to Mary one does not know, since her mother passed on before Mary had turned thirty or had an opportunity to get started with the tasks that would occupy the latter half of her years. It isn't at all beyond belief to assume that her mother, being a religious woman and one who may have thought her childbearing years were behind her, had attached special importance to the fact that she was to be a mother one more time.

Mary grew up in a busy farming household in which each of the members had their tasks to perform. Besides her brothers and sisters, her father's mother, Mary Ann Baker, lived with the family. The three-generation family was common in New England in the nineteenth century, as was the custom for unmarried daughters, not prepared to provide a full existence for themselves under the customs and laws of the day, to live either with parents or later with their married siblings' families.

Counting Mary's generation, some part of the Baker family had already been in America for six generations. A great-grandfather of Mary's own grandfather had settled in Charlestown (now a part of Boston) as early as 1640, just a decade after the first settlement of the Massachusetts Bay Colony and two decades after the landing of the Pilgrims at Plymouth. It was this great-grandfather's great-grandson, Joseph Baker, who came to New Hampshire some years before the American Revolution. He was a solid citizen – serving as deacon of the church and as selectman of his town (the selectmen in New England are the governing body of each town) – and it was his youngest son, Mark, who was to become Mary's father.

Mary's other relatives came from similarly solid pioneer backgrounds, although they had not all been in this country for as long as the Bakers. In fact, in her autobiographical work, *Retrospection and Introspection,* she seemed unaware of the long lineage of the Baker family in America, writing that "Joseph Baker and his wife, Marion (Mary Ann) McNeil...could hardly have crossed the Atlantic more than a score of years prior to the Revolutionary period."[2]

However, coming from stock that had already been settled in America for some time did not equate with wealth. Pioneer life was still lived in an extremely simple manner. When one compares the fine houses and elegant furniture that were built in Philadelphia and Boston by the time of the American Revolution with those in the New England countryside, it is apparent how much simpler the styles were in rural New England than in the comparatively rich Middle Atlantic area of the new nation or a seacoast trading center such as Boston.

Yankee styles may still have shown the heritage of a hardy, religious folk who did not find it proper to vaunt their material possessions. But they also reflected the economic facts of life. If one lived off the land, New England, with rocks and boulders left behind by the last glacier only fifteen to twenty thousand years earlier, was the hardest place on America's Eastern seaboard in which to eke out a living. The farther one went from Boston and the few other urban centers, the simpler life became. Mary's father had to work hard to supply his family's simple needs. While the Bakers would certainly not have been considered poor, their manner of living in the early nineteenth century would leave no room for sentimentalizing about the good old days. Moreover, as one went north from Boston, the winters quickly became longer and colder. In fact, they still do today. But there is a difference in the perspective. Whereas today, when people living in New York or Boston listen to the ski reports to find which mountain in New Hampshire or Vermont offers the best weekend skiing, two hundred years ago the same cold and snow conjured up a picture of livestock to be cared for through the winter, wood piled high for the stoves, families sitting by candlelight close to the hearth to read or talk with each other, and frequent illness.

It was in this communal setting of the small farmhouse in Bow that Mary attained her early impressions of the world. And, like the impressions we all receive as small children, they remained with her. One factor that entered into her own character was the apparent marked difference in temperament and tone between her mother and father. Mark Baker, the hardy New England farmer, was also a devout Calvinist. He clung to the traditional Calvinistic belief in predestination; there was little leeway in his attitude regarding salvation. Moreover, he appears to have enjoyed the religious argument for its own sake – a not unusual phenomenon in the New England Calvinist tradition.

The late twentieth century is erroneously apt to consider the Puritans of New England as the counterpart of the fundamentalist movement in America today. This is not an entirely erroneous comparison, but it has more to do with the earnestness of both groups than anything else. Both groups also based their appeal to authority on the Bible. The Puritan, however, also held a genuine, high regard for learning and the life of the intellect.

The Puritans differed from the Anglicans they had left behind in England in maintaining that the Bible alone was the ultimate source of truth. However, it never would have entered their minds that what they considered the fundamental truths about the universe as set forth in the Bible could be at odds with the discoveries of the sciences. Although evolution had not yet been generally discussed (Darwin's voyage on the Beagle did not begin until 1838, when Mary Baker was seventeen years old), the Puritans, at least in their day, would not have disputed the kind of scientific evidence with which fundamentalist believers in the literal scientific accuracy of the Bible have to contend.

Valuing the life of the intellect as an important adjunct to religious understanding, one of the first acts of the Puritans in the Massachusetts Bay Colony had been the establishment of Harvard College in 1636 for the training of future ministers. One can imagine, in the long, cold winter evenings when Mark Baker would occasionally argue over religion with the local minister, that there was a kind of pride in being able to hold his own in matters of the intellect. And as for the kind of church services the likes of Mark Baker enjoyed, this description by Horace Bushnell, a mid-nineteenth-century Congregational minister, of his home church in Connecticut would also suffice for New Hampshire:

> There is no affectation of seriousness in the assembly, no mannerism of worship; some would say, too little of the manner of worship. They think of nothing, in fact, save what meets their intelligence and enters into them by that method. They appear like men who have digestion for strong meat... Under their hard and... stolid faces, great thoughts are brewing, and these keep them warm. Free-will, fixed fate, foreknowledge absolute, Trinity, redemption, special grace, eternity – give them anything high enough, and the tough muscle of their inward man will be climbing sturdily into it; and if they go away having something to think of, they have had a good day.[3]

There was a connection between the necessarily lean living of the Yankee colonists and their descendants, at least up until the time of the Civil War, and an independence of outlook that could claim that, however little one had, he had achieved it through his own efforts. Mary wrote of her father in *Retrospection,* "My father possessed a strong intellect and an iron will."[4] Nowhere, though, does she speak of him with particular affection, although this is no indication that she had anything but love and respect for the authority figure he represented in her young life. The fact that her father remarried many years later, after he had been widowed and when Mary Baker herself was already a young widow living at home, undoubtedly had some effect on her feelings about him and her later memory of him.

If Mary's father represented the Old Testament God of judgment, her mother seemed to exemplify the unconditional love of Jesus as portrayed in the New Testament. "Of my mother I cannot speak as I would, for memory recalls qualities to which the pen can never do justice,"[5] she was to write when she was seventy years old. It was natural for her to feel closer to her mother, if only from the division of responsibilities that belonged to farm families of her day. Her father was presumably out of the house most of the day, while she helped her mother with the cooking, laundering, and sewing. Beyond that, her mother's character was seen by all as being exceptional. At her funeral, the minister eulogized, "She possessed a strong intellect, a sympathizing heart, and a placid spirit. Her presence, like the gentle dew and cheerful light, was felt by all around her."[6] Yet in the long daily prayers the entire family had together, it was Mark, the father-figure, who did the praying.

To many Americans living at the end of the twentieth century, and perhaps even more to non-Americans who are not familiar with the religious history of this country, it should be emphasized that, whatever the "fierceness" of the particular theological belief that was held to, religion in America, at least by the time Mary was growing up, had a voluntary nature to it. People adhered to a religion because they believed that it gave them strength to be whatever they were. Religion was not a burden, but a freeing activity. No one caught hold of this phenomenon better than the Frenchman Alexis de Tocqueville, who in his tour of America in the 1830s seems to have been more discerning of Americans than most of them were of themselves. De Tocqueville wrote:

> Upon my arrival in the United States, the religious aspect of the country was the first thing that struck my attention; and the longer I stayed there the more did I perceive the great political consequences resulting from this state of things, to which I was unaccustomed. In France I had almost always seen the spirit of religion and the spirit of freedom pursuing courses diametrically opposed to each other; but in America I found that they were intimately united, and that they reigned in common over the same country.[7]

❖ ❖ ❖ ❖

Nowhere was the difference between the approaches taken by her parents more apparent than in the disturbance the young Mary felt over the doctrine of predestination. Nor is any other event of her childhood years as suggestive of the direction her own life would eventually take. When a child (or adult) was to become a member of the Congregational Church of those days, it was customary for him or her to be examined regarding her state of thought – most particularly, regarding her theological beliefs. There has been some confusion for years as to whether the incident or incidents related here occurred when Mary Baker was twelve years old or seventeen. She remembers the event as happening when she was twelve; however, this is from an account she wrote when she was well along in years. The records of the local church show that she actually joined it when she was seventeen. What is most probable is that she had similar discussions with her parents beginning at roughly the age of twelve years and that not every part of the incident occurred in the same year.

Her father had explained to her Calvin's doctrine of predestination. As she tells it in her autobiography:

> Before this step [joining the church] was taken, the doctrine of unconditional election, or predestination, greatly troubled me; for I was unwilling to be saved, if

> my brothers and sisters were to be numbered among those who were doomed to perpetual banishment from God. So perturbed was I by the thoughts aroused by this erroneous doctrine, that the family doctor was summoned, and pronounced me stricken with fever.
>
> My father's relentless theology emphasized belief in a final judgment-day, in the danger of endless punishment, and in a Jehovah merciless towards unbelievers; and of these things he now spoke, hoping to win me from dreaded heresy.[8]

In this incident one can see that Mark Baker was not an uncaring father. When Mary fell ill, it was he who ran to fetch the doctor to care for her. The doctor sensed what was wrong and, according to one account, even told Mark that he must not worry Mary about such theological issues again.

She continues:

> My mother, as she bathed my burning temples, bade me lean on God's love, which would give me rest, if I went to Him in prayer, as I was wont to do, seeking His guidance. I prayed; and a soft glow of ineffable joy came over me. The fever was gone, and I rose and dressed myself, in a normal condition of health.

Later, (and this may have been when she was seventeen) the minister of the church, "an old-school expounder of the strictest Presbyterian doctrines," examined her.[9] She told him that she could never join a church if she had to assent to the concept of predestination.

> Distinctly do I recall what followed. I stoutly maintained that I was willing to trust God, and take my chance of spiritual safety with my brothers and sisters, – not one of whom had then made any profession of

> religion, – even if my creedal doubts left me outside the doors. The minister then wished me to tell him when I had experienced a change of heart; but tearfully I had to respond that I could not designate any precise time. Nevertheless he persisted in the assertion that I had been truly regenerated, and asked me to say how I felt when the new light dawned within me. I replied that I could only answer him in the words of the Psalmist: "Search me, O God, and know my heart: try me, and know my thoughts: and see if there be any wicked way in me, and lead me in the way everlasting." [10]

She was received into the church, notwithstanding her rejection of one of its main tenets.

One of her biographers of fifty years ago, commenting on the difference in natures that had to be accommodated within the Baker household in Bow, wrote that "the adjustment demanded in the coming together of these two heritages was tremendous, only exceeded in difficulty by the task of making the adjustment in the soul of a single individual [Mary]." [11] If there was any conscious juggling in Mary Baker's thought between the stern father-figure of Mark and the compassion that Abigail expressed, it is worth noting that it took place not only on the stage of Mary Baker's personal life but also, later on, in the very concept of God that gradually unfolded to her: that of a loving, compassionate Father-Mother, who, because of His/Her omnipotence, is also a Principle that is equated with Love and that expresses itself, when turned to, as inviolable law in men's affairs. Men and women are held, as it were, in God's arms, in security and harmony – if they only drop the beliefs that deny that fact. But this is to jump many years and many life lessons ahead of the trembling girl who stood before her "minister-priest" in the orthodox Congregational Church and maintained her independence of judgment.

Mary's intense excitement over a confession of faith and joining the local church was in part a foretelling of her own orientation toward God, to a religious "framework" or center for her entire life experience; it also indicated an unfortunate susceptibility to illness. To some degree this has to be understood as a phenomenon of that period, or of any period in which religious emotionalism is allowed to become confused with religious commitment. Elizabeth Cady (Stanton) had an experience at the age of fifteen similar in some respects to Mary Baker's. Sent away to a girls' boarding school in New York State, Elizabeth came under the influence of the revivalist Charles Finney during the Great Troy Revival in 1831. As she described the experience, "Owing to my gloomy Calvinist training in the old Scotch Presbyterian Church, and my vivid imagination, I was one of the first victims."[12] She experienced a personal conversion. Then she became so upset over her alleged sinful state that she had to leave the school and return home. Her father, Judge Cady, recognized the cause of her disturbed state and frequent nightmares at once, and Elizabeth was soon restored to a more normal mentality. In her case, the experience had the effect of cutting off any interest whatsoever in the religious life and of pointing her thought in other directions. "Her experience initiated a decade of religious indecision. His [Finney's] preaching had called into question all her Calvinist training and helped her reject it. She accepted Finney's imperative that she had a choice to make, and in the end she chose skepticism."[13]

Mary was also more than normally sensitive to the thoughts of those around her. In later life her cultivation of a spiritually based sensitivity made it possible for her to virtually read the thoughts of others, or at the very least to discern the motives that lay behind actions before they became as obvious to her associates as they were to her. Whether or not the kind of sensitivity she had as a child had any relation to her various illnesses, it is a fact that her health became a nagging problem.

About the very early years there is not much of a record. However, in the mid-1830s one of her brothers, George Sullivan, left home and moved to Connecticut. The letters that flowed between brother and sisters reveal a family in which all were interested in each other's welfare, as well as a degree of worldly concern that indicates most of the children as having escaped Mark Baker's strict vigilance. Abigail wrote to George, for instance, not to make love to the girls in Connecticut before he returned to New Hampshire. They also show the lighthearted side of life at home, as when Martha describes the scene one evening when she was trying to write:

> Mary is reading and Abbie sits and orders me what to say but I shall not regard her. Sullivan they do act so bad it is impossible for me to write and I wish you could make them behave for they keep shaking the table and making me laugh all the time…[14]

It is possible, though not certain, that George left home to settle in the slightly milder climate of southern New England. One of the first letters of the period indicates some concerns about his health. Most, if not all, of the Baker children endured periods of ill health; this condition was apparently accepted in some degree as an inevitable part of the harsh living conditions in New England. However, this same letter, written from Mary to her brother, also indicates that her own health was already, or still, in a fragile state:

> There is one thing if I have not improved it aright I have learned from experience to prize more perhaps than ever I did before that is *Dear brother* the *friendly advice* and *council* you was [sic] ever giving me and the lively interest you ever manifested in my welfare but now when I sit down to my *lonely* meal I have no brother Sullivan to encourage me as formerly but there is no philosophy in repining I must extend the thought of benevolence farther than selfishness would permit and only add my health at present is improveing slowly and I hope by dieting and being careful to sometime regain it.[15]

Mary closed by saying that this was only the second letter she had ever written (she was then fourteen). The "you was" was still an accepted colloquialism at the time.

1835 was also the year that saw the rest of the Baker family move from the farm at Bow to the small town of Sanbornton Bridge. Bow was only five miles south of Concord, while Sanbornton lay some twenty miles north of the New Hampshire capital. Bow, however, was hardly a town; it was certainly no place for the Baker girls to socialize in, and the five miles to Concord in the winter could seem like a long trip. Mark Baker may have had in mind living where his girls were apt to find suitable husbands, but he may have also realized that farming in the marginal, rocky soil of northern New England offered uncertain future prospects, what with the opening up of the lush farmlands of the Middle West and the new passage to the American heartland offered by the Erie Canal in New York State. Whatever the combination of reasons, Sanbornton Bridge was a town in which the three girls could make more friends, and also a place where Mark and Abigail themselves could live an easier life as they got on in years. Sanbornton Bridge was situated on the Winnepesaukee River. It had several mills that were powered by the river's current and was one of those New England towns that would thrive for the next couple of generations.

In 1837, just about the time Mary turned sixteen, Martha wrote to George that Mary was seriously ill:

> She was taken ill again...and her disease of that nature, which for a time, gave no signs of her recovery. In addition to her former diseases her stomach became most shockingly cankered, and an ulcer collected on her lungs...but she has a good deal recovered for two weeks past, and this morning was carried out to ride; 'tis possible she may yet enjoy her usual degree of health, but not without the utmost care, and exertion. [16]

Three weeks later Martha reported that Mary's health "at present, is about as it was when I wrote you last, and we have some hope that she will yet regain it." [17] Later that fall Martha was writing that she herself had stopped going to a school, for which her brother was paying her tuition, because she had become ill from the unheated classrooms. Then, "Mary's health is gradually advancing on bread and water." [18] This indication is the first one that part of Mary Baker's health problems had some connection with her digestion; later on she was to become for awhile a disciple of the Graham method of diet. (Graham, 1794-1851, was a Presbyterian minister and reformer. He recommended a vegetable diet as a cure for intemperance, but the part of his cure that Mary apparently followed was the use of coarsely ground whole wheat flour for her bread.)

Later in 1837, probably referring to the summer-long illness, Abi, her older sister, wrote to George: "Mary spent the last week with me and appears quite comfortable, but the poor girl can never enjoy life as most of us can should she live any time, and this is altogether uncertain. It surely is with all of us but it seems to be more so with her, since she retains life only by dieting and brushing, and all such simple expedients." [19]

In one of the first years the Bakers lived in Sanbornton Bridge, the town had a religious revival. This period saw the close of the Second Great Awakening in New England, a theological counterthrust to the deism of the Enlightenment and to the rationalistic branch of the New England Congregational Church, a portion of which had culminated in the Unitarian denomination. These revival meetings went on for several days; people would come from farms and surrounding towns as well. Mary's brother, Albert, heard that she had been influenced by the revival, and was concerned that she be overly stimulated by the emotional content of the meetings. (One sees shades of Elizabeth Cady's emotional experience here.) Albert wrote to Mary that he had heard she "had been brought to embrace the doctrines of that religion, the strange influences of which have thus far puzzled philosophy to solve. . .One thing, do not allow yourself to be suspected of, bigotry or fanaticism. They are as distinct from true religion, as from true philosophy – its very antipodes."[20]

Three years later, when Mary was approaching her nineteenth birthday, she was still having difficulties with her health, although not necessarily the same ones. Albert, who was by that time practicing law elsewhere in New Hampshire, wrote to the other sisters: "But my joy was saddened, upon reading in your postscript, that Mary's health is again in danger. I Pray she will be careful. I fear she has exposed herself. Don't breath [sic] these awful frosts. It is enough to break up the health of the stoutest. I have suffered from them, of late, but am recovered."[21] In the same month he wrote to Mary, and the letter suggests that ill health was nothing new to her: "I hope your usual fortitude may not have deserted you; & that amidst the depth of your sufferings, you may receive the satisfaction, to feel, that however great may be your afflictions, it is for your good – that the chastisement is inflicted by that Hand which is never laid upon us but in mercy, though it may appear in anger."[22]

Much of the language of letter writing at that time suffered from a formality that gives it a ring of artificiality to today's ears. Beneath the quite obvious sincerity of his solicitude for his sister Mary, however, there also appears the orthodox Christian view of that day that human suffering, if not in actual punishment for some deserved sin, was at least the working of God's inscrutable will. Years of ill health, which had already begun to affect her experience in childhood and adolescence, were to awaken in Mary a rebellion against the notion that life was meant to be lived for any reason other than to glorify God, to be His witness.

Mary's fragile health as a child and young adult, whatever the physical circumstances actually were, had another result: it dictated that she not have even the rather limited formal schooling that was then available to young females. The first finishing school that would offer a curriculum somewhat comparable to what boys of the same age were offered was Emma Willard in New York State. In fact, it was at Emma Willard's school that Elizabeth Cady finished her own formal education. And Clara Barton, born the same year as Mrs. Eddy in Massachusetts, even taught in local schools for ten years before going to an academy in New York State where she herself could become better educated.

Mrs. Eddy wrote of her own early education in *Retrospection*: "My father was taught to believe that my brain was too large for my body and so kept me much out of school, but I gained book-knowledge with far less labor than is usually requisite." [23] Actually, a great deal of education was carried on in the family in American homes of that generation. To anyone familiar with the patterns of early American life, there was nothing inferior about this kind of education. (There is a case at hand in our own family. My wife's great-great-grandfather came to the western-most frontier of Missouri from Virginia about the time Mrs. Eddy was growing up. *A History of Cass and Bates Counties, Missouri,* published in 1883, says of him:

> When he was nine years old his parents moved to Missouri. His early education was chiefly confined to the parental roof, at least until his eleventh year. At home he obtained an early knowledge of the primary branches of an English education, and with examples of reading and study before him he early imbibed a passionate fondness for reading and chiefly of the mathematical studies. He was familiar with the Latin grammar before his tenth year. By his twelfth year he had become familiar with Plutarch, Rollin, Walter Scott's histories; those of the United States and of England he was familiar with.")[24]

Mary Baker was also what we call today a quick learner. It is clear from the later reminiscences of those who knew her as a child that she had an active intellect and was quick to master anything that caught her attention.

Her main books in her self-education at home were Lindley Murray's *Grammar* and his *English Reader.* Murray had been a New York lawyer who reversed the flow across the Atlantic and settled in England later in life. The *Reader* he compiled was largely a collection of eighteenth century authors, which goes some way to explain the particular writing style Mrs. Eddy adopted in her own writing. But the *Reader* also contained passages from some of the Greek and Roman classics, as well as from the Bible. Murray was also concerned with the issue of slavery, and Mrs. Eddy may have read her first antislavery essays in the *English Reader.* The *Reader* was not the equivalent of several years of college literature courses, but neither was it a mere smattering of literature. As for grammar, Mrs. Eddy later wrote that she was as familiar with Murray's *Grammar* as she was with the Westminster Catechism. "And the latter I had to repeat every Sunday."[25]

The other main source of Mrs. Eddy's home education was her brother Albert, whose letters about her health were quoted above. Besides her mother, Albert was the closest family influence. The second son, born in 1810, he was already eleven years old when Mary was born. Apparently more intellectual than the other sons, he alone went off to college. When Mary Baker was old enough to begin learning serious subjects, Albert was finishing up at Dartmouth College in Hanover, New Hampshire. During his college years, he would help Mary with her learning when he was at home during his numerous college vacations. She wrote, "From my brother Albert I received lessons in the ancient tongues, Hebrew, Greek, and Latin."[26] One would doubt that she had a thorough knowledge of any of those languages, but she must have learned something about etymology, which helped her convey her meanings with such precision when she later honed the language of her metaphysical system. She also became a part-time student at one of the female academies in Sanbornton after the family moved there, and she noted in a newspaper article written in 1903 that as part of her education she had studied "Comstock's Natural Philosophy, Chemistry, Blair's Rhetoric, Whateley's Logic, Watt's `On the Mind and Moral Science.'"

Albert served as more than surrogate school teacher, however. In *Retrospection* she spoke of him as "next to my mother, the very dearest of my kindred. To speak of his beautiful character as I cherish it, would require more space than this little book can afford."[27] Albert served to open up Mary's world to more than just the close family around the Baker hearth or even to the community of Sanbornton Bridge. After Albert graduated from Dartmouth, he read law in the offices of Benjamin Pierce in Hillsborough, New Hampshire (along the road that went from Concord up to Dartmouth). Benjamin was the father of Franklin Pierce, who would be elected President of the United States in 1852. Once Albert began to practice law, he started to travel outside his home state. He also became a state legislator in 1838, and very likely would have gone to Congress as a representative from New Hampshire after the election of 1842, but for his untimely death in the autumn of 1841.

The Baker family letters show that Albert, as well as Mary's sister Martha, had various bouts of serious illness during the 1830s. Whether they were related to the problems Mary had is less clear. Albert was ill at various times from overwork. It was also not uncommon in those days for people to have more respiratory difficulties because of the lack of proper creature comforts in their houses, or from the severity of their conditions of travel during winter. There is nothing in the family history or in the correspondence to indicate that they were a pampered set of children, or that they exaggerated their several difficulties. In any case, when Albert died in the fall of 1841, a major prop in Mary's world was suddenly pulled from under her.

Albert had been a major influence in widening her intellectual interests and more generally in bringing a broader world into view. Some of his college essays, which she read, show that he had passed beyond the Calvinistic beliefs of his family and was more or less a deist. The deists of the nineteenth century were persons deeply influenced by the advances of the physical sciences. Their conception of God was that of a being who could not intervene in men's affairs through either whimsy or will, but was a kind of watchmaker who had set the watch (the world) in motion and then left it untended. Yet God seems to have remained a reality to Albert, even during his halcyon college days. An essay he wrote called "The Heresy of Reason" contains sentences such as these:

> The Being whom we adore, and a knowledge of whom we would fain attain, combining in himself all that is holy and perfect, the nearer we approach him and the more intimate our acquaintance, the purer will be our love and the stronger our attachment... But while we would concede the infinitude of the Divine Mind [God], we would maintain the ability in man of an infinite increase of knowledge; and though he can never reach perfection, he may forever approximate...[28]

Although Mary may not have read all her brother's college papers, this was the kind of language the two talked together; in fact, one even finds traces of some of what was quoted above in Mrs. Eddy's writings as a Christian Scientist. Some of Albert's college writing is at odds with his references to God's will in the letter to Mary quoted earlier. The language he had used in that letter may have been partly the expected language of polite intercourse at the time, particularly when speaking about illness, or Albert himself may have been tempered by his several bouts of severe illness during his short career as a lawyer.

But one should not get the impression that all of Mary's life consisted of illness in the family. The years after 1835 in Sanbornton Bridge gave Mary an opportunity to get a limited amount of formal schooling. She was probably a student sometime in 1838 at the Holmes Academy in Plymouth, New Hampshire, a small town north of Sanbornton Bridge. It was here that she met Augusta Holmes and developed a friendship that can be traced in some surviving letters. The letters to today's ears reek with sentimentality, but overlooking this element, one can see the genuine concern that Mary had for her health and future outlook:

> Can I *ever, ever* tell you my health will permit of my again enjoying one of the richest of heaven's earthly blessings, "the society of friends?"
>
> ...surely Augusta, I could say with Biron [sic], "it be hardly life, to bear within myself this barrenness of

spirit" was it not for *absent friends,* and those near me too, and *this sweet, cherished* remembrance, comes oer my spirits like a spell, and the *only* cloud that can forego this, is the thoughts of a *lingering disease.* To die, is almost *denied* me! But what complain? Will not he that tempers the wind to the shorn Lamb, be mindful of me also?"[29]

In 1842, when Mary either was or was about to become twenty-one, she was a student at the Sanbornton Academy, which was located in the town where the Bakers had been living. This was another of the girls' finishing schools of the day, which were the highest form of formal education then open to young women. In later years, she was remembered not only as being a good student, but also as being the one to whom the head of the academy would turn over the class whenever he had to leave the classroom. In 1902, the son of her teacher recalled his father saying of Mary: "Bright, good, and pure, aye brilliant! I never before had a pupil with such depth and independence of thought. She has some great future, mark that. She is an intellectual and spiritual genius."[30]

This bright but somewhat fragile woman had also become an attractive young lady. Around the turn of the century, some sixty years later, when the burgeoning popularity of Christian Science resulted in a kind of backlash aimed at belittling the background and reputation of Mary Baker Eddy, a muckraking journalist plied the town of Sanbornton Bridge, by now renamed Tilton, to gather information about the young Mary Baker. Even those who had resented her popularity at the time gave a uniformly positive physical description of her: slender, full-figured, lovely chestnut hair, deep-set eyes, probably gray-blue (although the color of her eyes seems to have been the subject of many a disagreement among her associates over the years).

❖ ❖ ❖ ❖

Abigail married in 1837, their sister Martha a year later. The move to Sanbornton had provided the girls with a more active social life and had aided in the completion of their education. Abigail married a Tilton, a member of a mill family whose local prominence was apparently the reason for Sanbornton Bridge eventually being renamed Tilton. Martha married Luther Pilsbury, who helped manage the New Hampshire state prison. Mary was alone now, but would also soon become a married woman and begin a new part of her experience.

What did she bring with her out of her childhood and early maturity? Each individual making life's journey leaves his or her own trail across the field of human experience. For many individuals, the marks that are left behind look almost indistinguishable from each other. For those whose names and deeds are remembered, there is something along the way that starts them down a path that no one else will follow. In the case of a religious leader such as Mary Baker eventually became, many thousands would eventually try to follow the path to spiritual development that she laid out, but that would not be the same thing as having her own life experiences. These would remain unique to her, as the individual experiences we all have are unique to each of us.

If one accepts the concept of a spiritual reality, of spiritual consciousness, it is quite straightforward to say that the most important parts of her experience can be explained by the high degree of spiritual receptivity, sensitiveness, insight, and humility she had developed by middle age. But quite apart from this, there were also elements in her first twenty-one years of living that made the path of her life begin to diverge from the more common paths others would be following – elements that, in retrospect, can be seen to have been essential parts of her particular life story.

The first is the pivotal place in Mary Baker's life of her religion. At this point, the religion that meant the most to her was the tender love, the practical evidence of Christianity, in her mother's life. However, her father's fondness for religious dialogue and the old Calvinist sense, not that God Himself could be explained, but that one's religious position should be intellectually solid, would assure that whatever religious position she eventually took would be one that was not built, as the religious revivals were, on emotionalism. For the moment, there was of course no inkling that she would become the religious figure she did. Yet it is significant that she had been the only one of her six brothers and sisters to make a formal confession of faith. She approached adulthood with the thought of God and her own relationship to Him close to both head and heart.

Sadly, she also carried a memory of illness and weakness into adulthood. Whatever her ailments, they had started early with her inability to have normal schooling with her sisters and continued through her teen years, as her letters to and from her brothers show. She was clearly not constantly ill, as her attendance at the Sanbornton Academy in 1842 indicates. Nor could she have appeared a sickly person, or the man she was about to marry would not have found her so attractive. But there had been enough experience with illness for her to become preoccupied with finding a way to overcome chronic illness and to enjoy normal health – and with questioning why one should have to waste even part of a life in inactivity. Moreover, Albert's untimely death at the age of thirty-one had certainly left doubts in her mind regarding her own prospects for a normal life.

Thirdly, she had already demonstrated a strong sense of independence. The biographies of the other women mentioned at the start of the chapter – Stanton, Anthony, and Barton – all show beginnings with some similarity to those of Mary Baker Eddy's. Stanton was raised a privileged child of the town judge, but the others came from backgrounds as humble or even simpler than Mary's. However, the kind of Puritan spirit that infused the New England household was not limited to the male members. There is never a suggestion with any one of these women that she felt her role in life should be less influential or important because of her sex. They would, it is true, find barriers to what they wanted to do that were gender barriers, but more important than that was the independent spirit that each already possessed as part of her heritage. In Mary Baker's case, this had been amply illustrated in her standing up to her father and her minister on questions regarding her own salvation.

Finally, as a subtheme throughout her long life, she had a strong attachment to family. The letters she wrote as her siblings moved away or married were not only indicative of the sentimentality of the generation. They also indicated a genuine sense of loss of family. This need to belong to someone, to some group, was soon to be fulfilled by her becoming a mother. But when the normal experiences of motherhood were later denied her, she still yearned to be a mother and to have her family. This she would indeed have, but it would come closer to being the family of man than the tight-knit family group of Bow.

Entr'acte 1

Puritanism in America

In telling the story of Mary Baker's youth as concisely as possible, there is insufficient room within the narrative itself to elaborate on the major significance of her Puritan background.

For the benefit of readers who are not familiar with American history, it needs to be said that Puritanism went a long way toward defining the meaning and purpose of early America.

Mary's father was a stern Calvinist, as has already been noted. The major theological tenet for which Calvinism is remembered today is its emphasis on predestination – that is, the belief that God knows beforehand who will ultimately find salvation and that nothing man can do of himself can gain him salvation. For most people approaching the Bible stories today, it seems little short of incredible that the few verses in the New Testament around which this theology draped itself could have supplied the stage set for what became a major part of Protestantism, particularly in the American colonies. Yet it is no more beyond belief than the manner in which Augustine in the late fourth century succeeded in redirecting the course of Christianity for at least a thousand years. At that time, its early message of redemption, freedom, and spiritual equality, which largely accounted for its early growth, became obscured by Augustine's emphasis on the alleged fall of man (stemming from the Bible story of Adam and Eve in the second chapter of Genesis) and man's inherent depravity.

The fact is that the appeal and tenacity of Calvinism did not hang on the tenet of predestination alone. Taken as a whole, it was able to satisfy the religious needs of several generations of Christians. Nor did Puritanism remain a static concept. American Puritanism needs to be approached, first, as a continuation and development of Puritanism in England. The English Reformation began less as a religious reform than as a political dispute between Henry VIII and the Pope. Once begun, however, it resulted in a long-fought contest over the nature and extent of religious authority. In one way or another, England underwent the throes of reformation from Henry's break with the Church of Rome in 1534 until the Glorious Revolution of 1689 settled William and Mary on the throne of England.

The English Reformation was initially about matters of church government and appropriate liturgy. As it developed, however, it concerned itself increasingly with matters of religious belief, of theology. The entire century from 1560 (Elizabeth ascended to the throne in 1558) to 1660, the end of the Puritan commonwealth, is viewed by some historians as one of Puritan ascendancy. There were gaps in this ascendancy, as in the reign of Charles I after 1625, which had a good deal to do with the first major wave of Puritan emigration to Massachusetts in the 1630s.

Puritan thought continued to develop in America, not at all unaware of what the Puritan theologians at Cambridge University were thinking. But religious thought and life were also affected by a new set of conditions in the American colonies. The early Puritan communities in Massachusetts had been attempts to set up "holy commonwealths." The aim of these communities was not the establishment of religious freedom, but the realization of the kind of community a Puritan reading of the Scriptures led them to think they should create.

By the end of the 1600s, this early concept of a "city on the hill" (what today would be called a local theocracy) had been challenged by the facts of life in the new colony. The embers from the inner fire of the first generation no longer cast a strong enough glow to keep the vision alive. The harsh facts of life in New England called for a degree of cooperation and compromise among all the settlers that the Puritans had not counted on. And the growing presence of other religious strains imposed a degree of competition among the churches that had also not been foreseen. Instead of a parish church, to which all members of a community belonged, the "gathered" church of those who chose to belong would become the American pattern. Thus it was more by accident than design that the concept of religious freedom came early to America. Certainly religious freedom, which is such a strong part of American values, was not part of the Puritans' agenda. They came to America to have the freedom to practice what they considered the only correct religion.

However medieval the general outlook of at least the early Puritans may appear today, one must bear in mind that theirs was a serious, well-articulated religion. Sydney Ahlstrom, a Yale professor of religious history who spent his entire career studying and explaining American religious history, wrote in *A Religious History of the American People* of the early Puritans: "Doctrine, moreover, was almost always felt to stand in need of support from both philosophical reason and common experience. Puritanism, in short, is generally marked by careful thought; it is an intellectual tradition of great profundity."[1]

Besides the Puritan respect for learning, already mentioned in the preceding chapter, Puritanism had other tangential effects on American culture that have been at least as long-lasting as the remnants of its religious beliefs. And when Mrs. Eddy noted that she came from a long Puritan background, she was surely as aware of these other, secular effects of Puritanism as she was of its religious tenets.

The Reformist tradition had little respect for the monastic life. All Christians must give witness of their calling. This concept gave men and women new pride in their work, whatever it was. Success at one's career, moreover, while it was definitely not a means of earning entry into heaven, was seen at one point as a sign that one was among the elect. Thus, for a few generations at least, the visible signs of election became important. After the religious connotation had passed, the national devotion to hard work was well established.

The Puritans also emphasized the role of law, beginning with God's inscrutable will as they felt they had seen it in the Bible.

This emphasis on the law as a guide to all human activity and a restraint on man's destructive impulses "helped to create a nation of individualists who were also fervent `moral athletes,' with a strong sense of transcendent values which must receive ordered and corporate expression in the commonwealth."[2] The democracy of local church government in New England also made the early American eager, as well as somewhat prepared, to govern his own civic affairs also.

The process of religious conversion itself, which became an important element in American Puritanism, emphasized the strength one could experience from reliance on God. Charles Cohen, another modern historian of them, writes, "Puritans were preoccupied with the limits of human power. Without faith, they thought, humanity wallows in sinful debility, but conversion changes helpless unregenerates into puissant Saints. The new birth was their initiation into potency, and belief the vehicle of their strength."[3] As for the way in which these people of such strong religious persuasion were viewed in their communities, Cohen says:

> . . .they earned their neighbors' enmity for divisive scrupulosity and hypocritical self-righteous zeal. To friends they seemed militant soldiers in the army of the Lord; to foes, officious busybodies disrupting village camaraderie, but on at least one point all observers could agree: *to be a Puritan meant living a life distinctively ardent.* [italics added][4]

As the religion became attenuated, the reliance on and complete submission to God's will that had been its basis was replaced by a kind of sturdy self-reliance – a perversion, no doubt, but still an independence that encouraged men not to take orders from anyone else. Thus, Puritanism made a strong contribution to the development of the concept of equality in the new democracy.

By the nineteenth century, when our story takes place, what was left of Puritanism had divided into two main religious strains: the more rationalistic outlook of the Unitarians, and the evangelicalism of nineteenth-century Protestantism. The latter was the strain more familiar to the young Mary Baker, although in the small towns of New Hampshire Puritanism itself lagged a few generations behind its evolution in larger commercial and intellectual centers. This fact explains the dilemma Mary had in her adolescent years over the doctrine of predestination – a doctrine that would have survived longer in areas not as readily influenced by current intellectual ferment.

On the secular side, Mary's family shared in and expressed all of the secular values that the Puritan culture had inculcated: the love of democracy, the independence of the individual conscience, the rule of law, the value of hard work, and a seriousness for whatever one had to face in life. While one might express all these traits without having been a Puritan, their particular development in American life as a group of characteristics common to the populace as a whole can be explained only by the religious culture of early America and, particularly, of the colonies in New England. This leads Ahlstrom to conclude in his opus, "Few cultures are so intractable to purely secular categories of historical interpretation." [5] This also explains why, when Mrs. Eddy referred to her Puritan background, that reference tells a good deal more about the way she was prepared to face life than merely the name of the church she attended on Sunday or even the theological beliefs preached within its white walls.

Chapter 2

Twenty Years of Disappointment and Preparation

Over the centuries, entering into marriage has held various and sometimes contradictory connotations, ranging from security for woman to a kind of enforced bondage to another human being. Its parameters have extended all the way from its being the medieval troubadour's concept of romantic love to a business contract entered into for the main purpose of producing healthy male heirs. In Mary Baker's day, marriage usually followed and was itself a sign of entry into full adulthood. Females in particular in post-colonial America still married young. For several generations after Mary's day, until well into the twentieth century, most American women expected their roles in life to be defined mainly by their relationship with and support of a husband's career. There has been no more marked change in social expectations than that which has occurred in the role of women in the last generation of the twentieth century, when most women expect to be wage-earners for a good part of their lives and when a significant minority consider their professional lives potentially as important to them as the role of wife and mother.

For a young girl living at home with both parents, however, as Mary Baker was in 1843, with no expectation on society's part that females should be anything beyond wives and mothers, marriage definitely dated one's maturity. Mary had already known her husband-to-be for some ten years. George Washington Glover was the brother of the young woman, Eliza Glover, whom her oldest brother, Samuel, had taken for his wife in 1832. George Glover had playfully told Mary at the time that he would return to marry her when she grew up (she was eleven at the time and he was already twenty-one). He had been up to Sanbornton Bridge once five years later, and they had renewed their acquaintance in the year or two before they married.

They did not know each other well, though. George Glover had first worked with Mary's brother, Samuel, in his contracting business in Boston. Then Glover went south to be a builder on his own. From what is known about him, he sounds like a bit of a swaggerer, although he may have picked up that quality among the more easygoing Southerners. He had been made an honorary colonel on the governor's staff in South Carolina and was active in his Masonic lodge. All in all, he fits the description of the nineteenth-century American "joiner" – gregarious, industrious, probably a bit of a boaster as well. That he apparently fitted in as well as he did in the social caste society of South Carolina says something positive about his ability to get along with people. Whether he would have made the ideal husband for Mary one will never know, since the marriage was to be cut short in less than a year by his death.

For her part, Mary had not enjoyed a string of beaux. Her sensitive health may have cut into any incipient social life in Sanbornton, but her father's attitudes probably hemmed her in even more. There were a few instances when Abigail and Martha went to local dances after the family moved to Sanbornton. Mary did not go, nor would she probably have ventured to cross her father by any direct act of disrespect for his wishes. So, when George Glover asked her to marry him, she may have felt that she would not have unlimited choices ahead of her.

They were married on the tenth of December, 1843. After spending the night in Concord, they went on to Boston and spent some days there with her brother, Samuel. Eliza Glover had already passed on, and Samuel had a new wife. They sailed from Boston to Charleston, arriving there late in December. One can imagine the contrast Mary felt on arriving in conservative, sedate Charleston. There was the contrast of cultures, with black slaves in the household. She did not see the worst side of slavery among the house servants of Charleston families, but the mere existence of human slavery offended her sensibilities. There was the contrast of climate and the easygoing ways that the warmth of the South produced among all its citizens. And there was the settled, affable Charleston culture, which, apart from its dependence on slavery, was a shining example of the refinements of civilization on this side of the Atlantic. She could scarcely have endured greater culture shock than an American of today would experience going to a Third World country in Africa.

She was also not well as she settled into Charleston. Some of this may have been the return of her former physical problems; some may have been associated with pregnancy, for she had become pregnant during the first month of marriage. Some of her anxiety must have shown up in the first letter she wrote home, as can be seen in the answers of both her parents and Martha. She either did not suspect that she was already carrying a child, or may have felt constrained not to talk about it yet. (In the few letters that survive from her six months in the South, there is never a mention of the fact. These are all, however, letters written to her from various family members.)

Mary's father continued in his ways as the stern disciplinarian and rigorous Calvinist in the family. In light of this, it is only fair to quote his entire part of the letter the Bakers first wrote to Mary in February, after first hearing from her. It illustrates the rigid theological bent in his thought, but also the genuine solicitude he felt for his youngest daughter:

> Yours of Jan. 25th came to hand yesterday, the contents of which brings to our minds both sensations of joy and sorrow, and I can say with Job - the thing I greatly feared has come unto you. But commit your ways to the Lord and he will sustain you. My space to write is very limited. I will only say you and Mr. Glover have my best wishes both for life or death and for this I would say remember thy Creator in the days of thy youth. In answer to your request respecting the dealings of the Church, there has nothing especial occurred since you left. I will conclude my part of the letter by recommending to both of you to give your hearts to God and if it should be to quit that

> unhealthy clime and come to a better, it would be pleasing to me.
>
> – From your affectionate Father, M. Baker [1]

His theology obviously lay close to the tip of his tongue, and what he meant by the reference to what he had "greatly feared" is unclear.

Her mother's part of the same letter would not have accomplished much toward assuaging Mary's homesickness. She said, in part: "We miss your good cheer. I look out at the window and say how I wish I could see George and Mary coming over the hill, but I must not enter into particulars of feelings… Mary, everything reminds me of you, the house appointed by you and me is precious for I enjoy it."

It seems unlikely that Mary discussed her pregnancy in her letters, as a further exchange of letters three months later still contains nothing in them about the subject. Abigail wrote her daughter then (in May) with questions about her overall health. "Don't write too much for fear it hurts you. How is your health and how is your back. Can you lie down and rise again without a groan?… Have you an appetite? Does your food distress you? How do you recreate yourself? Are you able to sew or do anything? I hope you remember the Sabbath day." She also reminded Mary to think well of her father, "for many have been the prayers he has offered for you." [2]

Those who remembered Mrs. Glover in later years from her brief life in the Carolinas spoke of her as adjusting to the new life quite well. One recalls: "I saw her on the street, and in church. She was extremely beautiful, one of the prettiest young women I have ever seen… she began contributing rhymes to the local paper." [3] In fact, one of this woman's relatives parodied several of her rhymes in the same paper. Thus Mrs. Glover readily continued the habit she had already started in New Hampshire of writing without hesitation for local publications. Another said, "She was brilliant, beautiful, cultured, witty and charming, and always sincerely interested in those around her."[4]

Later in the spring George Glover had to go up to Wilmington, North Carolina, to attend to his business. He had contracted to build a cathedral on the island of Haiti and had been gathering the lumber for the project in Wilmington. Had he lived, Mary would possibly have had a trip to Haiti in the offing. One of her poems of the period looks forward to visiting the West Indies, so they must have discussed the possibility of her going with him.

It is also possible that one reason for being in Wilmington was to rebuild the Custom House tower in that port city. Wilmington had had a large fire in 1843 and another one in January 1844 that had destroyed the Custom House. Several builders had been brought in from other cities to work on reconstruction projects.[5]

Wilmington was having an epidemic of yellow fever, and George became ill with the disease. Mary was not allowed to nurse him because of her pregnancy, but she prayed steadily for his life. After Glover died, the doctor in charge of his case credited Mary's prayers with sustaining him for a longer time than he would otherwise have lasted. Fearing that the illness might end as it did, Glover made arrangements after he fell ill for fellow Masons to take care of Mary's return to New England if he should die.

Travel was extremely complicated before the day of the long-distance railroad. Mary had to return to New Hampshire by a combination of stagecoach, short rail journeys, and coastal ships as far as New York. The longest single rail journey she could take without changing trains was from Philadelphia to New York. Glover's fellow Masons arranged for Mary to be accompanied on the trip home as far as New York. Her brother George came down to New York to meet her and bring her the rest of the way home.

So, in little more than six months the marriage that was to have brought her fulfillment and a purpose in living was ended.

Furthermore, she was ill-suited, either physically or financially, to care for the baby that was about to be born. Glover had had a thriving building business, but had apparently not made a great deal of money yet. While they were staying in Wilmington, there was either a fire on the dock or his lumber was stolen. Whatever the case, his estate was left owing the bill for lumber that he no longer had. He may have had a household servant or two as a slave, but it is likely that any slaves he had were used to settle the bills of his estate. This was common practice at the time. In fact, Glover had jokingly written to Abigail Tilton that if she would name her first child after him he would send her a slave. (In later years Mrs. Eddy recalled that she had freed Glover's slaves upon his death, but there is no way to reconstruct the event. It would have been difficult to have effectively freed them, since there was no provision for free blacks in the South of 1844. There is no doubt that Mrs. Eddy *would* have freed his slaves if she had had the prerogative to do so.)

At the turn of the century, the then treasurer of the North Carolina Society of the Colonial Dames of America recalled that her grandfather and aunts had often spoken of Mrs. Glover at the time she was widowed. All admired her beauty and culture. "She was so young, frail, and lovely, and it seemed so cruel that Mrs. Glover should have had such a hard experience, and then to have been left penniless."[6] From the memory and social position of those who knew the Glovers when they were in the South as a married couple, it can at least be established beyond a doubt that the young Glover was well liked, regarded as competent, and a man who could get along with others (judging particularly by his being on the governor's honorary staff). As for Mary, it is also clear that, in spite of her pregnancy and possibly other unrelated physical problems, she was learning in a short period to enter into the social life of a people who at first seemed quite foreign to her previous experience.

Besides being widowed and left without any money, Mary also suffered a shock from Glover's sudden passing. The return or continuation of her old difficulties, combined with a difficult delivery, left her in no better condition physically than financially to care for young George Washington Glover II. Unable to care for him after his birth in September 1844, she had to let him be nursed and cared for by another woman in Sanbornton: Mahala Sanborn, the daughter of the local blacksmith and already a frequent helper around the Baker household. Thus, instead of the joys of marriage and young motherhood, Mary had been deprived in short order of both. And, in fact, she was never able to take complete charge of her son.

There were few outside events to give relief to the routine of Mrs. Glover's life from the autumn of 1844 until she married Daniel Patterson almost nine years later. She was in extreme pain at times, suffering both from some kind of digestive problem (which accounts for her following the Graham method of diet for a time) and from a spinal injury. The spinal problem may have stemmed from her son's birth, but there is no record of what in today's terms would be considered a reliable medical diagnosis of the physical ailment. Her father would at times even hold her and rock her in order to soothe his frail daughter.

Mrs. Glover tried a brief experiment in 1846 in organizing a kindergarten in Sanbornton Bridge. She was encouraged to do this by Rev. Richard Rust, a Methodist minister who was principal of the New Hampshire Conference Seminary, the successor institution to the Sanbornton Academy she had attended briefly before her marriage. Either her periodic ill health or her lack of formal preparation for teaching ended this experiment, although Rust occasionally called on her as a substitute teacher at the seminary itself.

She also continued to keep up her writing for local periodicals. Not all of her work was published, but several poems did appear in the *New Hampshire Patriot* (four in 1848 alone), and she did some writing for a Masonic magazine. She followed political affairs closely; the subjects of her writing were the political topics and actors of the day. In a poem she wrote, published in the *New Hampshire Patriot* early in 1850, she even reacted to the failed revolutions in the year 1848 in Europe:

> From o'er the wave a wail of woe
> Booms like the midnight gun;
> And shall our free-born souls forego
> Scorn for the Austrian crown,
> In purple gore of martyrs dyed?
> Life, liberty down-trod!
> Brave Hungary, thy tears be dried,
> Stretch forth thine arm to God.[7]

None of this provided an adequate income for her to live independently, though. Nor did it bring the kind of satisfaction she might have found in being a busy wife and mother. It was not surprising, given her upbringing and religious orientation, that she wanted to live a life of service. But how? This is shown in a letter she wrote to her brother George in Connecticut early in 1848:

> … yet George you cannot conceive what a strange spirit I posess in such things. About the time I should judge from your letter that you were sick, I dreamed of you three nights successively and always awoke in trouble; so it was last Autumn when I was at Boston…. Oh! if I could be near you when you suffer. I might prove by *acts* what it is no use to talk about….
>
> I think it will event as it did with Albert [apparently talking about her own expected early demise].[8]

A few months later she described herself to her sister Martha as "being again on the billow of my moonless sea, waiting for a gale more friendly, or a surge of sorrow to steer my course for the ensuing summer. I feel as if I must *begin* something this summer, if my health is sufficient. I am weary working my way through life from the *middle* to the *end*."[9]

One cannot be certain to what extent Mrs. Glover expected to eventually support herself as a writer. Writing and school-teaching were the most obvious careers open to women at the time, and her submission of poetry to various periodicals, even before her marriage to Glover, indicates a steady intent to be heard through the vehicle of print. One letter that survives does indicate that others did take her work seriously. It is from Townsend Abell, in Middletown, Connecticut. She had written something for the *Connecticut Odd Fellow* magazine, and he was soliciting her continuing contributions:

> … we must depend much upon the encouragements of good correspondents. May we consider you as one? To tell you that I have been greatly pleased with your writings (for I had before noted your name) would be superfluous after entreating your kindly remembrance of me.[10]

She also wrote, much later in life, that she had agreed for her son to be taken from her (in 1849) partly so that she would have her full time available to pursuing her writing career. Whatever the reason, the next year, 1849, saw several changes begin to take place in her material circumstances. George married her old friend, Martha Rand, early in 1849. Then her mother, who had been a bulwark to Mary in her years of widowhood and illness, fell ill. Abigail passed on toward the end of the year. In a letter that was heartrending and at the same time matter-of-fact, Mary informed her brother George:

> This morning looks on us bereft of a Mother! Yes, that angel on earth is now in Heaven! I have prayed for support to write this letter, but I find it impossible to tell you particulars at this time… Oh! George, what is left on earth to *me!* But oh, my Mother – she has *suffered long with me.* Let me then be willing she should now *rejoice,* and I bear on till I follow her. I cannot write more. My grief overpowers me. Write to me.
>
> Your affec' Sister,
> Mary

> Died last night at half-past seven o'clock; will be buried next Saturday. I wish you could be here. [11]

❖ ❖ ❖ ❖

Within a year of the death of her mother, Mary's father was to remarry. One can imagine the various family conferences that were held to determine what to do with Mary and her son George, who had also been living with Mary in the family's homestead. A stepmother could not be expected to automatically step in and care for a frail stepdaughter. Moreover, the arrangement with George, who was with his mother part of the time but not always under her care, had to be considered. The decision to have him live with his former nursemaid, Mahala Sanborn, now married to one Russell Cheney, was probably made partly out of a family feeling that his mother would not, in any case, live long enough to raise him to maturity. Mary's wish to be free to write was probably also one factor in the decision. Her sister Abigail agreed to have Mary move in with her. But Abi was also raising a young son of her own. She did not want to take on the responsibility for both a semi-invalid sister and a young child who was not particularly well-disciplined. (It would seem, though, for most families in a similar situation at that period, that it would not have been an unusual solution to have taken in both Mary and young George.) So the decision for Mary and George to live apart was agreed upon, as difficult as it was for Mary to see it through. She wrote of it years later in *Retrospection and Introspection*:

> I had no training for self-support, and my home I regarded as very precious. The night before my child was taken from me, I knelt by his side throughout the dark hours, hoping for a vision of relief from this trial. The following lines are taken from my poem, "Mother's Darling," written after this separation: –
>
> Thy smile through tears, as sunshine o'er the sea,
>   Awoke new beauty in the surge's roll!

Oh, life is dead, bereft of all, with thee, –
  Star of my earthly hope, babe of my soul.[12]

Mrs. Glover had very likely experienced one other major disappointment at about this time. During her years of widowhood she had attracted several of the young men in Sanbornton, in spite of her frailty. She seems to have discouraged all but one of them, John Bartlett. Bartlett was a local young man who had gone to Harvard Law School. When he graduated in the spring of 1848, Mary had traveled down to Cambridge for his commencement. Since she traveled very little in these years, that fact in itself would indicate that something deeper than a casual friendship had been established. Then, in 1849 he went out to California to establish his law practice in Sacramento. Just a few weeks after her mother's death, Mary received word that Bartlett had also died. In her scrapbook, next to the obituary, she noted: "He was engaged to marry Mrs. Glover when he left N. H." Was it a formal engagement? There seems to have been no recognition of it within the family. Perhaps they had agreed to marry as soon as he got established in California. In any case, another window to fulfillment seemed to have been shut in her face.

The fact that she was interested in Bartlett does indicate that she had not given up the idea of marrying again. And over the next few years, when she was living with Abigail and her young family, the desire to be free of even a well-meaning sister's domination must have caused her to give considerable thought as to how she could bring about a change. The "change" appeared in the form of one Daniel Patterson, a distant relative of Mark Baker's new wife, Elizabeth Patterson. Daniel Patterson had grown up in Maine and was either an itinerant dentist or one who could not make a consistent success out of his practice in any one locality for long. He had practiced in several towns in Maine and was living in Franklin, New Hampshire, just a few miles from Sanbornton Bridge, at the time Mary met him.

By the end of 1852 they knew each other well. One letter Mary wrote to Patterson about this time was signed, "Yours in

Toothless Trouble." On New Year's Day 1853 she wrote him that she had just read *Uncle Tom's Cabin,* but did not particularly like it. By the early spring of 1853 they had become engaged, and then disengaged. Mary may have been troubled by stories she heard about Patterson's wandering past, but what she wrote to him about was religion, and it was a wholly genuine concern on her part: "... *I* have a fixed feeling that to yield my *religion* to yours I *could not,* other things compared to this, are but a grain to the universe." [13] Patterson, however, evidently suspected that it was Mary's father who disapproved of both his Baptist religion and his character. After a brief interval, the letters commenced again.

One fact that would not automatically be known today is that at that time dentists were often practicing homeopathy on the side. The medical profession had little regulation as yet, and homeopathy itself was a new and promising branch of medicine. When Mary writes to him about her illness, it is partly from her growing dependence on his friendship and very likely also partly a sharing of information about a new approach to medicine that interested them both. She wrote in April that she had taken some morphine, the only regularly prescribed painkiller at the time, "which I so much disapprove." [14] She also wrote about consulting her cousin, Dr. Morrill, who was a homeopathic physician:

> I still now say I am sitting up two hours and my worst symptoms are greatly relieved. My strength is very much exhausted by my sufferings. I shall require time to restore this.
>
> I have not called a Physician but receive counsel of Dr. Morrill; the *practice* has been all my own, and considering the severe attack, my previous debility, and chronic complaints, I think we managed a little wisely for me to be on the list of recovery today. [15]

Dr. Patterson wanted to marry Mary for a variety of reasons to which one cannot assign a precise priority. In her healthier moments she was still an attractive woman, just over thirty years of age. Her family was well known in the area, and he may have thought that the Baker connection would not hurt him professionally. Mary's curiosity, such as her interest in homeopathy, may have also told him that here was a woman with whom he could enjoy discussing something more than the weather. But he made no pretentions to being anything but what he was. He wrote to her, "It is proper that you should know me thoroughly so that when we are married… you may not look for either a philosophic, or a Poetical letter from your husband… my Dear you will never find me better in this respect than I have exhibited myself." [16]

The only trouble was that he wasn't even a non-poetical dentist in a consistent enough way. They married in June 1853 and lived in Franklin for the next two years. Mary's health was not good, and her husband's dental practice slipped into decline. But the biggest disappointment for Mary was that she did not get to have her son George come back to live with them. She wrote in *Retrospection:*

> My dominant thought in marrying again was to get back my child, but after our marriage his stepfather was not willing he should have a home with me. [17]

Patterson may not have actually agreed to take George back. Or, Mary's poor health after the marriage may have made it plain to him that she was unable to care for her son. Whichever the case, Abigail intervened to help, or so she thought. (She also may have played a role in getting Mary together with Patterson in the first place.) The Tiltons owned a small house farther north in New Hampshire, in the town of North Groton. Abi offered the house to the Pattersons if they would assume the mortgage on the property. It included a saw mill, and Patterson got hold of some timberland. The idea was that the income from the saw mill, together with some income from his dental practice, should give them a decent living. Meanwhile, Mary would again be close to her son, who was living with Mahala Cheney and her husband in the same town.

Patterson, it appears, did not enjoy having the son come to visit. By this time, young George was close to being a teenager. He had not been well groomed, what with his being passed between two homes when he was very small and then living with the simple and uneducated Cheney family. Patterson also felt that George's coming into the house for a visit or to play was upsetting to Mary. So, when a year later the Cheneys decided to move out West – actually, to Minnesota – Patterson arranged for them to take George with them without telling Mary.

When she found out about this, she had a further relapse and more physical difficulties. For a year and a half Dr. Patterson attended mainly to her needs, so his declining dental practice was not entirely due to his own neglect of his profession. Martha wrote to her brother George, "Mary has been sick several months and I expect they are brought to absolute want! He has done no work and takes care of her *alone.*" [18] During this period, the mortgage on the small house also fell into arrears. Mary's sister, Martha, for some unexplained reason had now become the holder of the mortgage, and she was reluctant to foreclose on her own sister. One can sense the not uncommon web of crosscurrents in the relationships within the family in this letter from Mark's second wife, Elizabeth Patterson, to George Baker in the summer of 1856:

> You spoke of Martha foreclosing her business with Doctor Patterson. Your Father spoke to Col Kate about it he says the time is not up until next spring that she can do it but he thinks she is safe haveing enough in her hands to secure her. . .We do not hear one word about Mary's health when he has written lately to anny one he says nothing about her they do not write to us she wrote to some one that she wanted me to go up and take care of her but I thought she needed some one who had some wit even one tallant but it was no use for me to go as in her opinion I did not possess even that.

> We do not know what will become of them as it requires all his time to take care of her We pitty them. Mr. Cheney wife and little George was here about the time of Marys Death [Martha's daughter Mary died in 1856] they have moved to Minosoti they arived in safety in six days much pleased with the place.[19]

Martha did not actually foreclose on the mortgage until the spring of 1860, when she had given up all hope of getting payment. Mary's health had continued to deteriorate, and the family may have also decided it was better to get her out of North Groton.

In the interval, Mary had been aided not only by Patterson, but also by a blind girl, Myra Smith, to whom she became strongly attached. The blind girl could see enough to get about the house and be of use to Mary. When the weather was right, she would arrange for her bed to be moved to a porch or balcony where she could enjoy the sunlight. She stayed with the Pattersons the entire five years they were in North Groton and even went with them down to nearby Rumney when they were evicted from their property in 1860.

❖ ❖ ❖ ❖

In spite of recurrent and at times constant illness and pain, Mrs. Patterson read all she could during these years. Myra Smith's sister would be up at the house visiting frequently, and she said in later years that, whenever Mrs. Patterson was not too ill to read, she would have a book in her hands. It was during this period that Mary acquired her knowledge about homeopathy and performed the few homeopathic experiments she refers to in her writings. This acquaintance with homeopathic theory was as critical in leading her thought to the threshold of Christian Science as was her soon-to-happen acquaintance with the mesmerist, Phineas Quimby. However, partly because of the controversy that came to exist over Quimby, that relationship has been overstressed, and the homeopathic one has received less attention than it deserves.

During the middle years of the nineteenth century, homeopathy emerged as a serious challenger to allopathic, or regular, medical practice. Developed by S.C.F. Hahnemann, a physician from Meissen, Germany, homeopathy had been practiced in Germany since 1796. It was brought to America in 1825 and quickly spread. It was introduced into New Hampshire in the year 1840. Mrs. Patterson was most familiar with the theory through a book known as Hull's *Jahr* (actually, it was Hull's editing of *Jahr's New Manual of Homeopathic Practice).*

It may seem only academic in this era of microbiology and gene technology to mention the theory behind homeopathy. Actually, homeopathic practice made a major contribution to the development of medicine in America. The basic medical part of the theory lay in the concept that the same medicine, or drug, that could induce in a healthy patient the symptoms of the sick patient could be used to cure that sick patient. A corollary to the theory, although not a part of it in the beginning, was that this same drug could be attenuated and actually become more powerful through its attenuation. This was the element in the theory that most attracted Mrs. Patterson's attention. In the Christian Science textbook she relates the details of a case she personally handled during these years. In this case, Mrs. Patterson continued the medication that the woman's doctor had been using. She says:

> I began to fear an aggravation of symptoms from their prolonged use, and told the patient so; but she was unwilling to give up the medicine while she was recovering. It then occurred to me to give her unmedicated pellets and watch the result. I did so, and she continued to gain. Finally she said that she would give up her medicine for one day, and risk the effects. After trying this, she informed me that she could get along two days without globules; but on the third day she again suffered, and was relieved by taking them. She went on in this way, taking the unmedicated pellets, – and receiving occasional visits from me, – but employing no other means, and she was cured.[20]

In reading this, one must remember that the practice of medicine was virtually unregulated at the time. The incident doesn't tell us about any other relationship Mrs. Patterson may have had with the patient, or the kind of consulting she may have done with her dentist husband about it. It does very clearly indicate, however, the direction already being taken by Mrs. Patterson's thinking: the primacy of thought in governing one's health. She was still a good distance away from understanding the method by which thought could affect the body, though, or from distinguishing between the thought that is not much more than wishful thinking and the thinking that is based on what she would call a metaphysical fact. So she was not able to apply it consistently to her own chronic illness.

A link also existed between at least some of the homeopathic physicians and the Swedish mystic, Emanuel Swedenborg (1688-1772). Homeopathy had been introduced into America by a Danish physician, Hans Gram, and Gram himself became a member of Swedenborg's Church of the New Jerusalem. Homeopathy itself split into two "sects," the more mystic of the two emphasizing the mental element in administering the drug. Hahnemann had written in his textbook of homeopathy, the *Organon,* "It is only by means of the spiritual influence of a morbific agent that our spiritual vital power can be diseased, and in like manner only by the spiritual operation of medicine can health be restored."[21]

At the turn of the twentieth century, there were thousands of homeopathic doctors with several million patients in the United States alone. Homeopathy had found a more welcome home here than in any other country. To appreciate its standing at the time, one need only look back at what the famous Eleventh Edition of the *Encyclopedia Britannica* (1910) said in summing up its contribution:

> Hahnemann undoubtedly deserves the credit of being the first to break decidedly with the old school of medical practice, in which, forgetful of the teachings

> of Hippocrates, nature was either overlooked or rudely opposed by wrong and ungentle methods. We can scarcely now estimate the force of character and of courage which was implied in his abandoning the common lines of medicine. More than this, he and his followers showed results in the treatment of disease which compared very favourably with the results of contemporary orthodox practice.[22]

One does not know to what degree some of these homeopathic theories entered into Mrs. Patterson's thinking. It would seem obvious that she was more than vaguely familiar with them if she herself went as far as experimenting with homeopathy. This acquaintance with homeopathy may have been the one bright light – other than her constant companionship with her Bible – that came to her during the five dark years in North Groton. These years finally came to an end when the mortgage on the house was foreclosed. Abi again came to her sister's aid, arriving in North Groton in a carriage to fetch her and bring her down to the village of Rumney Station.

Rumney Station, today's Rumney Depot, was on the railroad that ran through New Hampshire. The area was thus not entirely isolated from civilization. Both the Rumney house and the one in North Groton are modest by today's standards, but they were solid buildings and entirely adequate for a married couple. North Gorton was at the top of a large hill. Much of the area was being cut for timber, so there would have been some vista of the New Hampshire mountains from some locations. The house Mary had lived in, though, sits at the edge of a noisy stream and, at that time, had a road running directly in front of it. Across the road was the sawmill, powered by water diverted from the stream. The sawmill was several times larger than the modest house and, whenever it was in use, would not have made the house a place for contemplation. Both locations, over the period of seven years spent in them, must have contributed to Mary's feeling of being cut off from all that mattered to her.

Each of the moves since she had remarried had seemed to foreshadow another dark period in her life. Patterson's dental practice in Franklin had not worked out, nor had he allowed her son to come and live with them. In North Groton she had, on the whole, been in a state of serious illness, and George had been removed from her. Again it was Abi who made the arrangements (and possibly provided the funds) for the Pattersons to board with a family in Rumney Station. After a short time Patterson found a small house in Rumney village (another section of Rumney), and Myra Smith, the blind girl, rejoined her as her housekeeper.

But this time a new problem arose. Within a year the Civil War had started, and Patterson saw this as an occasion to get away from the humdrum of home. He was not the first husband to get this idea, nor should one think that this was his sole motive. But in March of 1862, with a special appointment from the governor of New Hampshire, he set out with money collected from citizens of New Hampshire to aid Northern sympathizers living in the South. He went to Washington, and from there, to view the recent battle site of Bull Run in Virginia (just outside Washington). While reconnoitering at Bull Run, he and some friends were captured by units of the Confederate army. Mary first heard of this in a letter she received from him in April 1862. He told of his capture and asked her to help get him released in a prisoner exchange. However, at the moment there were no prisoner exchanges! He also wrote, "I left my travelling bag and a new pair of boots at 381 Pennsylvania Avenue, Washington, at Mrs. C. W. Heydon's." That was likely a local rooming house, but no further explanation was given. He signed himself, "Your affectionate Husband."[23]

However, if Patterson was not to be released immediately, his imprisonment indirectly led to the partial release of his wife. For what transpired next, she may have been able to accomplish only by being forced to improvise on her own. In Patterson's absence, Abi had again come to the rescue, bringing Mary down from Rumney to live in her house in Sanbornton Bridge once more.

With the possible exception of her unwillingness to take in young George at the same time Mary had come to live with her, Abi had looked after Mary as an older sister normally would. She had seen Mary's frailty since at least the latter's teen years. She had had a strong hand in many of the events of Mary's life: most probably, in her marriage to Patterson, in the decision to board George with the Cheneys, in her move to North Groton, in her rescue from there to Rumney, and now in taking her once more into her own home. Moreover, Abi had the sturdy personality of all the members of the Baker family. It would have taken a rare sister, certainly a more humble one than the strong-willed Abi, to have looked at Mary through any lens other than the memory of frailty and failure, even when the events in Mary's life eventually deserved a more positive assessment.

❖ ❖ ❖ ❖

Almost two decades had now passed since Mary Baker had married George Glover and started down the path of young womanhood. She was now back to where she had started, only instead of living with her parents she had become the virtual ward of her oldest sister. What had been accomplished? What was there to start her on the career that was, over the next forty years, to make her a world-famous personage?

There had been twenty years of almost continual disappointment. The brief but happy marriage to Glover had been ended in six months by his death. She had been unable to care for her own son, and he was now lost even to her occasional visits because of his removal to the West. Her health had definitely declined. While she had been unable to take care of her son in the 1840s, she had written occasionally for the newspapers and magazines of the day and had briefly tried to run a kindergarten. But since her marriage to Patterson, she had become a semi-invalid with no apparent prospects for ever enjoying a normal life again. Moreover, she realized that her marriage to Patterson had been a mistake, even though there could still be moments of genuine tenderness between the two. And now this disappointing husband was sitting in a Southern prison!

On the other side of her "ledger," she had had some personal experience with homeopathy. And the emphasis of one branch of homeopathy on the mental element in treatment had gotten her to thinking along new lines. She had also made a personal vow to God that, if she ever regained her health, she would spend the rest of her life trying to help others do the same.

Nevertheless, there can be no doubt that the end of this period of her life found her becalmed on a "moonless sea," as she had described her feelings years before in one of her letters to her sister. While she could not appreciate it at the time, she would later write that "every material dependence" had failed her. Once a widow, now married to a man who could not support her, bereft of the companionship of her son, a burden on her family, without an independent income or any income while Patterson remained in prison, and with seriously failing health, almost all the lights in the lamp of her human sense of existence had been extinguished. Was it, one may ask, actually an essential part of her life story that every normal path to health and happiness be closed to her in order to bring her to that singleness of purpose in seeing her way through what was about to begin in her experience? She was to write later in the Christian Science textbook:

> The author's medical researches and experiments had prepared her thought for the metaphysics of Christian Science. Every material dependence had failed her in her search for truth; and she can now understand why, and can see the means by which mortals are divinely driven to a spiritual source for health and happiness.[24]

But it cannot have been that obvious to her in the spring of 1862. The spark that did keep the lamp of life aglow was her trust in God and the strong sense of independence this had given her from her youth onward. Her acceptance of responsibility for her own life, in contrast to a "humble" acceptance of one's lot in life, which was the more common reaction to multiple disappointments such as hers, explains her continuous search for a solution to her ill health. And now that persistence was about to be rewarded in a manner that would carry her forward beyond what she or any of her family at the time could have dreamed.

While Dr. Patterson had still been living in Rumney with his wife, the two of them had heard of the curative powers of a magnetic doctor, Phineas Quimby. Willing to try anything for his wife's release from suffering, Patterson had written to Quimby in the summer of 1862, when he heard that the doctor might be traveling to Concord, New Hampshire:

> My wife has been an invalid for a number of years; is not able to sit up but a little, and we wish to have the benefit of your wonderful power in her case. If you are soon coming to Concord I shall carry her up to you, and if you are not coming there we may try to carry her to Portland if you remain there.[25]

But Quimby did not make a trip to Concord that year. However, early the next year Mrs. Patterson wrote to him herself, asking if he could visit her. She wanted to go to Portland, but did not have the means to get there. Dependent on her sister Abi for financial support during these years, she had to some extent to follow Abi's wishes. And Abi was suspicious of Quimby and his reputed mesmerism. However, Abi did agree to send Mary to a water cure in Hill, New Hampshire, run by a Dr. Vail, in the summer of 1862.

While Mary was undergoing the water cure treatment there, with no good effect, she heard several stories of the cures reputed to Quimby and became even more determined to get to Portland to see him. Finally, in August she wrote:

> 1. Dear Sir: I am constrained to write you, feeling as I do the great mistake I made in not trying to reach you when I had more strength.

> 2. I have been at this Water Cure between 2 and 3 months, and when I came could walk 1/2 mile, now I can sit up but a few minutes at one time. Suppose I have faith sufficient to start for you, do you think I can reach you without sinking from the effects of the journey? I am so excitable I think I could keep alive till I reached you but then would there be foundation sufficient for you to restore me - is *the* question. I should rather die with my friends at S. Bridge, hence I shall go to you to *live* or to them to *die* very soon. Please answer this *yourself.*[26]

After the turn of this century, Quimby's son, George, told one of Mrs. Eddy's biographers that he remembered having to assist Mrs. Patterson up the steps of the hotel in Portland where his father had his offices. She was too weak to climb them herself. She certainly could not at that moment have known the full significance that day would have for her. But her independence and perseverance had brought her this far — plus her resolute belief that God had not meant for her life to be wasted in ill health. It would still be a long road to Christian Science, but twenty seemingly wasted years were about to come to an end.

Entr'acte 2

Hypnotism
From Mesmer to Quimby

Franz Mesmer, the Viennese doctor who gave to hypnotism its first name, mesmerism, does not himself belong to the life story of Mary Baker Eddy. But to understand the role of Phineas Quimby in her story, it is necessary to make a detour in time and to briefly trace the lineage that runs from Mesmer to Quimby. The purpose of this exercise is not only to make the correct historical connections. The lineage also makes it abundantly clear that Quimby's practice and all the way stations to it from Mesmer's own time were founded on materialistic theories that were entirely antipodal to what became known as Christian Science.

At the same time, to trace this history is not to denigrate the experiments of Mesmer nor to label Quimby as a charlatan. Both men, though of very opposite backgrounds, represented a pioneering effort that, by its own lights, was an honest one. When approaching any kind of medical practice dealing with mental control or influence over others, one has an obligation to be particularly sensitive to the potential for the misuse of such techniques. That has become obvious in modern times through our awareness of the potential for either benefit or harm in the relationship between a psychiatrist and his patient. But leaving aside the question of the correctness of the theories of either of these men, the motives of both Mesmer and Quimby appear to have been to alleviate suffering. One, Mesmer, belonged to the well-educated elite of Europe at the end of the Age of Enlightenment; the other, Quimby, was a prototype of the rather poorly educated, but honest, hardworking New England stock of the early nineteenth century.

Mesmer, born in Weil, on the German side of Lake Constance, in 1733, began the practice of medicine in Vienna in 1766. He had already earned a doctorate in philosophy and had studied law before deciding to take up medicine. Some eight years into his practice, his attention was drawn to the possible healthful effects of magnetizing portions of the human body. The discovery was not his, but upon hearing of the practice and believing that it had worked wonders in a particular case, he decided to experiment with it. He in turn found that he could produce what he believed to be some remarkable cures by passing a magnet over portions of the human body. As his practice developed along these lines, he was made to feel unwelcome in Vienna, the self-satisfied, conservative capital and cultural center of the Hapsburg Empire. After some time spent at the royal court of Bavaria in Munich, he moved to Paris in 1778, staying there until the Reign of Terror during the French Revolution was almost upon him in 1792.

Even while he had been living in Vienna, he had discovered that the properties of the magnet actually had nothing to do with the cure. He did not, however, take the next step and discern that it was the influence, or suggestion, of the doctor himself that effected a change in the patient. Rather, he postulated the existence of a kind of magnetic fluid, which he termed "animal magnetism," which could be affected by the laying on of hands on the patient's body.

His practice in Paris became so popular and included so many of the pre-Revolutionary aristocrats (including the Marquis de Lafayette), that Louis XVI appointed a Royal Commission to look into animal magnetism. The commission included the American scientist, Benjamin Franklin. This commission conducted as thorough a study as it could, including attending some of the mass sessions at which Mesmer's patients touched hands and sat around a tub of water in dimly lit salons, while he created a mental mood further open to suggestion through the playing of music.

The commission, except for one dissenter, reached the conclusion that there was no such thing as a magnetic fluid and that, therefore, animal magnetism did not exist: "… the commission has unanimously come to the conclusion that there is nothing to show that the fluid of animal magnetism exists and that, consequently, this non-existent fluid can serve no useful purpose..." But its members had to admit that they had seen undeniable phenomena, some of which included highly negative states of consciousness. "There is undoubtedly some power at work, a power that influences men's actions and dominates them. This power is the property of the magnetizer himself."

Antoine Laurent de Jussieu, a second-generation member of a family of renowned French botanists, who was a member of the commission, was not satisfied with the official explanation that no magnetic fluid existed. Although he did not know how to describe some of the experiments he had witnessed, he allowed at least the possibility of there being some element or power "which is transferable from one human being to another and which often produces a visible effect upon the person to whom it is transmitted." It was this power, known at first as mesmerism and today as hypnotism, that was being exercised by Mesmer. For the rest of his days, though, Mesmer publicly clung to the notion of the magnetic fluid. The excesses of the French Revolution made it necessary for him to leave France in 1792. Finding Vienna as unfriendly as previously, he took refuge in Switzerland, where he remained for the rest of his long career. Toward the end of his life he was invited to come to the University of Berlin, but he preferred to continue his researches in peace in Switzerland. He died in 1815.

Mesmer's theory entered a new phase with the discovery by the Marquis de Puysegur that he could put patients into what we would call today a hypnotic state, in which he could direct their actions. Hypnotism thereupon entered a new phase: it became a fad. Demonstrations of a hypnotist's ability to put a patient into a waking sleep became popular, and the fad shortly spread to America. In 1837, another Frenchman, Charles Poyen, wrote a book called *Progress of Animal Magnetism in New England.* Poyen had been giving demonstrations of hypnotism for a few years, and it was probably through Poyen that Phineas Quimby first heard of hypnotism. Up until this time, Quimby had been a successful New England clockmaker. He began following Poyen from town to town, intrigued by his demonstrations of hypnosis and wanting to learn more about how he performed them.

It also happened that, just as a hypnotist likes to find a subject who is easy to put into a trance, Quimby knew a young man, Lucius Burkmar, in his own town of Belfast, Maine, who could be easily hypnotized. In this state, Burkmar became clairvoyant. One of his specialties, it seems, was his ability to "look" into a patient's body and describe what was ailing him. From 1843 to 1847, Quimby and Burkmar traveled around New England several times, demonstrating this talent that Burkmar exhibited. Then he was loaned out to another hypnotist, John Bovee Dods, who was trying to find possible uses for hypnosis in healing disease. After Burkmar would allegedly pinpoint the ailing organ, Dods would prescribe the medicine, often a very expensive one.

When Burkmar returned to Quimby, the latter, who had begun practicing on patients, questioned whether a cheaper medicine might not work as well as the more expensive remedies. From this, it was a short step to his own original contribution in this line of development, that the medicine itself did not matter; it was, rather, the confidence expressed by the doctor in what he did that seemed to have the curative effect. Beginning in 1847, Quimby embarked on his own practice without the use of Burkmar as a medium to tell him what was ailing the patient. For the next fifteen years, he developed a practice that certainly depended on mental suggestion and continued to use some modified form of bodily contact. But he had gone a long way from Mesmer and his Parisian salon practice.

Quimby's kind of medicine did not endure. When hypnotism is sometimes used in medical practice today, it is generally as a means of alleviating pain or helping a patient recall some past event. And without Mrs. Eddy's passing connection with him, Quimby would be only a minor byway, if that, in the history of medical practice in the United States. Most of the elements in his system were diametrically opposed to Christian Science. But there were superficial similarities, none of which is more important than the fact that Mrs. Eddy kept alive the term "animal magnetism," even while giving it a broader and wholly negative meaning within the context of her metaphysical system. To see to what extent Quimby's practice had developed in the fifteen years between 1847 and 1862, we may proceed with the story of Mrs. Glover on that eventful day in 1862.

Chapter 3

The Period Leading to the Discovery
Quimbyism Both a Catalyst and a Cul-de-sac

The first meeting of Mary Baker Patterson with Phineas Quimby deserves to be acknowledged as one of the steps by which Mrs. Patterson climbed the road to Christian Science. There is irony in this, in that Quimby did not consider himself a religious man at all, and the frail human figure that came to him for help had no premonition of where that day would lead her. Yet from that day forward, Mrs. Patterson's thought was so energized that she did not stop searching until the main positions of what came to be Christian Science had become clear to her. This process would take virtually a decade to complete, although the most important steps were to come in 1866 and the immediately following years.

But on this crisp autumn day in October 1862, Mary was to experience a temporary fulfillment of the biblical promise of freedom. The memory of these days in Portland, Maine, would strengthen her in her persistence to find the complete freedom that she felt belonged to her as a child of God.

After being helped up the steps of the International Hotel in Portland to the waiting rooms of Dr. Quimby, she was soon admitted to the room where he practiced. Quimby by this time had white hair and a white beard, which probably helped establish an air of authority. He was known for the kindly look on his face and the warm, yet piercing eyes he would fix on his patients. Although he did not practice hypnotism in the explicit sense of putting another person into a hypnotic trance, his kind of treatment could basically be described as one of mental suggestion. He himself referred to it as the "talking cure."

As the previous essay indicated, Quimby usually told his patients that he would tell them what was ailing them, and that his explanation itself would be the cure. Looking at Mrs. Patterson, who, it should be remembered, had given him some inkling of the state of her thinking and of her family affairs from the few letters she had already written to him, he told her that she was "held in bondage by the opinions of her family and physicians." He also told her that "her animal spirit was reflecting its grief upon her body and calling it spinal disease."[1]

Although Quimby did not literally hypnotize his patients anymore, he did include a few signs of physical manipulation as part of his practice. Ordinarily he dipped the hair of his female patients in water. Whether or not he did that with Mary Patterson, he did rub her head, in the belief he shared with other mesmerists that it helped the flow of electricity in her body. He also told her that she would be cured. This attitude of confidence on his part, combined with the expectancy with which she had come to him, had an immediate salutary effect on her body.

Before she had left his room, she felt strengthened. And within a matter of a few days, she climbed the 182 steps of the Portland city hall dome. She became so enthusiastic over her sudden influx of strength that she even wrote a letter to the local Portland paper praising Dr. Quimby in biblical terms: "As he speaks as never man before spake, and heals as never man healed since Christ, is he not identified with truth? And is not this the Christ which is in him?"[2]

However, Mrs. Patterson did not stay cured. Her health was to ebb and flow several times between 1862 and 1866, and by 1866 she had come to wonder exactly what Quimby had represented for her or taught her. The improvement in her condition in the autumn of 1862, however, was so dramatic that she felt at the time it must all be due to his method of cure, and she set out to find out how he had cured her. In another letter she wrote to the *Portland Evening Courier* later that fall, she said (in part):

> ...now I can see dimly at first, and only as trees walking, the great principle which underlies Dr. Quimby's

> faith and works; and just in proportion to my right perception of truth is my recovery. This truth which he opposes to the error of giving intelligence to matter and placing pain where it never placed itself, if received understandingly, changes the currents of the system to their normal action; and the mechanism of the body goes on undisturbed. That this is a science capable of demonstration becomes clear to the minds of those patients who reason upon the process of their cure... At present I am too much in error to elucidate the truth, and can touch only the key-note for the master hand to wake the harmony.[3]

In these two letters one can glimpse some of the elements that Mrs. Patterson would be considering over the next several years. She immediately had made a connection in her own mind between Quimby's healing work and the healing recorded in the New Testament. Quimby could talk about the Bible and its main characters because biblical knowledge was still a part of the typical New Englander's background. But there had been nothing in what Quimby had said to her so far, or even in the method he used to cure her, to indicate that he himself was making any link between his work and the healings of Jesus.

Furthermore, she sensed right away that the healing depended at least partly on the patient's own "perception of truth," as she had written in her letter to the Portland newspaper. And she felt that there must be a science behind it. If healings could be reliable, there must be a method, a way – hence the leap to the word science.

Quimby gave Mrs. Patterson a good deal of his time over the next two years. By this time he had gathered around him a small retinue of admirers. Among them were Julius Dresser and the woman Dresser would marry, Annetta Seabury. It was Dresser who had talked up Quimby's cure at Dr. Hill's sanatorium in New Hampshire and had made Mrs. Patterson aware once more of the work that Quimby was doing. (It was also Dresser who would sow the seeds of confusion about the alleged relationship between Quimby and Christian Science some two decades later when he heard of Mary's success in establishing Christian Science in Boston.)

Besides Dresser, there were two sisters, the Misses Emma and Sarah Ware, daughters of a United States Supreme Court justice. These individuals appear to have acted more as a staff of helpers and not to have been an active part of any reciprocal thought process that may have transpired between Quimby and any of his patients. From the start, his relationship with Mrs. Patterson was a special one and very likely unique in his entire practice. It involved a kind of mutual respect that was beneficial to them both. Mrs. Patterson's questioning of him helped him to better articulate his system, even though the confused pattern of thinking in the Quimby manuscripts (the notebooks that he left behind at his passing), with their combination of a discussion about bodily fluids and a kind of pseudo-spirituality, presents nothing that one can identify as a coherent explanation of any system – medical, mental, or spiritual. And over the many weeks of separate visits, which, when added together, stretched into several months of acquaintance with Quimby, Mrs. Patterson gradually, albeit sadly, came to the conclusion that Quimby indeed did not possess a science of healing to offer mankind. Neither had he claimed to have enough of a system to his healing to be able to pass it along to someone else.

Before and during the time these events affecting her own mental and spiritual growth were taking place, her day-to-day life was also undergoing change. While she was still in Portland in November 1862, Dr. Patterson appeared at the hotel one day. She had already had word that he had escaped from prison in the South and was on his way home. When he found that Mary was not with the Tiltons in Sanbornton, he came to Portland to find her.

Early in 1863 they were both back in Sanbornton, with Abigail again providing temporary lodging and sustenance for them. Mary was in the midst of her early enthusiasm over Quimby and persuaded Abi to go to Portland with her son, Albert. Albert, it seems, had developed the smoking habit and was also drinking too much. Mary persuaded her reluctant sister to try to let Quimby heal him. Abi had none of Mary's faith in Quimby, however. Nor did Mary yet understand that it was her own faith that she could be healed, aided by Quimby's assurance that she would be cured, more than anything else in Quimby's method that had led to her own dramatic improvement.

After a failed visit to Portland, Abi was more confirmed than ever in her belief that Quimby was a quack. This led to her increasing uneasiness over her sister's interest in Quimby. Abi had controlled or at least exercised a major role in most of the events of Mary's life for the past twenty years, and here was a development occurring outside her "jurisdiction." She was losing control over her little sister, whom she most probably still regarded as an essentially weak woman who would eventually become dependent on her once again. Her own sense of respectability, as the wife of one of the leading businessmen of Sanbornton Bridge, was also offended by Mary's interest in this magnetic doctor.

From this point forward, Patterson faded as a major figure in Mary's life. By the summer of 1863 he had moved to Lynn, Massachusetts, just north of Boston, to go into dental practice there. Mary went with him, but their life together was virtually ended. Patterson's personal life had come into question in 1853 before he married Mary. Whether or not questions about him had been based on more than rumor, it appears that after his return from prison in the South he began a series of flirtations with other women. He and Mary did take a vacation together to Saco, Maine, where his brother lived, in September 1863. But increasingly he lived his own life and she lived hers.

Although Mary could not have known it at the time, the move to Lynn with Patterson did mark an important step in her preparation for her own future. It transplanted her from the succession of small towns in New Hampshire, where she had been living with Patterson for the previous decade, to a thriving industrial city on the Massachusetts coast and also to the vicinity of New England's business and intellectual capital, Boston. It also removed her permanently from "home," from both the protection that Abi could have offered her and from the potential control of her life that went with the promise of family shelter.

This was not an easy period for Mary. At first she had been enthralled by Quimby's cure, but at least some of her old troubles had soon recurred. She was not only distancing herself from what remained of the Baker family; there was also the mutual distancing between her and Patterson. Whether or not she had a sense of being on a definite mission yet, as she would have after 1866, she was intent on understanding if there was anything in Quimby's method that deserved further research or development. For his part, Quimby found her interesting enough to continue giving her a substantial amount of his free time for discussion. She returned to Portland in the winter of 1863, when Abi brought her son to Quimby. She also spent part of that summer there, part of the winter of 1864, and the month of May 1864. She paid her last visit to Quimby in April 1865, just nine months before he died. His own health had been failing for some time, and for about the last year of his life he withdrew from his practice and lived quietly with his family in Belfast, Maine.

❖ ❖ ❖ ❖

Three unrelated events in the 1862-66 period stand out as evidence of what she had already learned and as a kind of foretaste of what would follow: her writing for the Portland newspapers, a talk she gave in Portland, and her visit to Mary Ann Jarvis, a patient of Quimby's.

From even before the time of her marriage to George Glover, Mrs. Patterson had written for the press or for popular magazines. At first it had been mostly an occasional poem. These creations were not literature, but they were an outlet for her desire to communicate with others and to share her feelings about issues of the day. During 1863 she wrote several times for the *Portland Daily Press.* These articles were often excerpts from a journal she kept, commenting on the sights to be seen around Portland. While she did this partly to earn a small amount of money, there were countless other women who faced similar choices who did not try to write for others. Her desire to be heard – even more, her desire to share thoughts that she felt deserved sharing – had been with her from the time of her early womanhood. What she wrote in 1863 or 1864 was of no particular significance, but it was indicative of the route she would eventually follow to share Christian Science with the whole world. Not only does this remark refer to her eventually writing the Christian Science textbook, but it also refers to the fact that, from an early age, she was accustomed to using the press to publish her views.

Mrs. Patterson worked out her metaphysics and did her praying in the privacy of communion with God, whether she happened to be living in a boarding house or eventually more amply in a house with servants. Yet at the same time she took full advantage of all available public means to be heard. This was one of the legacies of growing up in America. She never doubted that her views had a right to be heard. And although she wrote frequently, including in the Christian Science textbook, about the unequal treatment given women under the law, she shared, as a child of the ethos of nineteenth-century seaboard America, the assumption of other women leaders that their voices were as important and as deserving of consideration as the voice of any male.

The second thing she did in these years follows from her writing. She gave a few speeches in Portland and in Warren, a small town farther up in the state of Maine. She was not yet an accomplished speaker, but she felt that she had something to say and again took advantage of any proper forum to say it. A local paper reported with restrained politeness:

> This lady is not in the habit of public speaking… She possesses a symmetrical and graceful form, and her manners were modest and unassuming. Her intellec-

> tual culture appears to be good, and her spirit touched to very fine issues, but she spins an exceedingly fine, silken thread, and her thoughts run closely on the borders of refined and highly sublimated transcendentalism which ordinary thinkers fail to comprehend… she reasoned so high above the ordinary plane upon which we stood that we failed to comprehend her meaning.[4]

The third event of note is the first instance of her "practice" – i.e., healing through prayer, whether audible or silent. She would later date the advent of Christian Science from 1866, and this incident occurred in 1864. Yet she included the account of it in the Christian Science textbook, apparently feeling that it was illustrative of enough of the elements of true practice to be considered in line with Christian Science.

Mary Ann Jarvis, a patient of Quimby's, had several ailments, but the one that Mrs. Patterson remembered healing her of during her two-month stay was a tendency to become ill whenever the east wind blew. As she described it years later in *Science and Health:*

> A woman, whom I cured of consumption, always breathed with great difficulty when the wind was from the east. I sat silently by her side a few moments. Her breath came gently. The inspirations were deep and natural. I then requested her to look at the weather-vane. She looked and saw that it pointed due east. The wind had not changed, but her thought of it had and so her difficulty in breathing had gone. The wind had not produced the difficulty. My metaphysical treatment changed the action of her belief on the lungs, and she never suffered again from east winds, but was restored to health.[5]

This was the first time she had used what she understood to be Quimby's method and seen a resulting healing. But she had also suffered herself in the process of healing Miss Jarvis. One of the peculiarities of Quimby's method of practice had been his belief that he himself was susceptible to taking on the symptoms of the patients he was treating. If disease was caused by thought, there could be a kind of negative thought transference as well as a positive one. And now Mrs. Patterson found that she had the same tendency. So she wrote to Quimby for help for herself: "...you know her body of belief 'is full of wounds and bruises' which in getting her out of I stumble, ..."[6]

This instance of helping Miss Jarvis was evidence that she was already keeping the promise she had made years before to give her life in service to others if she could only be healed of her own incapacities.

❖ ❖ ❖ ❖

Mrs. Patterson's partial dependence on Quimby for help during this period is proof enough that she had not yet had the spiritual insight that came to her in 1866. After she had cured Miss Jarvis, she wrote to Quimby of the healing, but ended the letter with, "Dr., won't you continue to help me by thinking of *myself.*"[7] Then, five days later, she wrote in apparent answer to his mental treatment:

> I received your gift of the "comforter" last Thursday, and to my amazement Miss Jarvis grew at once gay even, and has not been very sad a moment since. Your *power* put *me* to *sleep* and I have not felt nervous since, and the relief in other respects was entire, so I am well now for me.[8]

Three weeks later she wrote to Quimby again. The letter indicates the direction her thinking was taking her, and although she is still depending on him, it also shows her doing some independent questioning:

> Jesus taught as *man* does *not;* who then is wise, but you. What is your truth if it applies only to the evil diseases which show themselves... Dr, I have a strange feeling

> of late that I ought to be *perfect* after the command of science, in order to know and do the right.... I can love only a good, honorable and brave career; no other can suit me.... Please attend to my case when you get this; dyspepsia and constipation; two bug bears that Miss Jarvis has just got rid of and saddled on to me.
>
> Ever in hands of Fellowship.[9]

She was evidently not getting the aid from Quimby that she had at first thought he could provide. Another three weeks passed, into May of 1864, and she was writing, "Enclosed please find a `penny for your thoughts' and come to my relief in these respects restless nights and spinal pain and heat."[10]

It was also in May 1864 that Mrs. Patterson spent several more weeks in Portland. This was the fourth of her lengthy trips there and the last of any substance. She wrote later that Dr. Quimby let her read some of the material he was working on, and she in turn shared her thoughts with him. At this point in time, her thoughts in the main were presumably her interpretation of what she thought Quimby meant. In the years that followed, Julius Dresser was to claim that Mrs. Eddy had stolen Christian Science from Quimby. That charge is clearly not correct. Yet there were grounds for some misunderstanding, especially among later scholars who, because Quimby's jottings had not been published, knew little of his practice and did not take the time to try to understand Christian Science.

The basic premise of Christian Science is a theological one: the allness of God, who is defined, among other terms, as Spirit and Mind, and the consequent nothingness of the phenomenal world as interpreted by the limited material senses. There is nothing this bold or even hinting at this simplicity in the turgid prose of Quimby. Mrs. Patterson was not even thinking in these terms herself during the years she visited Quimby. It took several years after 1866 for her to find the right language to express the spiritual simplicity of the insight she had had on what might otherwise have been her deathbed in February 1866.

Yet Quimby had the important influence in her life that a catalyst has in producing a chemical reaction that would not occur in the absence of the catalyst. He reinforced the belief she already had that there must be a system to mental healing. Quimby's own use of biblical language, though without the theological underpinnings of the Bible or the moral demands of the Ten Commandments and the Sermon on the Mount, caused Mrs. Patterson to become even more interested in finding the science she had first thought resided in Quimby right in her King James Bible. Prior to her coming to Quimby for help in 1862, her Puritan Christian upbringing had remained the anchor in her life. Yet there is little substantial evidence during the dreary years of widowhood or when she was married to Patterson and being moved around New Hampshire that she thought the Bible itself contained the key to solving the problem of her invalidism. She had continued to read it for its comfort, while at the same time she was experimenting with homeopathy or depending in some periods on the Graham diet to sustain her existence.

If one takes the Quimby manuscripts, which were finally published in the 1920s, or even the "Questions and Answers" and the first volume of his journal, which are probably all of his notebooks that Mrs. Patterson actually read, what is most striking is not that the man was a hypnotist, but that he kept comparing his work to that of Christ Jesus. It was true, as his son later maintained, that Phineas Quimby was not a religious man. But this statement, as his son used it, applied mainly to his lack of formal religiosity. Quimby felt that the "priests and doctors" had sold mankind a false bill of goods. One can picture this largely unlettered, optimistic American of the mid-nineteenth century writing, "The priests and doctors conspire together to humbug the people, and they have invented all sorts of stories to frighten man and keep him under their power." (The pejoratively used word "priests" was meant to apply to all men of the cloth and not only to Roman Catholic clergy, as the word is more commonly used today.) Then, speaking directly of the orthodox interpretations of the Bible, he wrote:

> The knowledge of man puts false construction on his wisdom and gets up a sort of religion which has nothing to do with Jesus' truth. There is where the fault lies. If you do not believe the Bible as they explain it then you are an infidel. So all who cannot believe it as it has been explained, must throw it away. I do not throw the Bible away, but throw the explanation away, and apply Jesus' own words as He did and as He intended they should be applied, and let my works speak for themselves, whether they are of God or man, and leave the sick to judge.[11]

Yet even with this reference to the Bible, one could never conclude that Quimby's method of curing people was God-centered. It certainly had not developed from a study of the Bible or Jesus' healings. It was, as we have seen, a method in which one human mind tries in some way to reach another human mind and affect its thoughts. Where Quimby was in advance of his time was in recognizing that thought processes had, at least under some conditions, primacy over what the medical profession considered to be autonomous, materially controlled bodily processes.

Quimby did write about God, but there is no sense of spirituality or of a transcendent deity in his thought. He at times identifies God as Truth and also as Wisdom; the capital letters may belong to one of the later copyists and may not have been his own idea. (The Ware sisters acted as the faithful copyists of his notes.) There are even faint reminiscences of Quimby in the early editions of *Science and Health.* In the first edition of the Christian Science textbook, for instance, Mrs. Eddy does not yet give Mind as one of the seven synonyms of God, although the other six are already there. Instead, she refers to God as Wisdom, the term Quimby had used.

There are also many references to familiar Bible characters in Quimby's "Questions and Answers" – to Jesus many times, to Paul, John, and Peter. Many of the Bible verses that Mrs. Eddy later used to elucidate points in her teaching are touched upon by Quimby: Jesus telling his disciples to inform John of his healings as proof that he was the one of whom John had prophesied; being wiser than serpents and harmless as doves; the truth being revealed unto babes; and Jesus' reference to the temple being rebuilt in three days. In one section, Quimby tries to show a distinction between Jesus and the Christ, a point that was to be central to Mrs. Eddy's elucidation of the Bible. Quimby's explanation, however, is difficult to follow or to fathom; yet the ground is laid for someone else to take up the work, as Mrs. Eddy later did. Thus there is a recognition by Quimby of Jesus' works and of the role that a healing religion could play in people's lives. It was religion only in a going-to-church-on-Sunday sense that Quimby wanted no part of. At the same time, Quimby showed no recognition of the moral demands of genuine Christianity and wrote in one place that a man's morals were of no concern to him. If one asks himself whether Quimby had ever pondered the entire meaning of Jesus' teaching and healing, he would have to answer no.

Quimby noted a difference between the "natural" senses and spiritual sense, but his writings never make clear exactly what he means by either term. What he means by spirit seems to come closer to a refined, or more ethereal, materiality. In spite of the small beginnings he had made, he had gone far beyond what was then orthodox practice in the medical arts. In Mrs. Patterson's experience, he as well as the homeopathists had put an end to the notion that there was only one road to health. There is no way of being sure how many of his notebooks Mrs. Patterson actually read. One must also remember that some of Quimby's thoughts were probably put down after his discussions with Mrs. Patterson and reflected her own condition of thought as well as his. What one can say with some accuracy is that he represented one of the avenues through which her thought was opened to the possibility of a more wide-ranging interpretation of the Bible stories, and particularly of Jesus' life and works, than had ever existed in the mental landscape of the Bible laid out for her in the sermons of orthodox Congregational ministers.

For Mrs. Patterson, the closer her acquaintance with Quimby became, the more she realized that the route of mental suggestion, or mental transference, had something about it that was not only non-biblical, but was also the very antithesis of the method of healing Jesus must have used. Indirectly, Quimby turned her even more to her Bible, only she was now looking in it for the science she had at first thought resided in Quimby's method. Many of the superficial resemblances that Christian Science practice might later seem to have with Quimby –such as praying for those who are not physically present with the practitioner – would disappear when their actual content was examined.

Quimby also had a more general influence on Mrs. Patterson. While he did not permanently heal her, she had definitely emerged from the semi-invalidism of the 1850s and by 1866 was exercising an independence of action that would have been beyond the reach of her imagination a few years earlier. She had no secure livelihood. She could not depend on Patterson to support her after his return from the Civil War anymore than she could before the war, and she was even more distanced from her family because of her interest in an unorthodox form of medical practice. She had thought of being reunited with her son, but he had returned to the Middle Western prairies at the end of the Civil War. She was virtually homeless and turning forty-five years old in 1866. Her insecurity was still apparent in some of her occasional communications with her family. Yet, in spite of all this, she was in search of something that, while it still eluded her, she had become determined to find. If the answer did not lie with Quimbyism, she would continue the search.

And herein lies perhaps the greatest and most positive influence of Phineas Quimby, although it can never be proved outright. Had the kind magnetic doctor perhaps been the first male in her life since the death of her brother Albert to have appreciated her as a full human being? Her marriage to George Glover had been too brief to draw any conclusions from as to what extent Glover appreciated her. To her father and brothers and sisters she had represented mainly a young widow to care for and then – even worse – a semi-invalid. Patterson was by all accounts a decent enough person, but there was no hint of either intellect or spirituality about him, so he could hardly have identified or appreciated those elements in Mary. But here was Quimby, who by the 1860s had actually had several thousand patients come through his offices, finding this lonely but persistent invalid on his doorstep, and within weeks apparently appreciating her intelligence and her desire to learn from him. Whatever the limitations of his theories, there seems little question that Quimby had a large heart and that he was not in the business for the money. (In fact, he frequently refunded people's money when he felt he had not done enough for them.) The fact that this man took her seriously may, in the end, have done more to move Mary Baker Patterson ahead on her life's quest than did either the temporary cure he provided or the various specific subjects they talked about in his office. Although she was left to work out her answers alone, it was Quimby who had reinforced her sense of self-worth. Almost a generation later, she summed up the significance of Quimby as it then seemed to her:

> … I tried him, as a healer, and because he seemed to help me for the time, and had a higher ideal than I had heard of up to that time, I praised him to the skies… I actually loved him, I mean his high and noble character, and was literally unstinted in my praise of him, but when I found that Quimbyism was too short, and would not answer the cry of the human heart for succor, for real aid, I went, being driven thence by my extremity, to the Bible, and there I discovered Christian Science.[12]

Chapter 4

Years of Discovery
Early Practice – The First Class

New England winters have a well-earned reputation for being hard and long. Along the North Atlantic coast in New England, actual temperatures tend to be milder than even a few miles inland. But frequent northeasters, those gales that are whipped by a wind from the northeast, make up in severity for any warmer temperature they may bring. Snow, frozen slush, rain that freezes and adds to the icy surface – all these phenomena were as much present in the year 1866 as they are today. And by the end of January winter is at its severest, barely halfway over and the days only imperceptibly lengthening.

It was at just such a time in the winter of 1866, on a Thursday evening, February 1, that Mrs. Patterson set out to spend an evening at a temperance meeting. She was living with Patterson (who was out of town) in the small coastal town of Swampscott, and made her way presumably by some public conveyance to the larger center of Lynn. There, losing her footing, she had the accident that, along with the meeting with Quimby, was the second major event in this period. If the meeting with Quimby was significant, in that it marked the start of her emergence from the long period of invalidism and her research into the possibilities of mental healing, this accident remains the epochal event. Quimby had died only two weeks earlier, her own life would appear to be hanging by a mere thread, and what she could realize within her own consciousness would be the determining factor in the outcome. The short newspaper account from the *Lynn Reporter* of Saturday, February 3, reads:

> Mrs. Mary Patterson, of Swampscott, fell upon the ice near the corner of Market and Oxford streets, on Thursday evening, and was severely injured. She was taken up in an insensible condition and carried

> to the residence of S. M. Bubier, Esq., near by, where she was kindly cared for during the night. Dr. Cushing, who was called, found her injuries to be internal, and of a very severe nature, inducing spasms and intense suffering. She was removed to her home in Swampscott yesterday afternoon, though in a very critical condition.

Just as was the case with the Quimby "healing," the healing that Mrs. Patterson was about to experience was one from which she would have a partial relapse. But there was a vital difference. In the two days during which she lay in bed, she turned her thought to the Bible and to her lifelong reliance on God. On Sunday morning friends called on their way to church to see her. She told one of them that the next time she saw her she would be out of bed. Sometime Sunday during her prayerful individual communion with God, her thought fell on a Bible story (she recalled it later as the healing of the palsied man in the ninth chapter of Matthew). A vital sense of the presence of God came to her in a new way, which gave her the courage to rise out of bed on her own and walk across the room. She wrote twenty-five years later in *Retrospection and Introspection:*

> My immediate recovery from the effects of an injury caused by an accident, an injury that neither medicine nor surgery could reach, was the falling apple that led me to the discovery how to be well myself, and how to make others so.
>
> Even to the homeopathic physician who attended me, and rejoiced in my recovery, I could not then explain the *modus* of my relief. I could only assure him that the divine Spirit had wrought the miracle – a miracle which later I found to be in perfect scientific accord with divine law.[1]

Mrs. Patterson may or may not have had what would medically be called a terminal injury. There is little question, however, that she had been badly injured and that, along with her previous invalidism and still vacillating state of health, those acquaintances who knew her best thought it unlikely that she would ever again walk normally, if at all. Moreover, her quick improvement on Sunday, regardless of what she said or felt later, impressed upon her thought the immediacy of what she considered divine help if it could be appealed to understandingly.

Dr. Alvin Cushing, the homeopathic physician who treated her for her fall (actually just giving her painkillers), claimed in a statement he made forty years later that she had said nothing to him about being healed and that he had continued to call on her intermittently for another week or so. He also recalled from the space of a generation later that he had made no comments about the fall being of a life-threatening nature. It is worth noting, though, that Cushing was not disposed to be friendly toward the progress Christian Science was making in the early 1900s, so his personal views may have tempered his recollections. However, there seems no good reason to doubt the record in his appointment book that he did make some follow-up calls on Mrs. Patterson.

Some two weeks after this event, Mrs. Patterson wrote to one of Quimby's former patients, Julius Dresser, whom she had admired in Portland, saying that the fall had left her in a state as forlorn as when she first visited Quimby. She was shortly to recognize the unbridgeable gap separating the prayer that recognizes the presence of God, through the Christ-consciousness in every man and woman, from a strong human will that could be directed to another person and have an evil as well as a salutary effect. But this was not apparent at the time she appealed to Dresser for help.

Dresser turned down Mary's request, saying that he could not even help his own wife and did not know how to use Quimby's "system" to aid her. In retrospect, one may consider his response fortunate, because this episode was also one more of the turning points of 1866: it forced Mary to turn inward, or upward, to the spiritual resources available directly to her. Dresser's reply to her may have also influenced her in just a few years to emphasize her role in life as a teacher instead of merely healing others, although the available evidence indicates that she was a remarkable healer. But part of Dresser's response included this:

> Dr. Quimby gave himself away to his patients. To be sure he did a great work, but what will it avail in fifty years from now, if his theory does not come out, and if he and his ideas pass among the things that were, to be forgotten? He did work some changes in the minds of the people, which will grow with the development and progress in the world. He helped to make them progress. They will progress faster for his having lived and done his work. So with Jesus. He had an effect which was lasting and still exists.... He did not succeed, nor has Dr. Quimby succeeded in establishing the science he aimed to do. The true way to establish it is, as I look at it, to lecture and by a paper and make that the means rather more than the curing, to introduce the truth.[2]

At about this same time, she had published in a Lynn newspaper an ode to the memory of Dr. Quimby. It contained these lines:

> Rest should reward him who hath made us whole,
> Seeking, though tremblers, where his footsteps trod.[3]

Later in the summer, Mrs. Patterson petitioned the mayor of Lynn for damages: "Having suffered much, and still suffering, from the effects of that fall, she earnestly petitions your Honor for the recompense of justice in a pecuniary point, so far as that may atone for her injuries and loss."[4] The petition was not granted.

Sometime later in 1866, Patterson also apparently left Mary for the last time, thus leaving her to fend for herself or go back to her sisters for family charity. One of the more recent biographers of Mrs. Eddy, Julius Silberger writing in the genre of psychobiography, claims that until that eventful year she had depended on others for her sustenance. With the death of Quimby, he claims, she decided she could no longer depend on anyone else and would instead take control of her own life and eventually make others dependent on her. He writes:

> That was to be her remarkable accomplishment – that a helpless woman of forty-five, without formal training or serious preparation, would struggle with her feelings of helplessness so persistently and with such resourcefulness and opportunism that she would succeed both in creating a kind of security for herself and in disguising the emotional cost of the struggle from herself and from others…"[5]

Given the death of Quimby, the inability or refusal of Julius Dresser to come to her aid, and the desertion of her husband, one might not quarrel with the first part of that statement, although she had already been exercising a high degree of personal independence. But how does a dependent person suddenly pass from dependence to independence, particularly a person at mid-life or, in terms of the past century and Mrs. Patterson's own illnesses, a person well past mid-life? Such an assessment leaves out of the equation the most potent influence on and orientation of her whole life. This was her Calvinist Christian upbringing and the religious frame of reference that pervaded her entire thought process. Her search for relief from her chronic ill health had not been conducted with the thought of replicating Jesus' healings she had read about in the New Testament; but she *had* been convinced that the God she knew in the Bible did not mean for man to suffer. Moreover, while such a superficial view may fit some current psychological model of human behavior, it ignores the efforts she had been making to help herself through homeopathy and other means long before the 1860s, as well as the evidence that she was a normal member of a large family with normal adult desires to live a life of usefulness.

This psychological view of Mrs. Eddy, with which this author totally disagrees, not only omits some of the elements of her life up to that time. It also illustrates how different a person's life story may appear, depending on who the storyteller (the biographer) is. It would be extremely difficult for anyone who sympathizes with the role that her belief in God played in her life not to understand that her religious beliefs formed the core around which her experience was developing. In Mrs. Eddy's own brief sketch in *Retrospection,* she notes in the same chapter already quoted from above:

> During twenty years prior to my discovery I had been trying to trace all physical effects to a mental cause; and *in the latter part of 1866* [italics added by author] I gained the scientific certainty that all causation was Mind, and every effect a mental phenomenon.[6]

She also says on the same page that she withdrew from society for about three years "to ponder my mission, to search the Scriptures, to find the Science of Mind that should take the things of God and show them to the creature, and reveal the great curative Principle, - Deity." Before looking at these years, which were among the barest she was to endure in terms of physical hardship, perhaps even worse than the poverty of her life with Patterson in the small village of Rumney, one needs to look at just what Mrs. Patterson was actually finding as she "search[ed] the Scriptures."

❖ ❖ ❖ ❖

The full theology of Christian Science would be presented almost ten years later in the first edition of the textbook. But the most important tenet of the religion (which she was also a decade away from naming "Christian Science") was the allness of God and the implications this had for suffering humanity. That is alluded to in the quote in the above paragraph. She was eventually to describe Christian Science as the reintroduction of primitive Christianity. And as historical research is today making clearer about early Christianity, much of the appeal of the religion in its first years was due to the liberating effect on human life of acknowledging the power of an almighty, universal God, as well as the ethical responsibility this placed on man to live according to God's will, or law.

As she looked for the meaning of her own healing as well as the other events of 1866, she came to an unshakable conviction that she could act on the basis of the biblical statements regarding God's supremacy. Before her, the historical Christian church as a whole had taken one of only two apparent roads in reconciling the evil and disease in the world with the concept of an all-powerful God. The first chapter of Genesis presents an exalted view of God as making all things and seeing them as very good. And the experience of the Jews led them to some of the same heights by the time the Psalms were being written. But the church had said either (1) that God is ultimately supreme, but shares power for a time with a competitor (call him Satan), or (2) that God allows sickness, sin, and the assorted miseries of this world to teach man some kind of lesson – either to punish him for his sins or to teach him to submit to a divine purpose that may not be scrutable to mere human reasoning.

Mrs. Patterson intuited a third way, since neither of the two generally accepted theological modes of reasoning were compatible with her understanding of an all-powerful, loving God. She did not ignore the evil or disease in the world, but saw them as part of a wider misconception of the nature of the universe under God's control. Since God is all-powerful, His creation must reflect only His qualities, she reasoned. Thus, sin and sickness had to be a misconception of that which really exists. The foundation of this misconception lay in the belief in the reality of matter, of the whole phenomenal world as perceived by the limited material senses. If God was to be identified as Spirit, as the Bible so identifies Him, then what He has created must be, like Him, spiritual. The belief in a life based on matter and the evidence of the five material senses was at its core a belief in separation from God. And it was this belief of separation that underlay all the individual instances of human misery.

Years later, in a more developed statement of this theme in the textbook, *Science and Health,* she wrote:

> To seize the first horn of this dilemma and consider matter as a power in and of itself, is to leave the creator out of His own universe; while to grasp the other horn of the dilemma and regard God as the creator of matter, is not only to make Him responsible for all disasters, physical and moral, but to announce Him as their source, thereby making Him guilty of maintaining perpetual misrule in the form and under the name of natural law.[7]

Since the beginnings of Western thought, philosophy and religion had been dealing with dualism – spirit and matter, good and evil, life and death. While Mrs. Patterson was certainly no accomplished academic student of philosophy, she had had at least a smattering of philosophical reading in her general readers and was well aware of these basic dualisms. Each one of them is a set of contradictions, or opposites, which claim to be part of the human experience. It was her own search through the Bible, though, that led her to reject the notion of any dualism and to demand, somewhat as Calvin had demanded, that man keep his eye turned only to deity.

From the start, what distinguished Mrs. Eddy's discovery from anything preceding it was her rejection of dualism. Dualism was a phenomenon apparent only from a limited human perception of the universe. Thus, as the belief in the existence of two contradictory bases of being, spirit and matter, progressively disappeared in the individual human consciousness, the individual could comprehend her vision of the single, perfect universe created and still maintained by God. It was something like this kind of thinking that had brought Mary her healing from the fall on the ice and that would be responsible for the healings she would accomplish in the next few years.

In fact, without the concrete proofs of healing, this third way of dealing with the reality and power of God and the apparent evil in the universe would remain empty theory or, more likely, be perceived as a hallucination. There was no reason to deny what the material senses say is true if that denial did not have practical effects. Thus, from its very beginnings, healing became an integral and even indispensable part of the evidence that one understood at least something of Mrs. Patterson's approach.

Each individual would eventually have to see that the omnipresence of God, or Spirit, precludes the possibility of even entertaining the sense of a material universe; that the allness of God put into practice through prayer could annihilate the manifestation of evil; and that a God whom she identified as eternal Life itself would make possible the ultimate demonstration of the fact of eternity in individual experience (a fact basically incomprehensible to the thought basing everything on what the senses recognize – i.e., the space-time continuum). The claims of evil and disease, as well as the belief that life ends in death, were all part of the human misconception of existence that must eventually be overcome. All this and much more gradually dawned on her thought as she pursued further what it meant to be aware of the actual presence of this almighty God.

❖ ❖ ❖ ❖

After Patterson left his wife sometime in the fall of 1866, Mary boarded with at least two families in Lynn, the Philipses and the Clarks. During this period of 1866 there were several instances in which she effected a quick healing of others – instances that reinforced her conviction that there was a science, or method, to healing, and that it was going to become even clearer to her. The Philipses had a son of about fifteen years of age who had an infected finger. This infection had been active for several days, and he was in pain from it. Agreeing with Mrs. Patterson's request not to look at the finger, he put a bandage on it and went to bed for the night. In the morning the bandage had fallen off, and the finger itself was already normal.

Shortly after this incident, a visitor from Boston who was staying with the Oliver family (relatives of the Philipses) was healed very quickly of a fever that had made him delirious. And Mrs. Winslow, the wife of a retired Unitarian minister, was healed of her inability to walk. Mrs. Winslow had been confined to her chair for more than fifteen years and was soon walking on her own.

In each of the situations into which her dire economic circumstances now introduced her, Mary would have opportunity when sharing the common boardinghouse meal to at least broach the subject that compassed all her waking hours. Indirectly this led to the first informal student she would have, a young man by the Yankee-sounding name of Hiram Crafts. Crafts was a cobbler who came for part of each year to work in the shoe factories in Lynn and then return home to East Stoughton, a small town southwest of Boston (since renamed Avon). He became so interested in Mrs. Patterson's discussions of mental healing that he persuaded her to come to East Stoughton with him and his wife when they returned there in the late autumn of 1866. Mrs. Patterson agreed to teach him how to heal, in return for which she would get room and board and have the freedom to further refine her thoughts. During these years she was writing incessantly. Most of what she then wrote is not extant and is believed to be her own exegesis of Scripture. The small manuscript from which she taught her first formal classes in 1870 had not yet been written, and she would not even begin to write *Science and Health* until 1872. Yet all her writing in these early years of discovery was leading her to the eventual clarity of expression that would mark her finished work.

In the spring of 1867, Crafts decided he was ready to announce himself as a mental healer. The family, along with Mary, moved to Taunton, and he placed an ad in the local paper claiming he could cure "consumption, catarrh, scrofula, dyspepsia, and rheumatism..."

Mary felt she was making progress in her work, but she was also still feeling the hurt from being left by Patterson. This is apparent from two letters she wrote to her sister Martha in early

1867. In February she wrote, mentioning Crafts, "I hope you are better and that the little leaven I left will leaven the whole lump, for Martha dear, this leaven of Truth is not the leaven of the Scribes and Pharisees." [8] Yet two months later she wrote to Martha, despairing over Patterson:

> ...it is of no use for me ever to hope or fear in that direction, but one experience ever awaits me, disappointment and tears. My life is just as sad as it can be. I have no joy, but a sort of martyr courage and submission to my fate. Then I have a God to love and lean upon, and hitherto he has delivered me from the "lions" and "furnace" and I must trust that unseen love and wisdom and which I daily endeavor to do, calmly awaiting the blest moment that shall free me from the fetters of pain and sorrow which I have ever worn, and still wear in this mortality. [9]

Then, in a shift of tone, she told Martha hopefully that "the Doctor [Crafts] here is just beginning at great expense in a new place, and of course in no way to pay me yet, and when he will he is altogether uncertain, but all that come to him sick he cures."

During the summer she made what turned out to be a final family visit in Tilton, although she returned there several times in later years on specific errands. Her only remaining brother, George, was blind and had come home to die. Martha had been widowed and was living in Tilton with her daughter, Ellen. Abigail's husband had been extremely successful with the woolen mill. Abi herself possessed strong managerial talents, which she would put to use in later years as a widow. There was no interest at "home" in Mary's theories about healing; there was, in fact, only embarrassment over them. Yet on this final visit with what remained of the Baker family, whose ties had meant so much to Mary and whom she would have liked more than any other people on earth to show some interest in her new purpose in life, she found no response. None, that is, except in Ellen, Martha's daughter. Ellen had been ill for some weeks with an infection of some kind, probably enteritis. A family member later recalled what happened:

> In a few moments after [Mrs. Patterson] entered the room and stood by her bedside, [Ellen] recognized her aunt, and said, "I am glad to see you aunty." In about ten minutes more, Mrs. [Patterson] told her to "rise from her bed and walk." She rose and walked seven times across her room, then sat down in a chair. For two weeks before this, we had not entered her room without stepping lightly. Her bowels were so tender, she felt the jar, and it increased her sufferings… When she walked across the room at Mrs. [Patterson's] bidding, she told her to stamp her foot strongly upon the floor, and she did so without suffering from it. The next day she was dressed, and went down to the table; and the fourth day went on a journey of about a hundred miles in the cars. [10]

The various members of the family, as glad as they were to see Ellen well again, were perplexed by the healing. As was to be the case with many of Mrs. Eddy's encounters, and is still the experience of Christian Scientists today, there was a reluctance to accept the simplicity of spiritual healing. This reluctance was often accompanied by a semiconscious realization that the pattern of the universe and physical laws that we each carry around in our heads had been interrupted by the healing. The manner of the healing, through prayer alone, might at times be a phenomenon more difficult to cope with than the illness that had just been healed.

In any case, Ellen wanted to accompany Mary back to the Crafts household in Taunton. This proved to be a mistake. When Ellen saw what simple folk the Crafts really were, and also walked in on a family that had been having its own debate about Mrs. Patterson while she had been away visiting, she was repelled. She left for New Hampshire, and whatever tie she had had with her aunt Mary was broken. It was at about this time that Mary wrote a poem that was found in her papers at the time of her passing. She was used to expressing her heartfelt emotions in verse, and these verses, under the heading "Alone," indicate the degree to which she felt the doors of home, that concept that had been so unfulfilled in her life ever since she first left the family hearth to marry George Glover, closing even further on her:

> I've sought the home my childhood gave –
> A moment's shelter from the wave –
> Then those when sick, whose pain I bore,
> A *Sister!* drove me from the door?
> O weary heart! O tired sigh!
> So wronged to live. – Alone I'd die.

Yet even this sad refrain was balanced by two stanzas of hope at the end. In one of them she wrote:

> Thy love can live in Truth, and be
> A joy, and immortality;
> To bless mankind with word and deed, –
> Thy life a great and noble creed.
> O glorious hope, my faith renew,
> O mortal joys, adieu! adieu![11]

As for the Crafts, their arrangement with Mary had come to a predictable conclusion while she had been away. Mrs. Crafts did not appreciate keeping house for both her husband and Mary and obviously did not share her husband's enthusiasm for spiritual healing. Cobbling shoes appeared to her to be a more dependable way to earn one's living. Thus, one of the longer lasting living arrangements Mary had during the latter half of the 1860s came to an abrupt end. Once more she had to find lodging and a way to manage her meager living while she delved further in her search of the Bible.

One of the families with whom she had been well-acquainted in Lynn were the Winslows. In fact, she had healed Mrs. Winslow of longstanding invalidism. It was to the Winslows, perhaps among others, that she returned now in search of a place to think and continue her writing. Mrs. Winslow suggested a friend in the seacoast town of Amesbury, up near the New Hampshire border. Mary went there immediately. The friend Mrs. Winslow had suggested was not able to take her in, but through her she heard of a Mrs. Nathaniel Webster, who ran a large boardinghouse. Mrs. Webster was a spiritualist, as were many of the so-called freethinking individuals of New England in that period.

For some of them spiritualism meant a withdrawal from their former churches, while for others it was simply something one engaged in while remaining at least nominally committed to traditional religious beliefs. In any case, when Mrs. Webster was told by Mary that she had felt "called" to come to her house, she heartily took her in, not knowing that the bundle of thoughts Mary was engaged in and the bundle of writings that she was now carrying with her were destined to disturb conservative New England much more than spiritualism had ever been able to do.

The stay with Mrs. Webster lasted almost ten months, until the early summer of 1868. Mary apparently joined in some of the spiritualist evenings, but not as a serious participant.

Spiritualism was the vogue in New England at the time. It was known primarily for the belief that a spiritualist medium could get in touch with those who had died and receive meaningful messages from them. In an era in which traditional Christian concepts were being challenged by the advance of the physical sciences, spiritualism served to prop up the belief of some people in a life after death as well as the existence of a kingdom beyond that cognized by the senses. Mrs. Webster herself was what was called a "drawing medium." Instead of interpreting messages from the dead, she drew pictures and then tried to find messages from the departed in the meaning of the pictures.

She had a special affinity for anyone interested in spiritualism, but also seems to have been a genuine philanthropist, taking in many indigent boarders. Her husband ran a mill in Manchester, New Hampshire, and came home only every other Sunday. Thus, she ran the house virtually as she pleased, with the exception that her widowed son-in-law brought his small children there every summer. Before bringing them up to Grandma, he would make an earlier inspection of the house and clear it of any characters he regarded as possibly objectionable for his children. On the annual "sweep" of his mother-in-law's house in 1868, he decided that Mary Patterson must leave. He had possibly heard some local stories about her healing activities. Like many another person who came into contact with the concept of spiritual healing, he may have been disturbed rather than intrigued by the concept. That would not be such an unusual reaction, in fact, since spiritual healing formed no part of most people's approach to either medicine or religion in that era.

In any case, Mary, who must have felt something of the mental control he was trying to exercise over his mother-in-law, refused to leave. So, on a sultry early summer evening, with a thunderstorm in progress, he packed her things into her trunk and physically ejected both her and her trunk from the house. With rejection by her family, ejection by the Crafts, and now by Mrs. Webster's son-in-law, one must wonder at Mrs. Eddy's later statement regarding these years of progress and discovery:

> For three years after my discovery, I sought the solution of this problem of Mind-healing, searched the Scriptures and read little else, kept aloof from society, and devoted time and energies to discovering a positive rule. The search was sweet, calm, and buoyant with hope, not selfish nor depressing. I knew the Principle of all harmonious Mind-action to be God, and that cures were produced in primitive Christian healing by holy, uplifting faith; but I must know the Science of this healing, and I won my way to absolute conclusions through divine revelation, reason, and demonstration.[12]

At every step during these years, Mary's needs were indeed cared for, but at a level of subsistence that most people reading her story today would find difficult to comprehend. What one must remember is that at any time, at least up until 1870 or so, she could have agreed with Abi's request that she give up her search for this science of healing that she talked about and come back to a life of physical comfort and relative abundance in Tilton. There is absolutely no hint that she ever even considered such a solution. Yet in the slight correspondence that exists from the period (as in the 1867 letters to Martha), there is equally no clear evidence that day after day she felt herself the mistress of her own experience, or that she was indeed certain of the outcome of her searching.

One has to surmise two things from these bleak years. First, there was sufficient evidence of her own healing ability and of her capacity to impart something of this knowledge to others to give her the encouragement to persevere with her work. The other element is, perhaps, the simple fact that she was a woman. Try as much as one can to imagine it, it is much harder to picture a man in as dire circumstances having the kind of tenacity – *combined with an inherent nurturing quality of thought* – to carry on for these three or four desolate years as she did. Deprived of the joys of normal motherhood, or even of a normal marriage, having seen the members of what had been her close-knit family pass on or turn suspicious of her, she had, in place of these normal harmonizing and fulfilling elements in life, a new idea that she was nurturing. She may not have been consciously doing this, but the instinct of the mother to protect and nurture what she had already brought forth is the only fact that even half adequately explains the way she almost literally plowed ahead – even when her very living arrangements were abruptly altered.

As it happened, on that June night in 1868, two other boarders at Mrs. Webster's also were either turned out by her son-in-law or, at least, decided that if Mrs. Patterson was going, so were they. The three of them huddled on the porch until the rainstorm had ended and then went down the street to the house of a well-bred but somewhat impoverished New England lady, Sarah Bagley. Miss Bagley was a spinster whose family circumstances had suffered a decline. But she was in possession of the family house, which she maintained in a neat fashion. She also happened to be a spiritualist.

One of the persons evicted from the Webster house, another woman, has no part in Mrs. Glover's story. But the other person, a young man of nineteen, Richard Kennedy, plays a major role. Before long, Mrs. Glover (she had about this time reverted to using her first married name, obviously a sign that she did not expect to have any further relationship with Patterson) was giving lessons in her method of healing to both Sarah Bagley and Richard Kennedy. Bagley quickly left her spiritualist leanings and became a healer. After Hiram Crafts, she may in fact have been the first person to go into the practice in a serious, full-time manner. She never followed Mrs. Glover all the way into the practice of spiritual healing that became Christian Science, but she supported herself for the next twenty years by using what Mrs. Glover taught her of her method in 1868 and 1869.

Mary passed the summer of 1868 in Amesbury at Sarah Bagley's house. Then in September she had an opportunity to go back to Stoughton to live with a family by the name of Wentworth. She had met the Wentworths when she was living with Hiram Crafts in 1866-67. The situation seemed to offer her the calm she needed to continue her Bible research and writing. Her room and board would be paid for by teaching her system of healing to the wife, Sally Wentworth, who was herself a kind of practical healer. Mary went to the Wentworths' in the fall of 1868 and remained until the spring of 1870. This was the most settled period of her life during these years, and the one for which she might have been expressing her gratitude when she wrote about the search during these years as being "sweet, calm, and buoyant with hope..." Mr. Wentworth was a Universalist, and while he did not formally study what Mrs. Glover had to present to his wife, there was no opposition to it on his part. He was also healed of a sciatic condition by Mrs. Glover while she was living with them.

The Wentworths had four children, three of whom were still living at home. The youngest, Lucy, became a fast friend of Mrs. Glover's. From the reminiscences of Lucy and her school chums in later years, one gets the clearest picture of what Mrs. Glover was like during these years of her spiritual development. Lucy wrote that, when Hiram Crafts had first brought her over to their house, "we just felt as if an angel had come into our house." Lucy described her:

> She was a lonely woman past her prime who at the time had seen much of life. In appearance she was very straight of figure, a little above the average in height, with shoulders rather broad for her small waist, small hands and feet, dark brown hair and gray eyes with a faraway look in them, that were very expressive, and under excitement seemed darker than they really were....
>
> Her wardrobe at this time consisted of a black and white plaid, also a few morning dresses. Her one best black dress was of very fine material, made after the fashion of that day and trimmed with narrow silk velvet ribbon. She kept her clothes very carefully. It made no difference what she wore, there always seemed to be a certain style about her. [13]

The comment about the clothes reveals much. Mrs. Glover had come not from a home of wealth, but from a family that was well provided for and, in American parlance, "on the way up" during the years in which she was maturing. And during her long years of invalidism in the 1840s and 1850s, to which were added the poverty to which she had been increasingly burdened while married to Patterson, she had not lost the touch both of femininity and of propriety that others often remarked about her. It would still be several years before she was moderately well-off, but she always managed to have a sense of good taste, even elegance, about her. She must have had an innate sense that she would not get a hearing in a man's world if she appeared in it or before it without the graciousness one expected of a woman. Yet, having conformed to the world's general expectations of what a well-bred woman should be like, it was never the superficial about her that attracted. Rather, it was the sense of authority about her with which she was able to reach others.

Living in a house with three almost grown teenagers, Mary had the kind of companionship with a younger generation that had been almost completely lacking from her life for the previous two decades. She would work in her room on her writing during the day. Then she would turn to her "family." Lucy wrote, "She would often come to meet me on my way home from school and we would go for a short walk around the neighborhood… After she had worked for hours she always relaxed and threw off her seriousness. Then she would admit us, my brother Charles and me, and sometimes a school friend of Charles's. The boys would romp in her room sometimes rather boisterously, but she never seemed to mind it."[14] Another friend of Lucy's wrote to Mrs. Eddy toward the end of the latter's life, "There, now I can feel your arms about me as they used to be in the Springtime long ago when we used to hunt the anemone and you told me of the beautiful May flowers of your native state. What a beautiful time that was! How we longed for your coming in those days."[15] Mrs. Glover even taught the Wentworth children how to play backgammon.

One gets the clearest idea of what was going on in Mrs. Glover's thought during the Wentworth period from the letters she was writing. She had taken on the education of Sarah Bagley in mental healing, and there were several letters to Sarah. In the fall of 1868, Mary's brother George finally succumbed. Mary went back to new Hampshire for the funeral. Upon her return she wrote to Sarah:

> I have the sad news to tell you of my brother's death.…
>
> Such is all our experience fulfilling the lesson this world is not thy home. The pleasant firesides made desolate – the family altar, where is it? Forever

> departed to me, but to the other two remaining, they have their pleasant homes.
>
> But I would not weary you with such details, my experience is, that the unfortunate are only thought to be bores – until by chance a change comes, then friends throng, and smiles multiply.[16]

The brief moments of self-pity in some of her letters in this period may have served to clear her thought of emotional baggage that could have kept her from what she saw as her work; for at the same time she was hard at work on her manuscript. By June of 1869 she was ready to talk about it. To one old friend, Charlotte Mulliken, she wrote:

> I have just sent a work to the press for publication entitled Science of Soul – I mean you shall read it sometime. I have written this and notes on the entire book of Genesis within the last year and this, besides laboring for clothes and other expenses with teaching I am worn almost out, have lost my love of life completely and want to go where the weary have a rest and the heavy laden lay down their burdens.[17]

At about the same time she wrote to Sarah Bagley: "My volume is finished, Sarah, and ready for the press and the outcry that will follow it; first the ridicule, then the argument, and lastly the adoption by the public but it may be long ere the public get it." In the same letter she also identified the elements in human thought that she thought must be transformed before any healing message as radical – and simple – as hers could become firmly planted: "When the great harvest comes which shall divide truth from error what a glorious time some body will have of it to live in that age; oh but the selfishness, the cupidity, the wrong of this time will take a severe cudgeling before then."[18]

Sometime in 1868 someone had given Mary a copy of Smith's *Dictionary of the Bible;* this was apparently her first Bible aid, and she made good use of it. But her study of the Bible was less in historical terms, or in any of the age-encrusted categories of Calvinist theology on which she had been raised, than in looking for the line of spiritual enlightenment that had healed her that Sunday morning in Lynn. At the same time, she had the remnants of the legacy of Quimby to lay aside. She had long ago recognized that the kind of mental suggestion or control over another individual represented by his practice was not in line with the method of biblical healing, in which it was the realized presence of God in human consciousness that effected a healing. But she had not yet gone completely beyond some occasional reliance on Quimby as an authority figure. She may have simply been seeing something in Quimbyism that she herself had put there. Or there could have been a residue of reliance on a man's name.

This may help to explain some correspondence of hers in July 1869. After she had already finished her own manuscript, from which she would begin formally teaching what she first designated "moral science" in just another year, she wrote to Sarah Bagley:

> ...you had without my consent or knowledge copies of the MSS. of Dr. Quimby which belong exclusively to me and to such students as contract to receive their instructions....
>
> But now I learn from your own signature that you have retained a copy of those MSS. This was a fraud for which I must hold you or any other person responsible who should commit such an act. Now if you wish for a private settlement I will spare your feelings and charge you 50 doll[ar]s only for the copy....[19]

The main similarity between the manuscript to which she was apparently referring and her own manuscript, entitled *The Science of Man,* was that both were written in the form of questions and answers. However, Quimby's was a mixture of pseudo-scientific explanations, none of which departed from the common-sense view of man as a material body with a mind inside that might in some way influence the body. Mrs. Glover's, on the other hand, however imprecise her early explications may have been, began with her definition of God. Her system of healing came directly out of her understanding of God and could not be taught except as part of a religious practice that included all the ethical and moral demands of Christianity. In fact, the questions and answers bear a remarkable similarity to the final set of questions and answers in the chapter of the Christian Science textbook called "Recapitulation," the chapter on which Christian Science primary class teaching is based.[20] Beginning with a definition of God as Principle, she answered the question, "What is Principle," with the statement, "Principle is Life, Truth and Love, Substance and Intelligence."

During her eighteen-month stay with the Wentworths, her questions and answers that eventually became *The Science of Man* went through at least five revisions (these were copied for her by Mrs. Wentworth). One problem in dealing with the evolution of Mrs. Glover's thought during this period is that she continued to make references to Quimby, even as her own explication of healing moved further away from what she may have taken into thought from earlier discussions with him. One of the inheritances she still put up with from the Quimby acquaintance was his belief that the healer sometimes took on the beliefs of the patient he was healing. She wrote more than once of feeling the effect of others turning their thought to her personally for healing.

Yet all through this period of discovery and growth she continued to take the cases that her early students could not cure. Mrs. Wentworth was asked to take a case of a man who was suffering from excruciating intestinal pain. Mrs. Wentworth, upon seeing the evidence of the man's suffering, felt unprepared to handle the case. She had the man's son get the horses hitched and drive his father over to see Mrs. Glover. Mary told him that if he would be quiet she would heal him. Within a couple of hours he was entirely free. This was typical of what some of her early students reported about her. Putney Bancroft, who was in one of her first classes in 1870, said that she was absolutely fearless in the face of any illness.

During this period of living in Stoughton with the Wentworths, she had obviously made great progress in explaining her discovery to herself and in writing about it for others. Now the time had come for her to branch out more than she was able to do in Stoughton. Exactly why she left the Wentworths when she did is unclear, but sometime during the winter of 1870 she went back to Amesbury to live briefly with Sarah Bagley again. During the period she had been in Stoughton, she had been corresponding with both Bagley and young Richard Kennedy. Kennedy was the young man who had left the Webster house with her when she had been turned out in the rain that summer night in 1868. He was now twenty-one years old, and felt that he was ready to begin practicing her method of healing.

Mrs. Glover had not yet worked out a satisfactory way to delve deeper into her discovery, to write about it, and at the same time have a modicum of financial security. Her boarding with others had for the most part involved giving them lessons in her "moral science," as she then called it, and supporting their first steps in its practice. This had been the case with Hiram Crafts and with Mrs. Wentworth. She now worked out agreements with both Sarah Bagley and Richard Kennedy that provided for her to receive a percentage of their fees from their healing work in return for her continuing to teach them what she knew. Although this arrangement did not last for more than a few years, it did provide her with the income on which to live while she wrote the first draft of *Science and Health* a few years later.

In addition to this, her natural inclination to be a teacher came to the fore. She had gained sufficient confidence in her ability to impart the knowledge of her healing method to the few informal students she had already had, to feel that she could teach more than one student at a time.

So, in the spring of 1870 Richard Kennedy went back to the manufacturing city of Lynn and rented rooms from a Susie Magoun, who had just started a private school for small children. He explained that he needed rooms in which a doctor could receive his patients and for an elderly lady who was busy writing a book. Kennedy agreed to pay Mrs. Glover a fee equal to ten percent of his practice income, in return for continuing instruction from her and for her at least implied support in his more difficult cases. Exactly what he was practicing is debatable, as would become apparent in the next couple of years, when the two came to an irrevocable parting of the ways. But he clearly had a winning personality and must have had a salubrious effect on his patients. In the first year of their arrangement, he paid Mrs. Glover close to $2,000, a sum that would be equivalent to at least ten times that amount in today's dollars.[21]

The other way in which she met her financial needs was through the start of formal teaching. In August of 1870 she had her first class of five or six pupils, charging them $100 each for a series of twelve lessons over three weeks. In December she taught another class, and this time raised the tuition to $300. She did not collect this from every student, and sometimes over the years taught students for no fee at all if she felt they were ready for what she had to teach them. But the $300 remained her fee for the twenty years she taught, and was the basis for the modest but stable financial security she was able to build for herself even before the textbook's sales greatly increased her income. In her first three years in Lynn, she was able to put aside some $6,000, most of that amount probably coming from the arrangement she had with Kennedy. Because she looked on herself as a teacher more than as an individual practitioner, or healer, she never had any substantial income from her healing. Moreover, if she were to progress in her project of giving "moral science" to a wider world through her writings, it was absolutely necessary for her to find a way to meet her basic needs.

She was aware in setting the fee that it was high in terms of incomes in those days. The average student who came to her probably would have earned $1,000 a year or less in a shoe factory in Lynn. Even for those who had more promising careers, $300 was a large amount of money. She recognized this. Writing twenty years later in *Retrospection and Introspection,* she said:

> When God impelled me to set a price on my instruction in Christian Science Mind-healing, I could think of no financial equivalent for an impartation of a knowledge of that divine power which heals; but I was led to name three hundred dollars as the price for each pupil in one course of lessons at my College, – a startling sum for tuition lasting barely three weeks. This amount greatly troubled me. I shrank from asking it, but was finally led, by a strange providence, to accept this fee.[22]

Even many of the early students who did not stay with her in the work felt the instruction had been worth the money. One of them who left wrote: "I will say, and always have said, that her teachings in spiritual science were beyond any money consideration."[23]

❖ ❖ ❖ ❖

December 1870. We have reached that point in Mary Baker Eddy's life story with which this book began. Almost fifty years of age, for all practical purposes without family around her, her years of illness conquered, roughly eight years since she first met Quimby and began the searching, she had reached that sense of confidence and assurance in the validity of her discovery to begin to formally offer it to others – and, eventually, the others would be the entire world. She was still prone to moments of weakness and weariness that she sometimes shared with others through her letters. But more importantly, she had grown to the point where her sense of mission to the world had overcome timidity or moments of physical weakness. At this point, already past what was considered middle age in the year 1870, she was launching forth on a public venture that would occupy her for the next forty years. These were forty years in which she would continue to grow in her own understanding and individual use of what she had discovered, and at the same time grow closer to such a total dependence on God that nothing would deter her from what she perceived to be her "mission."

What, then, was she teaching these first students of hers in 1870? It was not yet what would become the full doctrine of Christian Science. It was a system of healing more than it was a religion, although, unlike Quimbyism, it was firmly based on a metaphysics that started with the supremacy of God. She had advertised for her first class in a Lynn newspaper:

> Mrs. Glover, the well-known Scientist, will receive applications for one week from ladies and gentlemen who wish to learn how to heal the sick without medicine, and with a success unequaled by any known method of the present day, at Dr. Kennedy's office, No. 71 South Common Street, Lynn, Mass.[24]

We have seen in the opening pages of this story the effect she had on her students. As for the content of what she was teaching, it was a metaphysics that had not yet grown to completion. It was Bible-based and sprang from a total reliance on God. Before the classes began, she had her students read from what became *The Science of Man;* it was then titled "Questions and Answers in Moral Science." It began:

> Question: What is God?
> Answer: A principle: wisdom, Love, and Truth.
> Question: What is this Principle?
> Answer: Life and intelligence.
> Question: What is Life and intelligence?
> Answer: Soul.
> Question: Then what is God?
> Answer: The Soul of man and the universe.

From this identification of God as the starting point and core of existence, she proceeded to define man as the idea, or reflection, of this Principle. The language was not at all as clear as it would later become, but one can certainly see the outlines of the final system. Separating the perfect idea, man, from the mortal that calls itself man gave her the foundation for healing:

> Question: What is the man that is sick and mortal?
> Answer: We have shown you that the man that is harmonious and immortal is learned of Science, and reverses the belief we have held of him by holding life, substance and intelligence in the Soul... Now, the body, that we call man, that is inharmonious and mortal, is a belief that life, substance and intelligence are in the body, that the Soul is here, hence, intelligence and life are in matter. From these false premises flow the error that is mortal, and this error is man that is sick and mortal called the body of man.

She taught from the beginning the insignificance of belief as opposed to spiritual understanding. "It is dangerous to believe in God when we are instructed to 'acquaint ourselves with God.'" She taught that sin and disease belonged to the realm of false belief. Not being a part of the creation God made, they could be destroyed by understanding their unreality. "You must pluck the beam out of your own eye first; you must take away the belief to yourself of all the so-called laws of health, which are only the educated laws of belief, by which we suffer the penalty of a belief, instead of the punishment of Truth."

But she also linked this kind of mental labor with the moral demands of the Bible. For instance:

> Now, then, to advance most rapidly in this Science, you will cut off every offending thought or motive, all that is not Truth. You will not love money, beyond the appreciation of it as a means of usefulness. You will not lie or deceive. You will be just and merciful, and if you hold any habit, which places pleasure in sense, you will be rid of this, or how can you destroy

> it in others. For instance, never let a student of Moral Science think to succeed by ought but honesty.[25]

Through questions and answers, which were part of her method of classroom teaching, she was able to discern the thought of the student and correct what needed correcting. One of the students in her very first class, Charles Stanley, argued with her when they began discussing religious concepts; he had come only to learn a mental method of healing, not to have his religious beliefs challenged. She dismissed him during the second week, saying that students were there to learn, not to teach.

She was already well on the way to establishing her authority as the teacher of "moral science." There were mistakes made in these first classes, mistakes that came from some remnants of Quimbyism that still clung to her progressing thought. In the next few years, she would see what still needed to be done. But as 1870 ended, her career as teacher had been launched, and she had settled into a mode of living, healing, teaching, and writing in Lynn that would occupy her there for the next decade.

Chapter 5

The Lynn Years
Continuing Discovery by Experience; The Textbook Is Written

As 1870 came to an end, Mary Glover had taught two classes in "Moral Science." The reaction of those students who were able to grasp the spirit as well as the letter of her teaching had encouraged her, in what she was beginning to define as her mission, to spread the healing method she had discovered. It may indeed be fortunate that she as yet had little idea of the resistance she would encounter to her teachings, or of the specific personal trials she would face during the decade of the 1870s in Lynn.

By the end of the decade, there would be a few persons across the United States who had begun to hear of Christian Science, as it was called after 1875. And there would be a small church in Boston, organized with twenty-six charter members in 1879. But before reaching even that point, Mrs. Glover was to undergo an array of testing and learning experiences. Each one, it can be said, would cause her intense anguish, but would also be the source of some increase in her ability to deal with the human mentality – especially the unregenerate human mentality that she called mortal mind. As the years went on, she became increasingly confident that God had given her a mission. Without this supreme confidence, it seems most unlikely that she would have continued with her work.

To look ahead briefly at the decade in Lynn before discussing some of its events in more detail, Mrs. Glover had not learned all there was about the system she would eventually denominate as Christian Science when she began teaching in 1870. She had it firmly planted in God, and this emphasis in her teaching on a supreme power was what enabled others to go out and heal. But she had not yet forbidden the use of physical manipulation, and this was shortly to bring her to a parting of the ways with Richard Kennedy. She had also not delved as deeply as she would later into the dangers of mental manipulation, or malpractice, on the part of an unprincipled practitioner of the art. Her mental method was firmly planted in the biblical record of Christianity, as she understood it, even in the year 1870. But in the traditional language of the Bible, the ways and wiles of the devil were not as clear to her as was the basic grounding of her thought in the power of God.

Beyond the fact that she still had some basic elements of her science to learn before she would have it all complete, there was the simple element of human inexperience in dealing with others. She made mistakes with some of the people she trusted too much. In later years she said of this tendency, "It has always been my misfortune to think people better and bigger than they really are. My mistake is, to endow another person with my ideal, and then make him think it his own."[1] Overly generous or not in her estimation of other people, she could make the movement grow only with the human resources she had at her disposal. And in that early period in Lynn, she was working for the most part with young people of only modest education, humble background, and limited human horizons. She quite understandably tended to trust each one who was attracted to her teaching, but there was literally not a single one of them who was able to follow her own advance in thought during the decade.

Richard Kennedy, whom she came to regard as her bitterest though unseen foe during the 1870s, wrote sympathetically during his later years of this period in her life. Although his remark refers to her boarding around in the late 1860s, it applies in general to this entire epoch of her life (and she would again be a boarder from 1872 until 1875):

> It was an unfortunate fact that Mrs. Eddy with her small income was obliged to live with people very often at this time in her life who were without education and cultivation. It was never her custom to keep apart from the family. She invariably mingled with them and through them kept in touch with the

> world. She had a great work to do; she was possessed by her purpose and like Paul the apostle, and many another great teacher and leader, she reiterated to herself, "This one thing I do." Of course simple-minded people who take life as it comes from day to day find any one with so fixed an object in life a rebuke to the flow of their own animal spirits.[2]

While Kennedy's even partial tribute to her a generation later is remarkable in view of the split that occurred between them, his choice of phrasing – "animal spirits" – was an apt description of a portion of the problem that arose almost immediately between him and Mrs. Glover. Part of Quimby's method, apparently to make patients more receptive to what Quimby would suggest to them, was to rub their heads. In treating a female patient, he would first wet her hair and then rub the head. At the time Mrs. Glover gave her first two classes in 1870, Kennedy was just becoming established in his Lynn practice. He was still following this method of Quimby manipulation, and at the beginning of each class session, he would rub the head of each student and massage the solar plexus, an area behind the diaphragm. Given the sensitivity of both parts of the body, it is understandable that those students who knew nothing of the Quimby background could not fathom the connection between the massaging and Mrs. Glover's spiritual instructions that followed.

For a time Mrs. Glover herself did not appear to see the inconsistency, although she never used any kind of bodily contact as part of her own treatments. But she wrote, in defense of rubbing, to Putney Bancroft, "Now studying is the process belief employs to gain the scientific man, the same as rubbing the head is the process my students employ to rub out belief and therefore let the idea man appear in its harmony."[3] The simplistic idea behind the rubbing was that, since one wanted to reach the thought of the patient, rubbing the head got closest to the center of thought. What purpose was served by Kennedy's also massaging the solar plexus is less clear.

In any case, the objections of a few discerning students, such as Bancroft, apparently made her question the practice of manipulation more than she had previously. Then the question came to be resolved through the agency of still another person, Wallace Wright. Wright was a young man of twenty-five whose father was a Universalist minister. The young Wright applied to have class with Mrs. Glover in the spring of 1871 (this was her third formal class), but before taking class with her, he submitted a list of questions. He asked her what the basis of her system was. She responded that it was founded on "God, the principle of man." One of his questions was, "Has this theory ever been advertised or practiced before you introduced it, or by any other individual?" Mrs. Glover answered him in detail:

> Never advertised, and practiced only by one individual who healed me Dr. Quimby of Portland, Me. An old gentleman who had made it a research for twenty five years, starting from the stand-point of magnetism thence going forward and leaving that behind. I discovered the art in a moment's time, and he acknowledged it to me; he died shortly after and since then, eight years, I have been founding and demonstrating the science. [4]

Wright had class and then moved to Knoxville, Tennessee, where he began to practice healing. He was apparently successful for a short time, but began to question the teaching and to think it had been a form of mesmerism. Mrs. Glover unsuccessfully tried to reason with him by letter: "To be happy and useful is in your power, and the science I have taught you enables you to be this, and to do great good to the world if you practice this science as laid down in your MSS. Time alone can perfect us in all great undertakings..." [5]

However, Wallace Wright was not the first man of twenty-five to think that he saw all things rightly, and things went from bad to worse. As Mrs. Glover wrote to Sarah Bagley in the pungent prose that would mark many of her letters during the seventies:

> Wright is all wrong at present. He gave the strongest protestations of admiration for this Science when he was about to leave for the South and has come back and is going over his grand ranting about it with all his little capacity. When they told me he said he should ruin this Science here and at the South I told them to tell him to take a bucket and go for the Atlantic ocean and work to empty it and if he succeeded to try his next job on the purpose he declared.[6]

Wright came back to Lynn and demanded his $300 class tuition refunded plus $200 in damages. He attacked Mrs. Glover in the pages of the *Lynn Transcript;* she counterattacked. One cannot help but have some empathy with them both. Mrs. Glover had to make it clear that she was not teaching mesmerism: "Mesmer was the author of it, and never, to my knowledge, did he claim it was Moral Science; and I, who know no more of the practice of mesmerism than does a kitten... would be loath to steal his thunder, or to attempt to teach what I did not understand."[7]

But poor young Wright sounded as if he believed that the absolute spiritual statements of Moral Science left no room for the good that can be expressed and experienced on the purely human level. This "so-called science," as he called it, "tells us that man is a delusion; that man, the noblest work of God, the result of His creative genius, the flowers in the fields, the mighty forests, the hidden wonders of the world, are all delusions, and the work of imagination."[8] Mrs. Glover countered with the statement: "The idea that expresses moral science is physical, and we see this idea traced out in one continuous page of nature's bright and glorious character. Every blade of grass, tree and flower, declare, 'How manifold are thy works, O Lord! in wisdom hast thou made them all.'"[9]

Wright had not only misunderstood her teaching; he had also put his finger on what would be the intellectual sticking point for thousands of others who would turn to Christian Science in the future without the spiritual openness required to gain the meaning of her words. Matter was unreal, yes; but basing one's thought on the perfect spiritual creation of God did not take away one iota of what was good in human experience. Yet looking only at statements of absolute spiritual fact, without their application to the present human experience, might easily lead anyone into an intellectual dead end.

The controversy went back and forth; Wright challenged Mrs. Glover in print to raise the dead, walk on the water, and perform other miracles on demand. Mrs. Glover did not respond, but her students did. Wright's last rejoinder, again in the *Lynn Transcript,* was to the effect that "Mrs. Glover and her science are virtually dead and buried." [10] It was the first of many false obituary notices that would be printed or said over the course of a century.

The public controversy with Wright hardly served to lend dignity to the new movement. However, from the very start, Mrs. Glover was a public person. There were no secrets in her science. She was convinced that it had a future and that the public should be warned about anyone who had had some connection with her and later misrepresented what he had been taught. [11] At the same time, one can see how such notice in the press could easily degenerate into a kind of negative gossip among townsfolk who were not necessarily hostile, but who had no particular interest in knowing exactly what Mrs. Glover was teaching.

The most positive result of the Wallace Wright episode was Mrs. Glover's looking mesmerism squarely in the face and admitting that there must be no trace of it in her teachings. And this meant that Richard Kennedy would have to stop massaging his patients! Mrs. Glover asked all her students to remove from their manuscripts the one reference that permitted physical manipulation. Kennedy rebelled, and told her he would no longer pay her under the terms of their contract. She tried to work with him a bit longer, but by the spring of 1872 the partnership was over. (Thirty years later Kennedy's calling card would read, "Richard Kennedy, Masseuse.")

The struggle with Kennedy had not been over physical manipulation only. Mrs. Glover was in frequent contact with almost all of her early students, and through them she often heard about the practices of others. She had been aware that Kennedy had a high proportion of female patients, and she was also aware that Kennedy had a strong tendency to try to influence the thinking of his patients. But since he began his treatments with physical manipulation, Mrs. Glover could see the possible connection between this and mental manipulation, or control.

Psychology had not yet become an organized discipline. William James's *Principles of Psychology*, the first major American textbook on the subject, would not appear until 1890. [12] The study of the human mind was taking place under the aegis of the faculties of both medicine and philosophy. Mrs. Glover was aware of the background of mesmerism, of course, but her practice of spiritual healing was providing her with the same kind of practical proving ground that a medical doctor finds in a research hospital. She would never get to the point of writing or speaking about the action of the human mind in terms acceptable to (or compatible with) the new science of psychology, but she was covering the same ground the psychologists would cover for many decades to come.

The reason the two strands of thought did not meet at some point is that Mrs. Glover presented Christian Science as a religion. The God of the Bible remains the starting point of any discussion of mind or intelligence in Christian Science. The human mind, which is the subject of psychology, is considered in Christian Science to be a part of the mind-body continuum that actually misrepresents the real man.

At this point, after the public controversy with Wright and the more private one with Kennedy, Mrs. Glover began to consider mesmerism as a much larger phenomenon than merely putting one's patients to sleep physically. She had already had convincing evidence of the power of thought to heal when this thought was imbued with the Christ-consciousness, or a sense of the presence of God. Now she understood somewhat more clearly the power of thought, when not in line with the Judeo-Christian moral code, to impress, or intrude, itself injuriously on another person's thought. She began to see a pattern in the stories people brought to her about Kennedy, a pattern of attempted control of a patient's thoughts without the patient's being aware of it. The degree to which she may have built this, in the case of Kennedy, into something greater than it actually was is a matter about which there can be some area of disagreement. Mrs. Glover was ever the mother ready to defend her child, Moral Science and later Christian Science, from attack. But there was undoubtedly more than a casual attempt on Kennedy's part to turn people away from her or to control other people's thinking.

Thus, the period that began with her teaching Wallace Wright in April 1871 and ended with her break with Kennedy about a year later was a tumultuous one in her own development. To the old Quimby belief that the healer, or practitioner, could manifest some of the same symptoms of the patients she was curing had been added this new knowledge of the danger of mental malpractice or, as she more commonly referred to it, malicious animal magnetism. Some of her letters of 1871-72 highlight the mental turmoil:

> To a friend in July 1871, while she was on another solitary visit to Tilton, New Hampshire: The day after my arrival here I made my lonely way to the cemetery where rest the remains of my parents and brothers. I felt like a pilgrim on the way to Mecca and as I look forward to the land of souls, I know that my hopes, and joys, and affections, have gone thither, and it only needs the vail to be lifted to let me in to those glorious realities, and close the door of earthly ills and illusions... [13]

> To her student, Putney Bancroft, in 1872: Truth is, I am so tried by the malice of my students that up to this time or a little prior to it I have done nothing but love and praise, that I am losing my happiness and

> consequently my health in the dark labyrinth into which I gaze and stand upon the brink thinking momently, will my students plunge therein? [14]
>
> To Mary Ellis, February 1872: Why I suffer so much is because, if we cast pearls before swine they turn and rend us. [15]
>
> To Sarah Bagley, April 1872: The great cause that I have established in the minds of thinkers in many places and for which I have borne most of the blows given to it, is now placed in the hands of *lust* and *lies.* [16]
>
> To Fred Ellis, while she was visiting in Tilton, New Hampshire, in May 1872: I cannot tell you the fearful wrongs Dr. R K is doing me in Lynn. He has called Wright to his rooms and has entered into conspiracy with him against me and, this was the meaning of that dreadful threat.
>
> O, Mr. Ellis, do talk with me about God, about wisdom, love, and Truth. I am almost lost in this hour. I am so bitterly tried by such accumulating falsehoods. I can only think of Joan of Arc. I am surrounded on all sides by his mad efforts to put me down before I shall tell the truth of him and which I do not desire to do. [17]

But the saddest outpouring of them all was a letter she wrote to Putney Bancroft on Thanksgiving Day 1872 (the last Thursday in November). Thanksgiving in the United States has a tradition going back to the Pilgrim Fathers. It had been a national holiday just since the Civil War, but it had long been an important day for family gatherings in New England. She wrote to "Friend Bancroft" in terms that, he claimed, still evoked emotion in him fifty years later:

> They tell me this day is set apart for festivities and rejoicing; but I have no evidence of this except the

> proclamation and gathering together of those who love one another. I am alone today, and shall probably not see a single student… family ties are broken never to be reunited in this world with me.
>
> But what of those who have learned with me the Truth of Moral Science; where do they find their joys; where do they seek friendship and happiness? Shall I see one of them today?[18]

❖ ❖ ❖ ❖

However, 1872 did not end on this mournful tone. Something else had been happening since the Wright defection and the break with Kennedy. Mary Glover had decided she must get to work on a major text explaining her science, and it was with this thought in mind that she was able to write to Sarah Bagley toward Christmastime: "I have a very nice time this winter everything so quiet pleasant scientific and comfortable. I have a better opportunity to write than ever before.... I have never since my first perceptions of God in science gained the understanding I have this year past and been able to so sift the tares from the wheat."[19]

For many years Mrs. Glover had been in the habit of turning to her Bible, opening it at random, and finding a Bible verse that spoke to her present need. To someone who has had no comparable experience, there is something unbelievable about such a procedure; in fact, it sounds so eerie as to color one's impressions of the person indulging in such a habit. On the other hand, this happened many times with Mrs. Glover, often in later years in the presence of some of her household staff. One can only state the facts as recorded by her or others and leave it for the individual to decide. Mrs. Glover, of course, would have said that her constant attempt to live close to God gave her the messages she needed from His inspired book at the right moment. In this instance, she had opened the Bible one day during her period of altercation in the press with Wallace Wright. Her eye had fallen on this passage in Isaiah: "Now go, write it before them in a table, and note it in a book, that it may be for the time to come for ever and ever." She noted the date in the margin of her Bible.

There were, of course, other reasons to write a book. Since 1866 she had been carrying around a bundle of manuscript papers, although these were mainly her attempt at an exegesis of the book of Genesis. She had copyrighted the book, *The Science of Man,* in 1869, and she used a changing version of that manuscript for her class teaching. But she had not actually published that yet and would not do so until 1876. It would have gone through several redactions by that date. *The Science of Man* dealt mainly with the method of healing, although it began, as we have seen, with a definition of God from which the rest flowed.

The rest, however, did not yet flow! This small pamphlet was not a complete statement of the theology of Christian Science, and she realized during these early years of controversy in Lynn that she needed to set it all down. Moreover, she was approaching the point where she was ready to do so. She could not have been ready any sooner. As she wrote later of these years:

> From 1866 to 1875, I myself was learning Christian Science step by step – gradually developing the wonderful germ I had discovered as an honest investigator. It was practical evolution. I was reaching by experience and demonstration the scientific proof, and scientific statement, of what I had already discovered.[20]

Mrs. Glover realized, from her attempts at writing so far, that for the textbook to be a success she needed to have undivided time to devote to writing it. This involved still another change in lifestyle. In any case, the living arrangement she had had for the past two years, during her partnership with Kennedy, had ceased to be a haven. She stayed on at Susie Magoun's for several months after Kennedy's departure, but her income was again in question. She knew she would have to conserve what principal she had while she was writing the book. So, from sometime in the late summer of 1872 until early 1875, she again became a boarder in the homes of students or friends. She lived briefly with her student, Dorcas Rawson. Then she boarded for six months with the Clarks, with whom she had lived back in 1866. She lived with her student, Putney Bancroft, and his wife for half a year. Finally, she boarded with the George Allen family for about half a year.

Mrs. Glover's frequent moves during this period do not appear to have been caused by disruptions or disagreements with the members of the households in which she was boarding. In the earlier period before 1870, she had talked openly of her ideas and found either some reception for them or outright hostility. Now she was engaged in a more precisely focused mission: to complete a writing assignment, as she saw it. This was a more private time for her, and while she was undoubtedly sensitive to the mental atmosphere wherever she boarded, there is no evidence of mental upheaval occasioned by her talking about her discovery. In fact, Bancroft wrote that she left his house in Swampscott because she was considering taking a few students in late 1873 and did not want to disturb his and his wife's privacy. Bancroft later described this period when she was writing *Science and Health:*

> I have known her when nearly crushed with sorrow, but she wrote on. I have known her when friend after friend deserted her, but she wrote on. I have seen student after student bring ridicule and reproach upon her, but still she wrote on.[21]

Bancroft himself sits in a special chair when one considers the early workers in Christian Science during the Lynn period. A member of her second class in 1870 and a man who never turned away from her, he also never made the grade as a practitioner. Yet there is a gentility about his writing some fifty years later that allows one to see his good, honest human qualities, which made Mrs. Glover place so much hope in him during this period.

After the defection of Kennedy, Bancroft appears to be the one person in whom she had placed the highest hopes for a while. In 1874 she encouraged him to start up a practice in Cambridge, thinking that being in close proximity to Harvard College would help build some links between her science and thinking people in the university atmosphere. He opened an office in Cambridgeport (East Cambridge), probably too far from Harvard to make the hoped for connection. His practice was slow in developing, and early in 1875 he gave up. During the period he was in Cambridge she wrote to him frequently. She tried, apparently without enough success, to send patients his way:

> They [prospective patients] wanted me to take the cases but I told them if they would apply to you I would oversee the job, did this to get them to go.
>
> A Mrs. Sweetland of California has written for me to take her case there. I answered I would put it in your hands… [22]

She wrote to him on another occasion, "…have as much faith in Truth as the mesmerizer has in error and you can snap her out like the blade of an old jackknife." [23] But Bancroft did not have the staying power – certainly not financially, and probably, even more critically, not metaphysically – for the challenge. Yet when he wrote to Mrs. Glover to tell her he was abandoning his attempt at the practice, she did not break with him. Rather, she wrote sympathetically:

> Do not let it be thought you left because you were driven out. Call it your family, as it was in reality. Had you not laid up first your treasures in earthly things you would have been free to work on under difficulties… Few doctors could build up a practice in the *short* time you have tried, and yet I blame you not. [24]

This letter brings up a point that arose with several of Mrs. Glover's early students: their degree of devotion to the mission she saw herself engaged in, and the complexities that could arise when a spouse did not share the same commitment. In many cases, Mrs. Glover encouraged her students to – or beyond – their limits, in her own intensity to get on with the work. She knew from the beginning that she could not expect Christian Science to grow from her healing work alone, but sometimes at this period she expected more from some of her students than it was probably reasonable to assume. She was totally unselfish and totally committed to her mission herself, but there were few who were ready to follow as completely as she felt they should.

As the textbook neared completion, Mrs. Glover was without funds to publish it, and she could find no publisher who thought it a good risk. So, in one more example of the kind of help she felt it proper for her students to proffer, she accepted the aid of two of them, George Barry and Elizabeth Newhall, in advancing $2700 to pay for publishing. (Once again, the reader must make some assumption regarding the equivalent sum more than a century later.)

During the spring and summer of 1875, while she was waiting impatiently for the book to appear, there were three other developments. The first, in the spring of 1875, was that she held her first formal class since 1872. In it was a young man, Daniel H. Spofford, whose wife had been in her first class in 1870. Spofford already knew something of the healing method through his wife, and Mrs. Glover was impressed enough with his potential to offer him class without payment of tuition. For the immediate future, he strengthened the "cause" by taking up the practice successfully in a way that Bancroft had not managed to do.

Also, during the summer of 1875, her students held informal church services for the first time. While Mrs. Glover could not have had more than twenty-five or so formal (as well as loyal) students by 1875, the very first church service attracted more than sixty people. This gives one some idea of the degree to which her work was becoming known in Lynn. The services also attracted some people, including spiritualists, who used the question period during the service to argue with Mrs. Glover. She decided that the services should be discontinued. The desire of her students to have something resembling the kind of churches most of them had been accustomed to, however, hinted at the eventual organization of the church that would be the culmination of the Lynn years.

Thirdly, she came to have a home of her own. While rooming at No. 9 Broad Street in Lynn, she saw a 'For Sale' sign on the house across the street at No. 8 Broad Street. She was finished with her book, but needed a place for quiet proofreading. She was clearly weary of her many moves, and thinking of teaching again on a regular basis. She figured out that if she could rent out a good part of the house, saving room only for her classroom and a room for herself, she could make the payments on it. The house sold for a little more than $5000, and she put down $2800, taking out a mortgage for the rest. Anyone who remembers the experience of becoming a homeowner for the first time will know a little of what Mrs. Glover must have felt. Few people, however, have moved as often as she had in the years since 1866; so the feeling of being settled again, and by means of her own finances, must have been one of the more satisfying moments of those years. In fact, Bancroft comments that the summer of 1875 was one of the happiest periods he saw in Mrs. Glover's life during the twelve years he was closely associated with her activities.

The actual appearance of *Science and Health* late in 1875 has similarities with the first classes Mrs. Glover taught in 1870. Both were epochal events in her career. Her first formal teaching was evidence that she felt ready to impart what she had learned to a wider audience. Yet, as we have just seen, she had had much more to learn before she was ready to write *Science and Health,* so the teaching had not yet been complete in 1870. The first edition of what came to be known as "the textbook" was more nearly complete. It contained a theology as well as a discussion of healing. It was even more firmly anchored in the Bible and, particularly, in the need, as Christians have traditionally expressed it, for a complete regeneration of the human being.

The first edition of *Science and Health,* however, was far from being the mature statement of Christian Science that developed over the course of many later editions. Mrs. Glover's statements regarding God were much clearer than those about man. She still occasionally used the word Quimby sometimes used for man, *shadow.* Also, the clear differentiation between the mortal concept of man and the perfect, spiritual man, whom she recognized as the exact reflection of his Maker, was lacking. The omnipotence and omnipresence of God were well presented – otherwise the very basis of healing in Christian Science would have been missing. But, of the seven synonyms for God that the Christian Science textbook uses today (Life, Truth, Love, Spirit, Soul, Mind, and Principle), she had not yet identified Mind as one of them. Just as the concept of man as the exact reflection of God was not as well presented as it would be later on, the words *mind, intelligence,* and *wisdom* were used without the precision they would have in later editions. In time, she would make a clear distinction between the divine Mind, or God, and His perfect creation, expressed as ideas held in this Mind, and the human mind. The human mind she would identify as the basis of mankind's problems, because of its belief in the reality of matter and a creation separate from what God has made.

The textbook did not and even today does not have the same kind of development from chapter to chapter that one would find in a book on any subject studied in a course in school. Rather, in each chapter, and one can say on virtually every page, there is some variation of the theme of the allness of God, Spirit, and therefore the powerlessness, the nothingness, of matter. Some of the chapters, such as those on prayer and her interpretation of Jesus' life and works, stand very close in content to the way they appear in the final work over thirty years later. On the other hand, many of the metaphysical sections were more sharply honed over the years. To read them in this first edition, one can understand why a casual reader may not have gotten very far.

There is also the hint of borrowing from other sources, although this was more commonly done one hundred years ago.

The trial of a sick person, in which "personal sense" is first tried in the wrong courtroom and then gets justice in the court of spiritual sense, is a lengthier version of a similar trial in one of the Quimby manuscripts, which she may have seen (or even contributed to!). Several of the allusions to outside events, such as to a felon who died when medical students played a trick on him by dribbling warm water on his arm and making him think it was blood, also appear in Warren Evans's *The Mental Cure.* Evans had been a Quimby patient who developed his own system of mental suggestion, and the above title, the first of many books he wrote, had appeared in 1869. But whatever she had read and digested from others she had made her own by the time she wrote *Science and Health.* The originality of the work was indubitable.

The textbook of 1875 was not a bestseller. Barry and some of her other young students went from door to door trying to sell it. After many months, only two hundred of the one thousand copies had been sold. Mrs. Glover sent copies to ministers and to thinkers from whom she hoped to get some attention. The most positive response she received was from Bronson Alcott, who by this time was an elderly man living in Concord. Known for his receptivity to new philosophic ideas, and particularly for his earlier experiments in education, he responded warmly to the textbook, writing to Mrs. Glover in January 1876:

> The sacred truths which you announce, sustained by facts of the Immortal Life, give to your work the seal of inspiration – reaffirm in modern phrase the Christian revelation. In times like ours, so sunk in sensualism, I hail with joy any voice speaking an assured word for God and Immortality. And my joy is heightened the more when I find the blessed words are of woman's divinings."[25]

Alcott's interest was great enough to get him to make a trip to Lynn to meet Mrs. Glover and to come again for an evening with some of her students. He spoke well of *Science and Health* to what remained of the Concord group of philosophers. Emerson was still living, but he did not seem to have grasped the radical spiritual import of what Mrs. Glover had seen. His own exalted sense of man did not rise above the physical base from which the material senses make their estimate of life. When he and Mrs. Glover finally met some years later, she found that he accepted with equanimity the weakening of his mental powers as he aged.

The interest shown by Alcott did not result in making Mrs. Glover's science acceptable to any academic group of thinkers or speculative philosophers. But the fact that this man, who was sensitive to a spiritual approach to life, had been reached by the book certainly gave her the most tangible proof she was to receive at that moment that what she had to teach could be done with the textbook. Incidentally, the textbook uses the words "Christian science" several times, but only at the end does it capitalize both words in one sentence. Over the next year, however, Christian Science would come to be adopted as the final descriptive phrase for what she was teaching.

❖ ❖ ❖ ❖

Whatever the immediate success of *Science and Health,* Mrs. Glover felt a recurrence of her prior tendency to be affected by the thoughts of others – in this case, by the thoughts of those who were reading the book. These were not malicious thoughts, but merely the thoughts of those who were silently turning for help to her personality instead of to what was in the book. Much of her correspondence during 1876 indicates that this was another uncomfortable period for her, and is also a very helpful, even if only partial, explanation of her unexpected decision to marry again at the end of the year.

She wrote to Benjamin Atkinson, a student and the mayor of Newburyport, Massachusetts, sometime during 1876: "… the growing cares and toils unfit me to do more than I am doing. I have to treat myself now, and the additional weight of the sick, beyond what I must inevitably support in the general mind is more than I can sustain; for the year past the touch of mortality, I have not been able to bear at times."[26]

Also during the course of 1876 she confided several times in an unmarried cousin, Hattie Baker, who was living in Boston:

> February: I feel the weight of sick folks terribly since my book is at work.[27]
>
> May: ... unless the sick relieve me of so many minds calling on me alone for help I shall finish my work here soon. I rose from the grave as it were when I got up by means of my discovery, and never since have been able to keep myself in health under the pressure of the minds of the sick. It takes me down every time; hence *I chose the calling* that *I could follow and that was teaching* [italics added]... If you knew what I suffer for the sick by this constant call on me that I have every hour through the mail and otherwise, you, I think, would pity me.[28]
>
> July: The day after my return home I had a violent seizure, I had been in the atmosphere of the sick too long for my belief.... Mrs. B ran for Dr. Eddy, he came when I was unconscious and immediately broke the spell!
>
> I was astonished at his skill, he was calm, clear, and strong, and so kind I *fell* in love with him. Never before had I seen his *real* character, so tender and yet so controlling.[29]

When she wrote the guileless line about falling in love with Eddy, she very likely meant no more than that she had been pleasantly surprised by all the elements of his character that had come to the fore at a moment of intense crisis for her. Yet when she did take the step of marrying again, her choice would be Gilbert Eddy, one of her students.

This period immediately after the publication of *Science and Health* was a very heady one for her. No sooner was the book out than she wished to make improvements in it. This she could not do until the first edition was sold and her share of the proceeds available to help finance a second edition. At the same time, she felt the stirring that the book was causing. As she looked about her for help, it was clear to her that she was operating within a predominantly male world. She did have some women students. Mrs. Spofford, who had been in her first class in 1870, had gone off to practice successfully in Knoxville, Tennessee. But not until she took a woman from Connecticut by the name of Julia Bartlett as a student in 1880 would she begin to have the kind of women about her upon whom she felt she could rely.

At the time Gilbert Eddy had instruction from her in 1876, she looked to Daniel Spofford as one of her ablest students. Spofford had established himself in practice as a scientific healer after taking instruction from her in a class in 1875 and was by this time separated from his wife. One of her letters to him in October 1876 indicated her trust in him, when she said, "My joy at having *one* living student, after those dozen years of struggle, toil and defeat, you at present cannot understand, but will know at a future time when the whole labor is left with you." [30] There is also evidence that she used him as her personal practitioner at some point during the autumn of 1876.

Meanwhile, she was reaching out to help her other students develop. She wrote a metaphysical treatment for lung disease to a Colonel Smith in Washington. [31] She wrote to another gentleman, recommending the textbook: "What that book teaches, gave me the only rest I ever found." [32] Then toward the end of the year she had a personal crisis with Spofford. Although the circumstances still remain a partial mystery, she wrote to him on December 30 to turn his thoughts away from her. "I never was worse than last night and you say you wish to do me good and I do not doubt it then won't you *quit thinking* of me." [33] She also indicated that she could not trust having a male student in her household ever again. Then, apparently later the same day, she wrote to Spofford, asking him to take a note to the Unitarian minister, Samuel Stewart, whose church she had been attending occasionally since 1870, requesting that he marry her and Gilbert Eddy on New Year's Day.

If one were writing about some ordinary citizen, one would be tempted to say that even in the nineteenth century there was a holiday syndrome at work. The holidays, particularly those that are fraught with family sentiment, are alleged to be difficult for those who have family problems to deal with, without the risk of some kind of crisis. But there was no long holiday period then as there is now. In fact, the entire year of 1876 had been a trying one for Mrs. Glover. We may never be privy to the details of all that transpired in those few days before year end. But it is possible that, as she looked forward to the new year and to the challenges she faced – marketing the first edition of the textbook, getting to work on a second edition, furthering the mental and spiritual progress of her students, taking on more students in more classes – that she wished more than ever for the kind of closeness of association that could come only through marriage. Moreover, Spofford had shown a romantic interest in her, as had several other men. Although in her mid-fifties, she was still extremely attractive.

Whatever it was about Spofford that had made her wary of him as the year ended may have turned her thought to the comfort that she might get and the help it would bring to her work if she had the assistance of an understanding husband. In sharing some of these thoughts with Gilbert Eddy, as she may well have done, it is immaterial whether he or she first broached the subject of marriage. The assumption, of course, is that he proposed to her. Given the teacher-student relationship and his reputed meekness, however, it is not inconceivable that the idea of marriage was first expressed by Mary.

She had described Gilbert Eddy in the letter quoted earlier as "calm, clear, and strong." He certainly did not have a personality that thrust itself on another person. Prior to having class with his future wife, Gilbert Eddy had been a sewing machine salesman living in East Boston with a family by the name of Godfrey. Mrs. Glover had healed Mrs. Godfrey overnight of a badly infected, festering finger, and the grateful Mrs. Godfrey had subsequently sent several patients to Mrs. Glover. Eddy himself had a chronic physical problem. Mrs. Godfrey sent him also to Mrs. Glover, who healed him. He very soon had class instruction with Mrs. Glover and entered into the public practice of Christian Science. The few descriptions of him from that time indicate a man of more than usual meekness and of a quiet disposition, but someone who would act from strong conviction. This combination of qualities must have seemed to Mrs. Glover to be the very ones that would calm the waters around her and also end any other incipient male competition for her attention.

Their marriage on January 1, 1877, simplifies all further references to the subject of this biography. From being Mary Baker to Mrs. Glover to Mrs. Patterson and then back to Mrs. Glover, it was now Mrs. Eddy for the remainder of her years. Her usage of intermediate initials and names changed somewhat, from Mary Glover Eddy to Mary B. Glover Eddy to Mary B. G. Eddy, and finally to Mary Baker Eddy. But it was Mrs. Eddy from this time forward, just as the healing system that she felt had gradually been revealed to her was denominated Christian Science after 1875.

The marriage proved a source of immense strength to her for the five and a half years that Eddy lived. These were some of her most trying years, and she had reckoned correctly on the stabilizing and strengthening influence Gilbert Eddy would be. Bancroft wrote of it later:

> [An earlier biographer] describes the married life of Mr. and Mrs. Eddy as one of "tranquil domestic existence." To my recollection it was quite the reverse. True, no inharmoniousness was apparent between them, but their life was one of great confusion, unceasing labor, and troublesome lawsuits throughout the five years they lived together as husband and

> wife… To my understanding, this brief period was the most trying and critical time in Mrs. Eddy's life.[34]

Moral support that he proved to be, it is also a fact that some of the trials she was about to have were brought on by reaction to the marriage itself. And that was an element she had very probably not counted on.

Almost immediately following the marriage, she wrote to Spofford (on January 3), whose professional services she still seemed to value highly, "I hope you will exercise a better feeling soon…. I have done what I deem the best thing that could be done under the circumstances, and feel sure I can teach my husband up to a higher usefulness, to purity, and the higher development of all his *latent noble* qualities of head and heart."[35] Toward the end of January her students gave her and Gilbert a wedding shower, which was reported in the Lynn newspapers.

More trouble was brewing, however, than she was aware of. Throughout the spring of 1877, she referred in much of her correspondence to the physical difficulties she was experiencing. She attributed this mainly to those who were leaning on her personally for their healing; as she wrote in one letter to Spofford, "...those who *call on me mentally* in suffering are in belief killing me!"[36] However, as sensitive as she believed herself to be to the thoughts of others, she may also have been feeling the rumblings of revolt from those closest to her.

George Barry, an early student, who along with Elizabeth Newhall had financed the first edition of the textbook, was affronted by her marriage to Gilbert Eddy. Young Barry would probably never have considered her in terms of marriage. But the role that gender plays at all levels of human relationships is vastly more complex than most people were aware of in the nineteenth century. Barry proceeded to sue Mrs. Eddy for every conceivable service he had rendered her while living at No. 8 Broad Street, even for carrying buckets of coal up to the upper rooms of the house. His suit asking for $2700 was not a frivolous matter, since Mrs. Eddy did not have such funds to pay out if she were to lose in court.

Then, more seriously, Spofford cooled toward her and eventually turned against her. Years later, in his small book already mentioned, Bancroft wrote that he had thought it a mistake for Mrs. Eddy to have placed so much trust in Spofford when he came to her class in 1875. In retrospect this was obviously easier to discern than it had been at the time; and once more, one must comment that Mrs. Eddy had only a limited number of people to turn to for assistance in these early years of what became the Christian Science movement. As late as April 1877, Mrs. Eddy was writing to Spofford about her physical condition, but sometime later that spring they had an open break. While it had an immediate cause, the underlying issue was almost surely Spofford's inability to separate his respect for Mrs. Eddy as teacher of the new science from his simmering resentment that she had married a man other than himself.

Among the names that crop up in these years are those of a Colonel and Mrs. E. J. Smith. The Smiths lived in Washington and had apparently come to have class with Mrs. Eddy. For many years Mrs. Eddy encouraged Smith to come and be part of her household, the group of earnest workers who came to support her metaphysically and to carry out whatever duties she asked of the young movement. Smith finally did come to Boston, sometime in the mid-80s, and appears to have lasted for only a month or so. Exactly what his deficiencies were, whether there was an abrupt falling out – these are minor questions in either the life of Mrs. Eddy or of her movement, but nonetheless questions that, if answered, might throw even more light on the kind of challenges Mrs. Eddy continued to face in her dealings with even her most promising students. As it happens, she wrote to Colonel Smith, in October 1877, one of the frankest confessions of her frustrations with her cause at that moment in time, and also of her relationship with Gilbert Eddy – a relationship she still must have felt pressed by other students to defend:

> … so far as I can spiritually discern the Divine purpose it is showing me I must not teach or suffer this science to be taught any further at present but wait for a little more fitness of the age and for more individual growth out of the old and more natural or easy approximation to the new way of salvation…
>
> At this hour in a spiritual vision I was directed to the 12 chap of Revelations to explain the hour and also I saw the terrible jargon of false students and their fatal power through mesmerism. …
>
> … I am convinced I have so far carried the introduction of this great Truth too much through my own spirituality… and there has not been sufficient of this in others to take the high trust and assume the high calling to which they have been assigned.
>
> Marriage with us is a union of affection and of high purposes. It is not a sexual union in this my husband coincides with me and is advancing rapidly towards God; but you cannot conceive how our influence is traduced and Truth vilified by some students.[37]

The immediate event that gave Spofford the excuse for his break with her was their disagreement over the terms on which he would undertake to publish a second edition of *Science and Health.* Mrs. Eddy wrote to him, in effect, that if he would not take on the job of publisher as she had proposed it to him, the textbook simply would go out of print. "If you conclude not to carry the work forward on the terms named, it will have to go out of edition as I can do no more for it, and I believe this hour is to try my students who think they have the cause at heart…."[38] Still upset over her marriage, he let his emotions get the better part of his judgment, as he wrote to the woman from whom he had learned whatever he knew of Christian Science:

> Nineteen months since the book was first issued and not corrected yet. . .and the "writing on the wall" is..." you have proven yourself unworthy to be the standard bearer of Christian Science," and God will remove from you the means for carrying on this work. . .I propose to carry it alone expecting no one but God to stand by me.[39]

Spofford may also have been smarting over the fact that Mrs. Eddy had had him transfer his growing practice to Gilbert Eddy, in order for him (Spofford) to give his full time to promoting the sale of her textbook. There is sufficient evidence that, whatever the full reason, Spofford began an attempt to wrest control of the fledgling movement from Mrs. Eddy, visiting many of her students to enlist them on his side. Whether he had done so or not, his arrogant assumption that he was fit to carry on the movement (possibly based on remarks Mrs. Eddy had made to him in 1876 in the context of carrying on the work after she was gone) were too much for Mrs. Eddy. The break became open, and she felt it as necessary to warn students about his influence as she had about Kennedy's five years earlier.

Events now went from bad to worse. Not only did she have Spofford's opposition to deal with, but a new student, who would eventually cause her as much agony as Kennedy and Spofford, entered the scene. This was a person by the name of Edward J. Arens, a German immigrant from Prussia, who was a cabinetmaker in Lynn. He took class with Mrs. Eddy in the autumn of 1877 and quickly gained her trust – a misplaced trust, as it later turned out. Arens had had some brushes with the law in the past; his name was associated with a gang of swindlers working the area from Boston up to the North Shore. Whatever degree of sincerity he evinced while having class with Mrs. Eddy, he very quickly gained her confidence.

Mrs. Eddy was also in need of funds to further the second edition of *Science and Health,* since the break with Spofford had occurred by this time. She must have told Arens a considerable amount about her arrangements with her students, because Arens convinced her that she should sue some of them on the basis that they had not paid her the percentages due her from their practice of Christian Science. Kennedy had also signed a note for $1000, in addition to his percentage agreement with her. Whether or not she gave Arens authority to sue in her name or actually assigned the notes to him, he unwisely engaged in a series of lawsuits in the early part of 1878, all of which were eventually lost.

In addition to these suits for money, he persuaded a Miss Lucretia Brown of Ipswich to sue Spofford on the grounds that he was mentally malpracticing her. Brown had been healed by Mrs. Eddy of a difficulty that had kept her bedridden for years, and her illness returned at this time (she was later permanently healed). The Brown case, tried in Salem District Court, became known as the modern version of the Salem witchcraft trials of 1692. When the case came up, it was quickly dismissed, the judge agreeing with the argument of Spofford's lawyer that the court had no jurisdiction over Spofford's mind.

The net result of all these minor lawsuits was not helpful to Mrs. Eddy's reputation or to her cause at the moment. She later regretted having allowed them to take place. Going to court to settle matters, sending students out to find patients, denouncing disloyal students to the press – these were all tactics that had seemed to have at least something to recommend them at the time. But as the decade ended, she was learning that the methods of Christian Science would have to be vastly different from the methods of society at large. This difference in approach to a problem applied not only to whether one resorted to traditional medical means or to a spiritual healer in the case of illness. In the area of human relationships, the tactics of human persuasion and argument would be undercut if one was to approach every problem from the standpoint of there being one infinite Mind governing every man and woman.

The final ignominy of the period, however, was yet to come, in the form of a lawsuit in which Arens himself was one of those sued. On October 8, 1878, Mrs. Eddy wrote to both Kennedy and Spofford, imploring them to stop what she had become convinced was a systematic form of malpractice against her and her students. In the letter to Spofford, she wrote:

> Your silent arguments to do me harm have done me the greatest possible good.... In order to meet the emergency, Truth has lifted me above my former self, enabled me to know who is using the argument, and when and what is being spoken, – and knowing this, what is said in secret is proclaimed on the house top, and affects me no more than for you to come and say it to me audibly....[40]

Just a week later Spofford disappeared from view. About ten days after that, a newspaper item noted that he had been missing since October 15. He turned up a few days later, thus making it necessary to correct an earlier newspaper story that his body had been identified in a morgue. Somehow a story had been concocted that Gilbert Eddy and Edward Arens had hired a Boston saloon keeper to do away with Spofford. The story is convoluted and belongs more to tales of the bizarre; on the other hand, the Boston papers took the tale seriously at the time. The *Boston Globe,* which, like many other big city newspapers, was highly interested in selling newspapers, printed the allegations as virtual fact, including the headline, MURDER HIM IN COLD BLOOD.

The incident gave the *Lynn Item* an opportunity to talk about the "notorious Scientists' home" on Broad Street, indicating the latent hostility that the small band of Mrs. Eddy's followers must have known was always close behind their every step. Eddy and Arens were jailed temporarily, and Mrs. Eddy had severe difficulty raising bail for them. Between the time the grand jury handed down an indictment against the two and the time the case would have come up, the lawyer the Eddys had hired managed to get a complete confession from an accomplice of the saloon keeper. The accomplice confessed that the entire tale had been fabricated. The two innocent victims were never exonerated in court, although the newspapers in later stories attempted to make up for their lack of sticking to the facts in the first instance. One story in the *Boston Globe* said, "Drs. Eddy and Arens are busy endeavoring to ferret and bring to justice the parties who caused the malicious persecution to be brought against them."

The mystery behind the suit has never been entirely solved. Kennedy had lost the original case that Arens brought against him, and the trial by jury that he requested came up while this conspiracy to murder case was at a high pitch. The jury found in Kennedy's favor. One biographer, Robert Peel, who considered all the known facts surrounding Mrs. Eddy's life at this period, reached the tentative conclusion that Kennedy himself had been the instigator. If so, it would have been only in connivance with Spofford, who was kept out of view for over two weeks. At the time, Mrs. Eddy felt that Spofford was the instigator, and she may have been right. He had refused to cooperate with her on the second edition of *Science and Health;* he also knew the projected timing of its appearance and the importance she placed on it. Twice she wrote to Colonel Smith that Spofford had been the villain, writing in March 1879, "The cause is prospering again, rising up slowly from the awful blow of malice and falsehoods dealt it last Autumn.... It was got up by Spofford to stop the sale of my Book..."[41]

No one has suggested that Arens conspired to be named a defendant. But it is not inconceivable that this man, who apparently had police and underground connections before coming to Mrs. Eddy for class, and who, in just three more years, was to act unethically toward her himself, had already hatched some scheme that would have made him look like more of a hero to her had her lawyer not been so successful in uncovering the whole fraud.

In any case, this was the worst in the series of incidents in the "Lynn years" that brought Christian Science into the public arena in ways that, to the casual, outside observer, would not have enhanced its attractiveness. Fifty years later, in the 1920s, a new director of The Mother Church who had just arrived in Boston visited with an acquaintance on Beacon Hill. This was the home of Boston's most distinguished citizens. This woman, a friend of his family's, told him bluntly that she did not know how he could be associated with Christian Science. She had come from Lynn, or had friends in Lynn, and she knew what kind of things had gone on in Lynn, she said.

The director left her with a copy of *Science and Health.* Sometime later, when visiting with her again, she recalled the earlier conversation. "I really don't know a thing about what went on in Lynn," she said. "I was only repeating what other people had told me. Since you were here I have read your text-book, and now I know that what they said could not have been true of the woman who could write that."[42] But such was some of the legacy of the Lynn years.

❖ ❖ ❖ ❖

During the entire first two years of the Eddys' marriage, 1877 and 1878, Mrs. Eddy was involved in getting her second edition of the textbook published, in realizing the depths of the defection of another student (Spofford) for whom she had had high hopes, and in these various lawsuits. These were not her only activities, to be sure. She taught a class in early 1877, but did not teach another until the spring of 1878, which indicates her preoccupation with other affairs. And she continued to shepherd the healing activities of her more active students, who remained unswayed by the shenanigans going on around them.

As the end of the 1870s approached, it was becoming clear to her that, if her movement was to flourish, it needed to move beyond the mental confines of Lynn. Some of the problems she faced were compounded by the small size of the group, its parochialism, and the overfamiliarity that this undoubtedly bred among some of its members. By this time, Mrs. Eddy had probably taught no more than fifty, or at the most seventy, students.

Not all of them had stayed with what they had learned, but others came for healing who had not yet been taught themselves. So there were many reasons for Mrs. Eddy to begin to look beyond Lynn for the focus of her activities. That she eventually settled on Boston may now seem like a foregone conclusion. It was the closest big city, and she already had a few students there. Boston had enjoyed its cultural heyday in the 1840s and 1850s; after the Civil War it went through a period of relative decline, somewhat eclipsed by the rapid growth of several Middle Western cities. This fact explains why Mrs. Eddy briefly considered even Cincinnati as the headquarters of her movement in the early 1880s.

She also had other considerations to take into account. Beginning even this early in the history of Christian Science, she often focused her thought on what the next step needed to be. When she decided on a direction, her students might not understand why. They had not been privileged to know the weeks or months of thought she might have given to a certain problem. That she had in mind an ultimate shape for her church as early as 1879 is clearly not the case. But she had begun to see, from the various calamities in Lynn, along with the continued success of those who had learned to heal, that her movement needed a protection that she personally could not always provide. This resulted in her taking two steps in the next few years: formally organizing as a church in 1879, and the chartering of the Massachusetts Metaphysical College in 1881.

Years later Mrs. Eddy told one of the members of her household, Irving C. Tomlinson, that Christian Science had not come to her all at once:

> Mrs. Eddy never claimed… that [1866] marked the fullness and completion of her discovery. To the contrary she said: "My discovery of Science was the result of experience and growth. It was not a case of instantaneous conversion in which I could say, 'Now the past is nothing – begin entirely anew.' I demon-

> strated each step of the way. In Christian Science we are not spiritual bankrupts with whom God has paid it all. We must work out our own salvation."[43]

She may have been speaking in this case mainly about the metaphysical system of Christian Science, but the remark applies as well to the steps by which she built an organization that could maintain her discovery after she was gone. She had not been certain originally that Christian Science should be organized along the lines of a church at all. She had mentioned to several students, and to one young man whose family she boarded with as far back as the late 1860s, that she would have a church of her own someday. But she had also written rather disparagingly of church organization in the first edition of *Science and Health:*

> We have no need of creeds and church organizations to sustain or explain a demonstrable platform, that defines itself in healing the sick, and casting out error.... The mistake the disciples of Jesus made to found religious organizations and church rites, if indeed they did this, was one the Master did not make.... No time was lost by our Master in organizations, rites, and ceremonies, or in proselyting for certain forms of belief....[44]

However, a few more years' experience had matured her thought and changed that opinion. For one thing, her students did not find an expression of their views or their testimonies regarding the efficacy of Christian Science welcome in their old churches. For another, Christian Science was performing the role in their lives that religion plays in any age or society. Not only was it founded on an explanation of the work of Christ Jesus, but also its worship centered on an expansion of what the presence of God should mean to each human being. Even more important, its attempt to give coherence to all aspects of life – in this case through denying the ultimate reality of matter and establishing the reign of Spirit in human affairs – fulfilled the purpose that every religion has of giving meaning to people's everyday lives.

Mrs. Eddy had also begun to preach in Boston during the winter of 1878-79. She must have seen from this experience that many would become interested in Christian Science if they were approached through the normal channels of churchgoing. She preached and answered questions in a Baptist church (with the minister present). After one such meeting she wrote to Clara Choate, a fairly new student whom she was to rely on somewhat for the next few years:

> I wish you could have been at the meeting at the Tabernacle last Sunday. My subject was "Christ's Coming" and I did twist the cords and make a lash for their backs that cut smoothly I assure you. . .three rose for questions. I answered, and *beat* them every time. . .I have lectured in parlors 14 years, God calls me now to go before the people in a wider sense.[45]

By the summer of 1879, Mrs. Eddy had decided it was time to formally organize as a church. (There had been, since 1876, a Christian Scientist Association. This, however, was composed only of her students, and its meetings were, in effect, an extension of their class instruction and were not open to the public.) A charter was granted for "The Church of Christ (Scientist)" by the Commonwealth of Massachusetts in August 1879. The church's purpose was "to commemorate the word and works of our Master, which should reinstate primitive Christianity and its lost element of healing." The church's location was given as Boston, although the members continued to hold meetings in various locations (including their homes) in Lynn, Salem, and Boston. There were twenty-six charter members.

At the same time this church organization had been proceeding, Mrs. Eddy had also been considering leaving Massachusetts entirely. In the autumn of 1879, she sent a new student, Arthur Buswell, to Cincinnati to investigate what the mental climate and legal situation in Ohio might be for the teaching of Christian Science. She intended to go out there and look around herself, but was persuaded by her students in Boston to spend the winter preaching in Boston. So, she and Gilbert Eddy let out the house in Lynn and made arrangements to live in Boston for the winter of 1880. The young church began to hold services in Hawthorne Hall, on Park Street in the heart of the city. She wrote to James Ackland, another new student who lived in Philadelphia, "...we ought to remain here this winter and I preach to the Pharisees one season to settle the ferment. I want to go to Ohio and I said I should go...." [46] Then, by the spring of 1880, she was writing to Ackland about coming to Philadelphia: " I think perhaps we had better store our furniture here at present. I am engaged three weeks longer in Boston. I am going to Phila. to rest a little at first. Please be reticent on business matters and tell no one I am a healer until I have a chance to be, if ever that comes again." [47]

Finally, she and Gilbert spent five weeks of the summer of 1880 in Concord, New Hampshire, close to her birthplace. She wrote to another student from Concord:

> Here is a good place for a student and *you are the student,* but the laws of the state prohibit all practice not recognized by the Medical faculty. I have recently thought our diplomas will not pass the ordeal required by state laws. [48]

In 1880 Massachusetts had considered and defeated a bill that would have been equally restrictive as far as non-medical means of practice. The fact that it had even been brought up for debate may have been one reason Mrs. Eddy considered leaving the state. However, she now found a way to stay in Massachusetts and, she hoped, to bolster the respectability of her system of healing and its protection under the law. An 1874 Massachusetts law allowed a minimum of seven persons to form a corporation "for a benevolent, charitable, educational, medical, religious, or scientific purpose." In June 1880 Mrs. Eddy decided to charter such an institution and call it the Massachusetts Metaphysical College. To help her incorporate, she enlisted the aid of two doctors, one of whom, Rufus Noyes, had just written a book extremely critical of the practice of medicine. He and the other doctor, Charles Eastman, had just started the Bellevue Medical College in Boston under the same provisions of law. Mrs. Eddy's Massachusetts Metaphysical College would become the locus of her teaching in the 1880s, the teaching that was to lay the groundwork for the spread of Christian Science across America.

The formation of a formal church organization and the chartering of the college were not all that she was involved in during the years 1879 through 1881. But just as the two preceding years had been occupied with lawsuits, it is clear that Mrs. Eddy was trying to see the way ahead during these years – and that she was looking far beyond what her small number of students at that time saw was needed for the future of Christian Science.

During this period she also found the time to write letters to her students, to lead, or sometimes coax, them to a more spiritual view of life, or to encourage them when their understanding seemed too small for the cases that were coming to them. To Clara Choate, whose ambitions in the new movement were at times matched by her reluctance to give up the most pleasant elements of her comfortable social life, she found it necessary to say:

> I hope dear one, you will in the far future reach the place of teacher and lecturer. It is a *humble* solemn, earnest, unselfish, perfectly *sincere* place that we must arrive at before we can be fit to impart God's direct commands. Now as before they must come from Horeb, the Mount of holiness. May the dear Father bless and keep you till you arrive at the full likeness.[49]

On the other hand, all she needed with another student, Julia Bartlett, was to write words of gentle encouragement. Julia had been healed of invalidism, which had afflicted her most of her adult life and, in 1880, at the age of thirty-eight, went through class with Mrs. Eddy. She immediately began to heal and was a teacher in the movement until the 1920s. That Mrs. Eddy could write as the letter below indicates shows her own deep immersion in the Bible. Her healing system by this time was firmly rooted in the ethics and morality demanded of every Christian. None of the events that had been making newspaper headlines for Christian Science during these years were more than whitecaps on the surface of a sea below whose surface the movement of spiritual healing was beginning to swell:

> The cases you named as more obstinate I hope have yielded before this and you have learned that time will conquer all error. Do not forget to be strong in the clear consciousness that you are able to heal and no counter mind can make you weak for a moment through fear or a lack of confidence in your power, or rather understanding.
>
> Remember God, Truth, is the *Healer* the balm of Gilead and our only Physician and can never be insufficient for all things.
>
> You will find at first cases that seem defiant, but *all is mind,* and they yield at last the same as a cherished malice or envy, they fall at length before Truth and that is the end of them. Some individuals yield more slowly if it is a moral question that separates them from the light that destroys darkness; to such, use the arguments that hit the mark and it will destroy the disease.
>
> Sometimes things very remote from what would seem the cause are what hold the patient from recovery. But remember the words of our Master Physician "Verily I say unto you ye shall not have gone over all Israel until some shall be saved." In other words, ye shall not have spoken unto all their beliefs until some shall yield up the ghost.[50]

❖ ❖ ❖ ❖

At the same time that Mrs. Eddy was finding a way to make her exit from Lynn to a broader and somewhat more receptive mental atmosphere in Boston, she had the first visit from her son, George, since he had been taken away from New Hampshire in the mid-1850s. After the Civil War, they had occasionally corresponded, but she had not actually seen him since he was twelve years old. The saga of George and his family's relation to Mrs. Eddy is a sad one, culminating a quarter of a century later in George's being used by men whose motive was to discredit Christian Science in a lawsuit against his mother. All her life Mrs. Eddy continued to long for the closeness of family ties. But the family hearth that was broken up when her brothers and sisters left home to marry was never to be replaced by any kind of permanent and satisfying family for her.

George's visit in the winter of 1879-80 was the first of several instances that made it clear that mother and son were on two separate tracks in life; knowledge of that fact, however, did not make the situation any easier for Mrs. Eddy or weaken the strong maternal feelings she had toward George. Earlier in the winter, when she had been considering moving the locus of her activities to Cincinnati, she had written to George and suggested that he meet her there. George traveled to Cincinnati, but when he found that she was still in Boston, he came all the way east to Boston.

During this particular winter, the Eddys had to move several times in Boston because of the opposition to what they were teaching (more probably, a prejudice against what people *heard* they were teaching). Mrs. Eddy strongly suspected that Richard Kennedy was behind some of the sudden turns of fortune for them. No sooner would they be settled in a new rooming house than the mood would turn against them, and they would be asked to vacate. This opposition to his mother bothered George, and well into the first decade of the twentieth century, he told a newspaper reporter that he himself had put a stop to Kennedy's interference with his mother. Mrs. Eddy must have mentioned Kennedy frequently as the cause of the opposition to her work in Boston. At any rate, George Glover claimed that one day he found out where Kennedy's office was, went to him on the pretext of being a patient, and when admitted to his office pulled a gun, held it to Kennedy's head, and told him that if his mother had to move again that winter he (Glover) would track down Kennedy and shoot him "like a mad dog." Kennedy, who was still living at the time (1907), denied that the incident had ever occurred. But even if Glover was fabricating the story, it indicated that he vividly remembered the opposition to his mother.

Glover, of course, did not fit into the Boston of 1880 – or very likely of any other year. This story about him, whether true or not, bears at least some resemblance to the vision one has of his father, the young builder in the South who may have had something of the youthful swaggerer about himself as well. Furthermore, George was untutored, almost illiterate. He had gone from farming to gold prospecting, a profession that would bring him to his mother's desk (by letter) many times in the future with requests for financial aid. He dressed like the archetypal Westerner on horseback, and with his high boots and cowboy manner he must have caused a stir in genteel Boston. His mother's innate love for him overlooked these sartorial details, however. His visit lasted for a good two months. In the end, his wife and children begged him to come home, and Mrs. Eddy's first reunion with her son was ended. Although he had little comprehension of what Christian Science encompassed, and Mrs. Eddy certainly recognized this, this fact did not prevent her from treating him with all the consideration one might expect a mother to have for her only child and even at times in the future confiding in him about her own emotional state.

❖ ❖ ❖ ❖

Mrs. Eddy had first preached in Boston during the winter of 1878-79. The next two winters found her residing there, although she did not make the final move until the spring of 1882 after she and Gilbert had spent two months in Washington. Before reaching that time, though, one climactic event in Lynn served as nothing else would to bring those years to a definite close – as well as to indicate why it was time for the Lynn period to come to an end.

There had been some degree of turmoil in every one of her years in Lynn, particularly since the publication of *Science and Health* in 1875. Mrs. Eddy could explain this as the opposition of the unregenerate human mind to a system of thought that was exposing that same mind as a fraud. Yet, at this point in time, she still saw or at least spoke about the specific attacks of error in terms of persons. In just a few years she would be taking pains to make sure her students recognized the impersonality of the carnal mind (St. Paul's phrase) and that, in their attempts to protect themselves from it, they themselves not engage in any kind of mental work against other individuals.

The trials of the late 1870s, however, had appeared in terms of individuals – the lawsuit of George Barry, the defection of Daniel Spofford, the various lawsuits instigated by Arens, then the "conspiracy to murder" episode, in which Arens and her husband had been falsely accused. Throughout all these trials, Mrs. Eddy had continued her work as best she could and, in the process, continued to make demands on the most promising of her students. But many of them did not see the complete challenge that Christian Science represented to the accustomed ways of human thinking, or sense the reason for the opposition it seemed to stir up. Moreover, Mrs. Eddy herself made no claim to being a faultless human being. She was a woman with a mission, and undoubtedly her singlemindedness and utter devotion to that mission did not carry all her students with her to the degree she may have assumed. In this kind of hothouse environment, where growth was being expected of all the plants in the hothouse, some of the plants seemed to think they would thrive better in a cooler atmosphere.

In the fall of 1881, Mrs. Eddy was about to begin her third winter of preaching in Boston. On the evening of October 26, eight of her students presented a petition at a meeting of the Christian Scientist Association, delivering their joint judgment on their teacher:

> We, the undersigned, while we acknowledge and appreciate the understanding of Truth imparted to

> us by our Teacher, Mrs. Mary B. G. Eddy, led by Divine Intelligence to perceive with sorrow that departure from the straight and narrow road (which alone leads to growth of Christ-like virtues) made manifest by frequent ebullitions of temper, love of money, and the appearance of hypocrisy, *cannot* longer submit to such Leadership… [51]

They concluded by withdrawing from the Association. Two of those who withdrew had been in one of Mrs. Eddy's first classes in 1870 and had withstood the turmoil of the 1870s until that moment.

Mrs. Eddy was temporarily stunned by the defections. After the meeting ended, she asked a couple of students to remain with her. The following morning her new student, Julia Bartlett, heard of the events of the night before and came to Lynn from nearby Salem, where she happened to be. Mrs. Eddy asked her, two other students, and Gilbert to stay with her for a few days. During this time, from later accounts, Mrs. Eddy went through a kind of personal transfiguration that gave her the strength to deal with this latest crisis. After hours of meditation, she began to quote from the Bible, seemingly at random, many verses that applied to the situation in which she saw herself and her movement.

Five days later the leaders of the "rebellion" were expelled from the Christian Scientist Association. More importantly for the future, the twenty or so remaining members met in Boston on November 9 and formally ordained Mrs. Eddy as pastor of the Church of Christ, Scientist. In a long resolution they passed, they spoke of Mrs. Eddy in terms reminiscent of biblical language:

> Resolved, That while she had had little or no help, except from God, in the introduction to this age of materiality of her book, Science and Health, and the carrying forward of the Christian principles it teaches and explains, she has been unremitting in her faithfulness to her God-appointed work, and we do

> understand her to be the chosen messenger of God to bear his truth to the nations, and unless we hear "Her Voice," we do not hear "His Voice."[52]

This was probably the first formal claim in writing to Mrs. Eddy's authority having anything to do with biblical prophecy. It was a reference that would cause Mrs. Eddy herself, and then increasing numbers of her students and followers in future years, to ponder the source of her authority. Many would find a convincing connection between the metaphysics and practice of Christian Science and the biblical promise of a Comforter.

But such considerations were not the order of the day for most of the early Christian Scientists. Nor were they uppermost in the thoughts of Mary and Gilbert Eddy, for whom the dark days of October 1881 in Lynn were about to be followed by the hectic activity of the move to Boston and two months of business in Washington.

Chapter 6

The Boston Years

A National Movement Forms

Mrs. Eddy's two-month visit to Washington and Philadelphia in 1882 marked the first time that she traveled outside New England for any extensive period of time since she had returned as a grieving young widow from Wilmington, North Carolina, in 1844. (She had made one quick trip to Philadelphia to the U.S. Centennial Exhibition there in the autumn of 1876.) Sometime during the previous year she had written to Colonel Smith, who had had class instruction from her in the late 1870s, to inquire about the possibility of moving to Washington. In a letter written in 1881, in which she complained that "although we are doing immeasurable good we are scarcely allowed a foothold on earth," she asked, "My especial object in writing at this time [is] to learn what the prospect for me would be in your vicinity."[1]

By 1882, however, she had finally settled on Boston as the permanent headquarters for her church, and her visit to Washington was prompted by two other considerations: to do what she could on a brief visit to develop interest in Christian Science there, and to give Gilbert Eddy an opportunity to better familiarize himself with copyright law. Arens, who had been a co-defendant with Gilbert Eddy in the 1878 conspiracy-to-murder case, had by now gone his own way, making use of some part of what he had learned from Mrs. Eddy. He was also plagiarizing her textbook.

While Gilbert went about his research into copyright law, Mrs. Eddy plunged into her own research: to ascertain the degree of interest in her system of healing in Washington. She also had those strong first impressions that come on any traveler, perhaps particularly so in the case of a nineteenth-century American seeing for the first time the physical grandeur of the city that the Frenchman L'Enfant had planned almost a century earlier. She was struck by the beauty of the nation's capital and wrote back to Boston that it must be the most beautiful city in the world. She wrote a note to a young friend, Alice Sibley, in which she said of Washington, "It seems to me quite a type geographically considered of the ancient Eden if the old story be true which I never doubted."[2]

But more important than her interest in the physical geography, she found interest in the "human geography" – in the minds of inquiring people in the capital. She invited those who were inquisitive into her rooms, just across the street from the Capitol itself, on First Street N.E., for lectures each evening. She wrote to Clara Choate at the end of February that she had lectured for fourteen evenings in a row, for three hours each evening. "Get to bed at 12, rise at 6, and *work.* I have a goodly number already enlisted in the work."[3]

Clearly exhilarated by the weeks in Washington, she then traveled with Gilbert to Philadelphia for some more meetings. Before leaving Boston, she had put her student, Julia Bartlett, more or less in temporary charge of church affairs there. The terms under which she gave this charge, though, would have been baffling to anyone having less humility than Bartlett:

> There should be a substitute for me to lead this people and now dear Student, I ask you will you take this place not that you can unloose the sandals of my shoes not that you can fill my place but only that I think you rather more fit for it than anyone whom I leave. Now do not yield to temptation and say you cannot…[4]

Julia apparently acquiesced.

It is interesting to note how, early in this period of what became the Christian Science movement, Mrs. Eddy used the positive qualities she found in her students and tried to work around the more negative ones, in the hope that further regeneration of character would correct whatever character traits were in need of change. Clara Choate, who was also mentioned in the previous chapter, did not possess the humility that Mrs. Eddy came to value in Bartlett. Choate was never willing to give up her social pretensions and cast her lot entirely with Mrs. Eddy, but she was also attracting students in the Boston area. And it was to Choate that Mrs. Eddy made one of her relatively few gender references:

> It is glorious to see what the women *alone* are doing here [Philadelphia] for temperance. More than ever man has done. This is the period of *women, they* are to move and to carry all the great moral and Christian reforms. I know it. Now darling, let us work as the industrious Suffragists are at work who are getting a hearing all over the land. Let us work as they do in love "prefering one another."[5]

This reference, in which she seemed to be giving preference to women over men in her movement, should not be taken at face value. It is more likely the reaction to whatever she noticed going on in Philadelphia at the time. She had already tried, without result, for more than a few years to get two of her male students, Colonel Smith in Washington and James Ackland in Philadelphia, to work as healers or, in the case of Smith, to come to Boston to help her. So she may have felt that women were readier than men to cast their lots for her cause.

While the Eddys were away, Julia Bartlett and Abbie Whiting held Friday evening meetings at rooms they had rented in Charlestown, one of the oldest parts of Boston. Julia Bartlett recounted later that she was seeing up to thirty patients daily, so the healing activity was definitely taking hold and news of it spreading. At the same time, Clara Choate was both holding public meetings and teaching Christian Science in Boston and Lawrence, some thirty miles north.

Mrs. Eddy may have been wary that Choate was attracting an audience as much through personal charm, or magnetism, as from the selfless spirituality she saw in Julia Bartlett. But she went along with Choate, for the moment at least, and when she and Gilbert returned to Boston in the spring, she allowed Clara to hold a reception for her in her home on Tremont Street. More prophetically than she could know at the time, she wrote of the reception to James Ackland, "This was my entry into Jerusalem. Will it be followed with the cross?"[6]

On the last Sunday in March 1882, the *Boston Globe* ran a multicolumned article about Christian Science. The article contained several accounts of healing attributed to Christian Science, preceded by seven layers of headlines, including "Disease a Belief, Not a Reality," "Startling Theory of God and the Bible," and "The Divine Mind the Power Which Dispels Sickness." The claims made in the article were bound to catch the attention of readers, and the next week the *Globe* ran another long article consisting of rebuttals from ministers and physicians. The publicity indicates that by 1882 Mrs. Eddy and her teaching and healing were certainly attracting a kind of interested attention they had not enjoyed in Lynn. The small movement was growing, and those who had been healed were eager to tell of their experiences. But the opposition expressed by the second article also indicated the two-edged sword represented by the press. From Mrs. Eddy's point of view, the publicity did little good if it could be contradicted by the publishing of points of view or misrepresentations of her position that she had no opportunity to counter. This experience alone must have had something to do with her decision just a year later to launch her own first periodical.

The Eddys settled down briefly in a townhouse at 569 Columbus Avenue in Boston's South End. But the settling in process was interrupted by the illness and death of Gilbert Eddy just a few months later. Dr. Eddy, as he was called, had taken to heart almost literally the controversies that had surrounded Mrs. Eddy since their marriage in 1877. Described as a quite capable but very mild man, he would have continued to be a good helpmate for his more volatile wife. But the final years in Lynn had been filled with lawsuits, and one of the reasons for their extended stay in Washington had been for him to ascertain what could be done to stop the plagiarisms of Daniel Arens against his wife's textbook. After the Eddys returned to Boston, Gilbert's health declined. Mrs. Eddy said later that she had known he was ill, but that he continually maintained that he was treating himself adequately through his own prayers. That she knew it was serious, though, is shown by a letter in which she instructed Putney Bancroft, her student from 1870, in how to pray for Gilbert:

> Please drop the treatment it does not meet the occasion, and substitute this. Treat my husband. Say to him "You can help your wife and they cannot prevent it, and they cannot make you sick in belief and she feel your symptoms of liver complaint and humour of stomach." ... All are going to try together once a day between 4 and 5:00 P.M.[7]

The note to Bancroft is revealing, not only for its information about Gilbert, but also for the state of Christian Science treatment at that time. Mrs. Eddy makes no mention of "multiple prayers" for an individual as being appropriate, as they might be in the case of a church congregation all praying together about a common situation. Yet there must have been some kind of joint effort involved in Gilbert's case. The other difference in treatment is that, at least toward the end of her life, Mrs. Eddy told one of her trusted followers that she would no longer give a "personal" treatment, one that tried to reach out to the thought of the patient. Rather, she came to see treatment as a rising of thought to the divine, in the contemplation of which neither the practitioner nor the patient could believe a lie about man's true condition of health and wholeness.

Gilbert Eddy succumbed on the night of June 2, 1882. That day he had felt well enough to go out for a ride on the Boston trolley. His death shocked the entire household. Mrs. Eddy herself went through the most outward emotional reaction she was to show for the rest of her life, although some of her later crises may have caused a degree of pain and stress that were not as obvious to all her household. But with Gilbert's death, she felt that the forces of malpractice, of malicious mesmerism, had achieved the kind of victory they had been seeking for years. The entry into Jerusalem indeed seemed to her to have been followed by a personal version of Gethsemane.

The doctor's autopsy, which she requested, showed that Gilbert had had a heart condition. Mrs. Eddy admitted that, when he had been examined some years before, a doctor had indicated something about his heart, but said it was not serious enough to be concerned about. Her own conclusion, which she talked about to a *Boston Globe* reporter, was that Dr. Eddy had been mentally poisoned with arsenic, and that he died from that mental poison as surely as if evidence of arsenic had been present. And, although she wisely did not name the poisoner, she felt it must be Arens. That same day (June 3) she wrote to Arens's father-in-law, who had gone through a class in Christian Science with her:

> With the cold form of beloved husband lying on his bier in my desolated home I appeal to you once more, and if you are not darkened to the sense of the awful crimes I know you will stop them by every influence in your power.[8]

In a letter written some ten days after the event to a newspaper editor, Mrs. Eddy laid out the situation as it appeared to her:

> This is an awful hour, the Revelator saw it and portrayed it. Mind has been liberated from some of its fetters, to do good, and on the other hand it has taken this greater freedom to do evil.
>
> One of the persons [Kennedy, presumably] who is committing these crimes said to me in 1872, "Nobody will believe you if you do tell of what I can do and mean to do in *mesmerism*"... The physician

> who examined him on his application to enter a Temperance Order in Lynn spoke of a heart difficulty but said it was *not sufficient* to ever *injure him*… The mental argument that always relieved him was, that arsenic could not inflame the mucous membrane of the heart or lungs.[9]

One of her students, Arthur Buswell, offered her the use of his farm in the hills of Vermont. There she retreated for about six weeks with the young woman, Alice Sibley, with whom she had carried on a kind of mother-daughter correspondence for some time. In Vermont she collected herself, after going through a period of grief that is not uncommon. Present-day Christian Scientists, as well as many others who view man's life as partaking of eternity, have demonstrated a considerable degree of calm at the passing of their most beloved family members. In trying to see Mrs. Eddy as she was at this period, one has to try to balance the fact that, while her teaching was more from inspiration than strong emotional exhortation, this did not rule out the possession of strong human emotions or their expression at many critical moments in her life. Moreover, Gilbert's death seemed to her at the time to be the work of former students who were trying to destroy Christian Science. This, coupled with the facts that he had been of great assistance to her during the more than five years of their marriage and that they had enjoyed a mutual affection, made the event seem nothing less than a full-scale tragedy for her. Thus, she wrote to Colonel Smith, who seems to have remained a confidant of hers throughout these years, "Words are vain, I cannot write my grief and you cannot have the least conception of it. I feel almost as if I never should be comforted while I stay away from my loved precious one that has gone before me."[10]

The letters that are preserved (there could have been others) indicate her closeness to the same individuals throughout this period – as well as, perhaps, the few of them in number she felt she could confide in. Besides Colonel Smith in Washington, there was James Ackland in Philadelphia. And the two women workers in Boston, as different as black and white, Clara Choate and Julia Bartlett. Mrs. Eddy had gone up to Vermont toward the end of June. By mid-July she wrote to Clara, "I long to return and the time will soon pass. I dread to return but the days glide by." [11] And a few days later, to Julia, "I can't yet feel much interest in anything of earth. I shall try and eventually succeed in rising from the gloom of my irreparable loss, but it must take *time. Long* after I shall smile and appear happy shall I have to *struggle alone* with my great grief that none shall know if I can hide it." [12]

But something positive was also happening to Mrs. Eddy while she adjusted to her widowhood. One can picture her studying her Bible and praying many times each day, trying to regain her composure and also to hear what she could feel was God's direction as to how to proceed. It must have occurred to her that the normal human sense of family was finished for her. Her ties with her own generation were broken, her son was going down his own track in life, and now a husband she had loved and depended upon for support was taken from her. It was becoming clear to her that she was basically alone – but alone with her God, which made all the difference. One can see how her thought was coming around in a letter she wrote to James Ackland at the end of July, as she was about to return to Boston:

> I would like more than ever to be myself again if only for one short year that I might establish our cause on a firmer foothold than ever yet it has been. But I question my ability to walk over all, only as God gives me aid that I never have had before… The world was for others. It was not for me. I was made a lone isle in life's desolate sea.
>
> …We shall return soon to the stately halls of my Boston home but the walls whisper a secret they tell me home is not there since Gilbert has gone. Adieu. [13]

There was no turning back after the six weeks in Vermont. Whatever Mrs. Eddy had experienced among the green hills she loved, much more happened to her than merely overcoming her shock and grief. After she returned, there seemed to be new vigor and purpose to her actions. In time, she would make it clear that her teaching regarding mental malpractice had also been clarified. But even before that, it became apparent that she was more determined than ever to press ahead with her cause. And for the next few years, that meant teaching classes and starting a publication that would serve the needs of a growing movement. The classes she taught in the six or seven active years of the Massachusetts Metaphysical College created the base of practitioners and teachers from which the movement had its rapid growth after 1890. And the magazine she launched in 1883 became the vehicle through which she kept in touch with a scattered field and tried to correct criticisms of Christian Science or departures from the integrity of her entire body of teaching.

❖ ❖ ❖ ❖

Before launching into a description of her major activities in the period from 1882 until 1889, when she left Boston, one might try to sketch a word picture of what this Boston of the eighties was like. For, while it is obvious that it was one of the major cities of America and that its population would offer her more opportunities to spread her teachings than had the small industrial city of Lynn, Boston presented its own unique contours. The old Bostonians were proud of their past: their Puritan heritage; the Unitarian breakaway from orthodoxy, best remembered in the name of William Ellery Channing; the transcendentalist phase (which had actually been centered twenty-five miles to the west in Concord); and the championing of the abolitionist cause before the Civil War. Not all Bostonians had been abolitionists, however; there was a Yankee conservatism and caution that had expressed itself in active opposition to such firebrand leaders of the abolitionist cause as William Lloyd Garrison.

Now in the eighties, many of these conservative Bostonians were more in tune with the Anglo-Catholicism of Phillips Brooks, one of Boston's great preachers of the decade. In 1877,

Trinity Church had been erected in Copley Square, just a few blocks from where the Christian Science headquarters and Mother Church buildings would eventually rise. Brooks was a man who tried to apply Christian principles to everyday life and to lead his parishioners in that direction. Many of his sermons, which emphasized that man is the child of God, could have been given by Mrs. Eddy had they included her insights into the practice of Christian healing.

Boston itself, or the "old Boston," had become effete. No new movements such as abolitionism had arisen to capture its attention. The nation's interests had turned westward after the Civil War, and new industrial cities were rising up across the Middle West. Even the intellectual capital had shifted westward. Van Wyck Brooks, in his book, *New England Indian Summer*, summed it up by writing, "Society had lost its vital interests, and the Boston mind was indolent and flaccid, as if the struggle for existence had passed it by." [14] Many of the intellectual types were estranged from the industrial development that came to America during the Gilded Age, and after shunning Europe and its ways for several generations, they turned there with a new fascination. To quote Brooks again: "They felt as if the labours of their fathers had been mocked, as if their country had been wrested from them; and they looked across the sea again, despairing of a nation that had passed beyond their powers of comprehension." [15]

To further complicate their outlook on a nation whose physical expansion dwarfed their cramped New England view, the Bostonians had to deal with immigrants en masse. Even before the Civil War, the influx of Irish immigrants had started. As early as 1849, the Boston Committee of Internal Health had issued a scathing report on the conditions under which the Irish had to live in Boston's North End. "The whole district is a perfect hive of human beings, without comforts and mostly without common necessities; in many cases huddled together like brutes, without regard to sex or age, or sense of decency...." [16]

After the Civil War, many of the Irish, who had fought along with those who had been Americans longer than they, began to organize. As a social history of Boston says, "Through the seventies and eighties, the Irish mass on the doorstep of Boston stirred and groped upwards. As prescient natives had feared, the weight of numbers was beginning to tell. With a high Irish birth rate and declining mortality, due to improved living conditions, the Irish fast approached a point where they composed half the city's population." [17] By 1885, just three years after Mrs. Eddy's arrival in Boston, the inevitable happened: the Irish won the mayoralty, with Hugh O'Brien being elected mayor of the city.

Viewed from the standpoint of religious affiliation, then, a large part of Boston was now Roman Catholic. Part of the older Boston was experimenting with more liberal, theologically open forms of Protestantism as well as with the High Episcopal Church. And on the fringes there was interest in spiritualism, mind cures (some of which represented themselves as coming from Christian Science), and Eastern religions. William Dean Howells may have had some of these types in mind when he wrote that the churches were full of people who "*hoped* that their souls were immortal, but *knew* that they were cultivated!" [18]

Mrs. Eddy correctly recognized that if her movement was to prosper, it would need to have a base in a larger center than Lynn. So the move to Boston, in retrospect, has the quality of being an inevitable event. But recognizing the cultural and religious melange that Boston had become, it should be clear that setting up headquarters in Boston guaranteed her only a wider audience, not any kind of automatic growth or approval for a doctrine of religion and practice of healing that stood in opposition to the thinking of most of the theological academy as well as the medical profession. The rebuttals to the first long, positive *Boston Globe* article that followed a week afterwards had been indicative of the kind of tempest Christian Science would stir up in its larger setting.

❖ ❖ ❖ ❖

Having made up her mind to return to Boston and continue her work without her husband's presence, Mrs. Eddy also took another step that remained a part of her *modus operandi* for the rest of her life. In 1881, at the time of the defection of the eight students in Lynn, a young man by the name of Calvin Frye, who had recently taken a class with her, was staying in her home. Frye came from a farm in northern New England and had become interested in Christian Science after Clara Choate healed his mother of insanity. Frye was a forerunner of the type of which Calvin Coolidge has been somewhat inaccurately caricatured – taciturn, parsimonious, withered. Looking at the letters he wrote from time to time and at what others have said about him, he deserves a more positive description. Although somewhat of a plodder, he definitely had some innate intelligence. His acquaintance with Mrs. Eddy had already changed his life. Before 1882, he had been living with an invalid father and his formerly insane mother. His own earlier brief marriage had ended with his wife's death. So, when Mrs. Eddy sent him a telegram to join her on the train back from Vermont, he answered her call. Already in early middle age, he became her private secretary, never leaving her for even a full day's vacation for the twenty-eight years she would need his services. It may be that only a person with no strong personal ambition or need to be heard by others could have stood by her side and worked for her as he did for almost three decades.

Besides Frye as her personal secretary, Mrs. Eddy had two or three other workers in the household with her. From the time she had bought the house at No. 8 Broad Street in Lynn in 1875, it had been her habit to have household help. Because of her earlier invalidism and her need to board around during the years after 1866, Mrs. Eddy had never experienced what would have been the typical lifestyle of a nineteenth-century homemaker. After she bought the house in Lynn and was established as a healer, teacher, and writer of the textbook, various students lived with her and earned their room and board by doing household chores. So, by the time she had settled down on Columbus Avenue in Boston, it had been customary for her to have a menage composed of several people. This continued for the rest of her days, with the duties of her help becoming more formally defined as the years progressed.

Some did the normal household chores; others worked there as Christian Science healers, or practitioners. But Mrs. Eddy carried the load of spreading Christian Science virtually alone for many years. It seemed enough for most of her students just to grasp the main threads of what she was teaching and to be able to heal others. To think of what steps to take next, to have any concept of what Christian Science might grow into, was just not their work – even if they had thought about it.

By late 1882, she was in full stride again. She taught her largest class to date in the fall of 1882 – some eight persons – and wrote in one letter, "The ship of science is again walking the wave, rising above the billows, bidding defiance to the flood-gates of error, for God is at the helm." [19]

The work that Mrs. Eddy did in the next six and a half years moved Christian Science from being largely a local phenomenon, the so-called Boston craze of the early 1880s, to the status of a national movement. She accomplished this through two major avenues: her own individual teaching, and the establishment of a monthly magazine, eventually called *The Christian Science Journal.* Beginning with her re-establishing herself after the death of Gilbert Eddy, she taught some thirty-five classes from late 1882 until the spring of 1889; these classes in total had slightly over 700 students in them. At first the classes were small. In 1882 the three classes she taught averaged only seven persons. (She taught one class in May, before Gilbert's death, and two that autumn after returning from Vermont.)

In these first years in Boston, she was not bashful about soliciting pupils. For instance, in the fall of 1883, she wrote to a prospective student, Sarah Heywood:

> I know of no way in which you can gain a thorough knowledge of it [Christian Science] but by studying it under my instructions. There are some others who claim to teach it but I was many years reaching a thorough knowledge of this great question of Healing

> through Mind, and no one can teach it who does not prepare himself by proper time and practice and study for a teacher....
>
> My tuition for a course that will fit you for a healer is $300. The length of time required in which you recite to me is three weeks. You can then begin a practice and have success as a healer.
>
> The best *time* to do good is *now.* You had better join my class at once.[20]

Mrs. Heywood was in her class of February 1884. Mrs. Eddy also wrote similarly to others, telling them that a class was about to open and inviting them to be in it.

As the healing practice grew, and as her magazine became a means of communication from her to her students as well as to a wider field, including many who first heard about Christian Science from the *Journal,* the numbers of those coming to her for teaching increased. During most of these Boston years, Mrs. Eddy taught five or six classes. Getting together the names of the most promising candidates for a class and preparing for it, holding it, and then starting the process all over again made it impossible for her to teach more than this number of classes a year. After she began teaching Normal classes (classes specifically designed to train future teachers of Christian Science) in 1884, the number of Primary classes dropped off slightly. The following table summarizes her teaching activity during the Boston years:

	Primary classes	Normal classes	Total no. of students
1882	3	-	21
1883	6	-	42
1884	5	1	89
1885	4	1	78
1886	2	3	106
1887	3	2	136
1888	3	1	131
1889	1	-	68

The Normal classes were generally smaller than the Primary classes. The number of students she took for the beginning course grew from an average of seven in the first years to twenty-five in 1886 and 1887, and forty for the three classes she taught in 1888. In the last Primary class she taught, in February 1889, she had sixty-eight students, far more than the number she felt she could adequately interact with as a teacher. Her teaching method was Socratic, probing the thought of the student. Without adequate time to sense the state of individual thought, the teaching could not have the same value. The growing pressure on her to admit greater numbers, linked with her inability to teach them in what she felt was an adequate manner, weighed more heavily on her as the decade advanced.

At the same time that she was carrying an increased amount of responsibility through her teaching, she was editing and writing for her magazine and answering correspondence from the practitioners she had encouraged to go out into the field. She sometimes came close to sinking under the burden, and there were occasionally uncomfortable nights when she wrestled with problems that she alone seemed to see.

One cannot assess how much of the burden she might have avoided had she handled particular people or circumstances differently. Those who have written about her without sympathy have typically portrayed her as being unduly sensitive or even imagining plots against her that did not exist. It is perhaps impossible to strike a neutral ground, because none may in fact exist. To anyone who, at some time in his or her own life, has felt resistance to a new idea (not necessarily in the field of religion, either, where reactions tend to be especially emotional and visceral), it is not at all difficult to empathize with the opposition Mrs. Eddy was feeling at times to what she was teaching. Nor did she have anyone close to her who in any large measure understood the kind of opposition she felt exposed to. Again, she unburdened herself to Colonel Smith:

> If only the warfare was *open,* and I had one strong nature like dear Gilbert's or your own to share my

> *cares* and burdens I could endure it better. As it is, I have all this superstructure of Christian Science resting on my shoulders and no *moments yet* of *rest.* I hope it all will not again go crashing down over my head and ears if I let go for a brief space, for if it does I shall not rebuild again at the awful cost of the past *two years.* [21]

She was writing this to Smith when the second of two challenges she was forced to meet in 1883 was at its height. This was her suit against Edward Arens to prevent him from plagiarizing her works. The first, earlier in the year, had been a newspaper contretemps with Julius Dresser.

Julius Dresser and his wife, Annetta, had been living in Colorado for some years. Julius had been one of the patients of Phineas Quimby whom Mrs. Eddy had first met in 1862, and to whom she had written in vain to ask for help during the period after her fall on the ice in 1866. Julius had never been in good health, and he and his wife had moved to the West partly in search of a healthier climate. [22] In the early 1880s, they began to hear of Christian Science and eventually made a connection in their own minds between it and the Mary Patterson they had known in Portland.

The Dressers came back to Boston to live, with their first order of business being to "expose" Mrs. Eddy for what they alleged to be her expropriation of Quimby's doctrines. It did not occur to Dresser that what Mrs. Eddy was teaching and practicing was not even a faint tracing of the Quimby pattern. But not understanding this, Dresser began a newspaper attack on Mrs. Eddy, to which she responded with a vigor and readiness for battle that were still her wont. This was only a repeat of the Wallace Wright kind of publicity she had endured in the early days in Lynn, and at the moment she still felt it necessary to face down her opponents in kind.

Dresser launched his attack on Christian Science and Mrs. Eddy with a letter to the *Boston Post* in February 1883, part of which said, "Some parties healing through a mental method, which they claim to have discovered, did, in reality, obtain their first thoughts of this truth from Dr. Quimby, and have added their own opinions to the grain of vision thus obtained, presenting to the people a small amount of wheat mixed with a great quantity of chaff." [23] Dresser used the pseudonymous initials, A. O.

Mrs. Eddy responded, signing herself in turn as E. G. She acknowledged that some of Quimby's patients had been cured, but she pointed out that Quimby had always included some physical manipulation with his treatments. She went on: "We were his patient, but he never gave us any further information relating to his practice, but always said it is a secret of mine, and I have thought best not to divulge it." She did say that he had kept notes on his cases and that she had seen some of his "scribblings." "He requested us to transform them frequently and to give them different meanings, which we did." [24]

The discussion continued through a second inconclusive set of letters. Dresser claimed that Quimby had left mesmerism behind and did his healing "by the application of truth." [25] Mrs. Eddy had learned by this time that mesmerism encompassed far more than putting a patient to sleep physically. She admitted in her second letter that she had at one time defended Quimby against the charge of being a mesmerist, but said she had now learned that mesmerism had a wider definition. "… if one manipulates the sick no matter what his theory is, it precludes the possibility of his practice being mental science." [26]

This flurry in the newspapers indicates that Christian Science had become a lively enough topic in Boston for newspaper editors to allow space for these letters. But Mrs. Eddy's attempts in a few paragraphs to set the record straight about Quimby, and particularly to differentiate what she was teaching from the various kinds of mind-cure beginning to be practiced, can only have concentrated her thought on finding and training a reliable core of Christian Scientists who could, by their practice, show what she was teaching them.

The other challenge she had to work through in 1883 was a lawsuit against Arens. Perhaps the charges about Quimby that she had just been answering made her feel even more keenly the necessity to defend the integrity of her writing. Anyhow, in early April, she sued Arens to prevent him from selling his work, called *The Understanding of Christianity, or God,* in which he plagiarized *Science and Health.* His defense was that Mrs. Eddy had herself plagiarized Quimby's writings, and therefore he was not quoting Mrs. Eddy. In the meantime, Arens, Julius Dresser, George Quimby (the son of Phineas), and the Ware sisters had been in some kind of loose correspondence. Quimby was for some reason reluctant to let his father's manuscripts be examined; in fact, he did not publish them until ten years after Mrs. Eddy's passing. He had sent them to Washington to the Ware sisters, who, as previously mentioned, had also been Quimby patients as well as his copyists.

The role of the Ware sisters in the affair has never been fully explained. However, one of the Ware sisters was living in Europe, and the sister in Washington sent the papers to the sister abroad. This action prevented any subpoena being issued for the papers to be produced as evidence in court. It would have been better for Mrs. Eddy if the papers could have been examined then, instead of remaining a matter of speculation for an entire generation. But it would also have lost Arens's case for him, since the basic structure of ideas in *Science and Health* is clearly not derived from Quimby. As it was, Arens did lose his case anyway, since he was in no position to prove his claim.

The extent of damage Arens might have done to Mrs. Eddy's fledgling movement if he had continued to misuse portions of her writing is hard to assess. Most of the mind cure artists of the 1880s quickly disappeared from the scene. (Julius Dresser himself was to become one of the founders of the New Thought movement, which has proved its viability.) However, Mrs. Eddy considered as one of her primary challenges during this period the need of maintaining the purity of any teaching that called itself "Christian Science." Even someone who does not practice Christian Science can well understand that its metaphysics stands as a whole unit. On the one hand, Mrs. Eddy had to try as much as the law would allow her to stop portions of her work from being stolen or misappropriated by others. On the other hand, she had to watch that those who claimed to be her steadfast students did not lapse into what she considered incorrect teaching within the growing Christian Science movement.

What she was teaching was not that difficult to grasp intellectually. The difficulty lay in putting off the old man, a phrase Paul uses in both Ephesians and Colossians (books of the New Testament). To Mrs. Eddy, this "putting off" implied a complete laying aside of the deeply held human belief in a material creation and a mortal man – the common sense view of life. Yet it seemed easier for many people first encountering her radical interpretation of reality to adopt some kind of mental clutter that would claim to accommodate both views of creation, both views of reality.

Two letters she wrote in 1884 indicate her thought at this period. To a minister, Rev. John Parson, who had written inquiring about her manner of church service and what kind of religion this was, she replied:

> We repeat the Lord's Prayer audibly and offer man's prayer silently....
>
> We are essentially an Evangelical order, the life and teachings of Jesus as contained in the four Gospels are our basis. We believe that healing the sick is essential to Christianity. We have *no doubt* of the inspiration of the Scriptures. We admit thoroughly the Godhead and divinity of Christ, but in more of a spiritual than a personal view do we understand the former as Father, Son, and Holy Ghost....[27]

Another minister, Rev. A. J. Swarts, left his former fold to engage briefly with Christian Science. He and his wife were in the class Mrs. Eddy taught when she went out to Chicago in May 1884. Like several other ministers whose assistance she tried to make use of in the 1880s, Swarts was not able to accept the simplicity of Christian Science or, very possibly, the leadership of a woman. Mrs. Eddy wrote to him in August of that year that she noticed that one of the people he had been teaching advertised "Treats by massage, magnetism, medicated agencies" at the same time that Swarts advertised that he was teaching Christian Science. Mrs. Eddy went on to lecture Swarts in these words:

> Now dear brother consistency is not only a jewel, but the imperative duty of a Christian Scientist *especially,* else, their theory and practice will be a kingdom divided against itself that cannot *stand.*
>
> I have laid the sure foundation of all my success in establishing so far the cause of Christian Science by strict adherence in my teachings and practice and writings to the one statement and its proof that all is Mind there is no matter! Hence no mixing with matter. This is a purely divine science, that is mental, and not *material* in its *methods.* Nor is it mixed with spiritualism or any *other ism.* It precludes the possibility of one mind helping another so-called mind....[28]

❖ ❖ ❖ ❖

The other part of the new course of action that she inaugurated soon after settling down on Columbus Avenue was to start a publication initially called *The Journal of Christian Science.* It commenced publication in April 1883 as a bi-monthly, but the frequency was stepped up to monthly after a year and a half, and its name was changed to *The Christian Science Journal.* In the first issue, Mrs. Eddy set forth her intended purpose for the *Journal:*

> An organ from the Christian Scientists has become a necessity. Many questions come to the College and to

> the practising students, yet but little time has been devoted to their answer. Further enlightenment is necessary for the age, and a paper devoted to this work seems alone adequate to meet the requirement.[29]

The periodical went through several evolutions, or more properly speaking, a continuing evolution, during the first decade of its life. Mrs. Eddy began as the editor and almost sole contributor to it. At various times during the 1880s she named others as editor, but the magazine never settled down until she found a dependable editor in the person of Judge Septimus J. Hanna in the early 1890s. Throughout the time she was living in Boston she kept firm oversight over the *Journal.* Considering some of the people she tried temporarily as editors, it was fortunate from her point of view that she did keep watch over the periodical.

The *Journal* fulfilled several purposes for Mrs. Eddy. It answered questions that were coming to her from her students. It also answered questions that arose from a still skeptical or misinformed public. Christian Science was becoming popular in Boston at the same time that spiritualism was at its height and various forms of mesmerism and mind-cure were competing for public attention. "Much interest," she wrote, "is expressed everywhere on this subject of metaphysical healing, but in many minds it is confounded with mesmerism and so-called spiritualism, so that the vastness of its power is lost where it is not correctly understood."[30]

Most importantly, she used the *Journal* to build a credible record for the honest investigator of Christian Science healing. She approached the subject of health from at least two unique perspectives. First, she felt that the medical profession tended to dismiss the evidence of spiritual healing. "We are often denied the results of our labors because people do not understand the power of metaphysics, and they think that health and strength would have returned naturally without any assistance," she wrote. This is similar to the remarks made one century later that incidents of Christian Science healing are "anecdotal." The evidence of healing to those who have been healed is no more anecdotal than it is to individuals who have come out of the hospital with medical cures. But the medical profession had a point then and still has today in claiming that healings in Christian Science do not normally take place under medically monitored conditions.

Mrs. Eddy's other point regarding the world of medicine was that the medical preoccupation of the public actually did them harm. "After looking over the newspapers of the day, very naturally comes the reflection that it is dangerous to live, so loaded seems the very air with disease."

In a tone of attack that would disappear in a very short time, the *Journal* printed reports of medical malpractice and even some items called "Humor," which were targeted at the medical profession. Item:

> TOO MUCH ACCURACY. A very accurate Chicago physician sent in a certificate of death the other day with his name signed in the space reserved for the cause of death.[31]

Leaving aside these signs of how embattled Mrs. Eddy was feeling at times, the *Journal* was intended mainly to build a written record of the viability and progress of Christian Science healing. Its masthead at first read, "Independent Family Paper, to Promote Health and Morals." The existence of the *Journal* gave Mrs. Eddy the means to reach beyond Boston and New England. She was preaching regularly at Hawthorne Hall in Boston, and she would still be teaching for more than another six years. But it was through her magazine that she could respond to current questions about and criticisms of Christian Science, and give continuing advice to those she had sent out into the field or to those who were first hearing about Christian Science on the farms and in the small towns of that still developing Midwestern landscape stretching from Ohio to Colorado. No longer the physical frontier of America, in terms of social intercourse much of mid-America was a generation behind the more settled Eastern seaboard. And given the sparse population of much of the area, medical help was often scarce or too far away to be depended upon.

In the early years, the existence of the *Journal* may have created the impression of a movement that was larger than it actually was. Certainly the existence of such a publication gave Mrs. Eddy the most effective means available in that day to continue giving definition to Christian Science.

Along with her teaching and editing, Mrs. Eddy was also a frequent preacher at the Sunday services of her church in Boston. However, she also sometimes used the assistance of ministers who were sympathetic to Christian Science. The services were held in the afternoon, so that those who were still attending their old churches but were interested in hearing about Christian Science could attend.

❖ ❖ ❖ ❖

Besides the new view of creation that Mrs. Eddy laid before the eyes of her students, there are two elements that appear frequently in the correspondence of the 1880s, which by their frequency indicate their importance to Mrs. Eddy: a slightly different approach to handling the belief of animal magnetism, particularly in the form of malicious malpractice; and the need she felt to impress her students with a selfless commitment to the entire Christian message.

In the third edition of *Science and Health,* for which Gilbert Eddy had written an introduction, there was a denunciation of some of the individuals who had been considered disloyal to Mrs. Eddy. Dr. Eddy himself wrote in not too guarded language about the plagiarisms of Edward Arens. By the time of the sixth edition in 1887, the forty-seven pages Mrs. Eddy had given to malpractice had shrunk to thirteen (and they would shrink still more, to only six, by the early 1890s).

The change may have been more a warning to Mrs. Eddy's students than a change in her own manner of practice. She wanted to make sure that in their mental treatment, or practice, students did not name the person who they felt was the malpractitioner. She directed her students, "We had better suffer for others' wrong than to misjudge a person."[32] To another, "Make it *nothing* now (you have rebuked long enough) just as you do sickness. Don't *answer back* at all but know there is but *one* Mind that can talk."[33] And Calvin Frye, almost certainly with Mrs. Eddy's approval, wrote to A. B. Dorman, who had had class with Mrs. Eddy in 1883, "When we have mastered the question of M., it is not necessary to continue to take it up as a personality, we have long since ceased to take it up so."[34]

As for the Christian message of humility and selfless love, she found too many of her otherwise promising students interested in the healing method of Christian Science without seeing the connection that she had found to be indissoluble between success in healing and the consistent practice of such traditional Christian virtues (enumerated by Paul) as "love, joy, peace, longsuffering, gentleness, goodness, faith, meekness [and] temperance." To look only for success in healing was like trying to pick out the purple threads from the seamless robe and, in the process, destroying the robe.

While in the first years in Boston Mrs. Eddy had still solicited pupils whom she thought promising, she took no one whose motives she questioned. To a man who had had class with her the year before and wanted his mother-in-law to study with Mrs. Eddy, she replied, "I should prefer not to take her until she appreciates this cause more in its *Christian* demands to leave all for Christ."[35] To another she wrote that what her students required to reach their full potential was "the whole substance of Science viz. Christianity; seen in unselfishness, *love,* cross-bearing, etc."[36] And to a woman who studied with Mrs. Eddy when she taught a class in Chicago in 1884, but whose intellectuality kept her from embracing the simplicity of Christian Science, "I have not been able to learn from your lips what your feelings are on the *Christian* side of this Cause. And that is the only side...."[37]

Many of these people who did not measure up to Mrs. Eddy's expectations for them remind one of Jesus' parable of the sower and the seed. Very little seed actually fell into good soil, while most seems to have been wasted along the roadside or to have fallen in rocky soil. Yet in partial defense of some of these people, it is probably true that the emphasis in teaching was to lay open to them the possibilities of healing through their acceptance of a spiritual view of reality. They may have felt themselves ready to respond to the opportunity to heal more than to all the requisite conditions laid down for consistent success in their practice. Many of them were young people, whereas Mrs. Eddy in the mid-1880s was in her mid-sixties. Her mettle had been so tested by the trials she had had, both before her discovery of what she would name Christian Science and in the years she had been trying to teach it, that she knew instinctively that one needed the protection of all the Christian qualities. Even in her own case, she was still going through a process of learning to practice a gentleness in her relations with the outside world that did not always come easily during these turbulent years in Boston.

One reminiscence of Mrs. Eddy by a young Bostonian who flirted with Christian Science and was committed to many worthwhile social projects reveals Mrs. Eddy's concern that her students should progress in their expression of humility and brotherliness. She wrote:

> Mrs. Eddy was very appreciative of my voluntary welfare work. . . .she admitted when I said the other half of Christian Science would demand human brotherhood practically applied in every relation of life. But she said the first thing is to implant firmly in human consciousness the Power of God to heal sickness, sorrow, etc. When that has taken hold of mankind, the other will in time follow as a necessary sequence.[38]

The necessary humility had not yet been planted in the heart of Clara Choate. Late in 1883, Mrs. Eddy decided that someone needed to go to Chicago. She was aware that Clara enjoyed a certain social position in Boston and that Choate was also the cause of some friction within the Christian Scientist Association. But she also thought enough of Choate's abilities to ask her to go a thousand miles on a mission. Clara feared that, if she was too successful, Mrs. Eddy would ask her to stay. So she opted to remain in Boston.

Mary wrote firmly to Clara in tones calling up biblical authority: "Before you ever heard of Christian Science I had been commissioned of God to lead his children out of the darkness of today. You never can do this until your life is changed as you well know. Those that talk truth in one thing must *live* it in all things to be fit for pioneers. I have done telling you to no purpose." [39] The next day she wrote to her again: "If you will not hear God's voice speaking through me they will conquer you and kill you just as they did Gilbert. I *know* it." [40]

A month later Mrs. Eddy asked her to withdraw from both the church and the Association, which she did, but the Association nevertheless formally expelled her at its next meeting. Choate certainly did not have the kind of total commitment to Mrs. Eddy's cause that Mrs. Eddy knew would be needed in the years ahead. There were very few who did. But Choate's social ambitions also did not sit well with many of Mrs. Eddy's simpler students, and Choate very likely was insensitive to some of her actions in dealing with others.

One outcome of the Choate episode was that Mrs. Eddy decided to go to Chicago herself in May 1884. She had not traveled so far since she had gone to Charleston as a young bride. Train travel by this time was becoming common and more comfortable, although the fast trains between the East Coast and Chicago would not generally be running until about 1900. Neither the prospect of this trip nor the later one to Chicago in 1888 seems to have daunted Mrs. Eddy in the least.

Judging by the people she was to choose to run the affairs of her church in the next twenty years, Mrs. Eddy did not show herself to be a social revolutionary. Where it was assumed a man should do the job, she chose a man. But there is virtually nothing in her life at any period to indicate that she held back because she herself was a woman. She felt disadvantaged at times, yes, but not held back.

Chicago was a great success. In May 1884, she taught a class of twenty-five persons, including three doctors and two clergymen, one a Methodist and the other a Universalist. She already had students in Chicago who had came to Boston to take her classes, but her trip to the Middle West gave her a new insight into the rapid growth there and the receptivity of the Middle West in general to Christian Science. She would have the same problems there as elsewhere with former students borrowing from Christian Science and adulterating it. But she would also see her movement make substantial progress there in the next few years.

Its progress in Boston was not going unnoticed either. There were still attacks from some of the clergy against what she was presumed to be teaching, and a particularly vitriolic one came to her attention early in 1885. A conservative minister by the name of A. J. Gordon, unlike some who dismissed the healing record of Christian Science out of hand, admitted that Christian Science was healing the sick but (in effect) by Beelzebub. Another minister, Joseph Cook, read a letter of Gordon's at a Monday lecture in Boston's Tremont Temple, and Mrs. Eddy, upon hearing about it, demanded the right to reply. Cook allowed her ten minutes the next week. Those ten minutes were an epochal moment for Mrs. Eddy, even if the event in and of itself was quickly forgotten. Just five years earlier, as Mrs. Eddy was getting ready to leave Lynn, Christian Science had received scant attention from the representatives of orthodoxy. Yet here, after holding classes in her Massachusetts Metaphysical College for less than three years, the bastions of religious orthodoxy were sufficiently disturbed to find it necessary to denounce Christian Science.

Mrs. Eddy spoke before a hall of two thousand persons, most of whom were hostile to her views. She was given the barest of introductions and told that she would be removed from the platform if she spoke longer than ten minutes. Gordon had written about her as the "lady apostle," scarcely hiding the extra degree of venom that the male ministry of that day could direct against a female who thought she had a new revelation. But Mrs. Eddy made the most of her ten minutes. In the most direct language, she answered questions she posed to herself. No, she was not a spiritualist; her God was not a personal God: "I know not what the person of omnipotence and omnipresence is or what the infinite includes; therefore, I worship that of which I can conceive, first, as a loving Father and Mother…." Yes, she believed in the atonement, although she did not elaborate on her theological differences here. Healing was accomplished not by any action of the human mind but by "Christ come to destroy the power of the flesh." Then, in conclusion, she answered the question, "Is there a personal man?"

> . . .To my sense, we have not seen all of man; he is more than personal sense can cognize, who is the image and likeness of the infinite. I have not seen a perfect man in mind or body, – and such must be the personality of him who is the true likeness; the lost image is not this personality, and corporeal man is this lost image; hence, it doth not appear what is the real personality of man. The only cause for making this question of personality a point, or of any importance, is that man's perfect model should be held in mind, whereby to improve his present condition; that his contemplation regarding himself should turn away from inharmony, sickness, and sin, to that which is the image of his Maker.[41]

The discussions among the Boston ministers continued in their denominational enclaves, with one Baptist minister later that spring commenting that if people were being healed in Christian Science, theological points were not going to prevent them from crossing over to the new religion. His advice to his fellow ministers is reminiscent of the lawyer Gamaliel in the

Book of Acts. Gamaliel, telling the Jews to leave the Christians alone, said, "... if this counsel or this work be of men, it will come to nought: But if it be of God, ye cannot overthrow it; lest haply ye be found even to fight against God." [42]

Mrs. Eddy must have looked on all the attention that Christian Science was getting as a two-edged sword. It drew the inquisitive and open mind to Christian Science. But most of the criticism showed the deep misunderstanding of what she was trying to say and do. She could accomplish only so much in trying to deal with the clergy. Their theological beliefs had driven such deep grooves into their thought processes that most of them probably were honestly incapable of comprehending her sense of God, or the distinction between Jesus and the Christ, or the new meaning she attached to the concept of atonement.

There was one place, however, in which she determined to make her meaning even clearer to those who really were honest and open in their inquiry. And that was in another revision of her textbook, *Science and Health.* For she could see that the numbers she could teach in her classes were limited, and that statement applied even to the teachers she had begun to send throughout the country after 1884. But the numbers she could reach through her book were unlimited. Furthermore, if she could not always be certain of the quality of teaching of her students, the textbook could be relied upon as the final word about Christian Science. She often spoke and wrote about the book as if it had been literally dictated to her by God.

She believed, increasingly as the years went by, that she had a unique mission. She was not reluctant to speak to her own students in terms such as these: "... it is not me as a person who is able for these things, but my blessed Father who has spoken, and does not cease to speak still through me to the age. Science and Health ought to convince you of that, also that all I advise always prospers when my advice is taken." [43]

While she looked on the concepts in the textbook as a divine revelation, this did not blind her to the fact that she was a human being with a particular background. That being the case, her expression of what she considered a revelation was to some extent a human activity that in some inescapable ways reflected her background. Yet, as the years multiplied and the editions of the textbook increased, she removed most of the early references that placed it – and her – in a particular time period. A reference to the "crimes" of Jefferson Davis, the President of the Confederacy during the Civil War, was removed, for instance.

In another sense, she realized that she needed a professional editor who might serve as a check on what she meant in particular passages and, more particularly, improve her syntax and punctuation. These had never been her forte, and she had no time or patience to work on them now. So, to this end, she made an arrangement with a retired Unitarian minister, James Wiggin, to work on a new edition of the textbook in the spring of 1885, shortly after her Tremont Temple appearance. Wiggin assisted her throughout that year in preparing what became the sixteenth edition of *Science and Health.* In the spring of 1886, she even invited him to be present in one of her classes, although it was as an observer and not a student. A debonair sort of man, who was at home in the Boston literary world and greatly enjoyed the theater, he was an unusual ally. He did not take up the study of Christian Science, although Mrs. Eddy's performance as teacher in class made a strong and positive impression on him – for her intellectual clarity, her insight into students' thinking, and her biblical knowledge.

It was a prickly relationship, but in it one sees the kindness Mrs. Eddy could instinctively offer to others and her respect for what they could do for her, even while being on guard to defend her own sense of authority. When she hired Wiggin, she wrote that she was sending him "the first volume of Science and Health from which many are stealing and many more are unconscious of anything in it worth stealing."[44] Hearing that he was not well one day, she sent a note around to say that she had hired a team of horses "to take you out in the cool of the day.

Now step right into it and leave all cares behind and tell the driver to take you into pleasant places as long as you care to drive. … Remember the City lieth foursquare and every side is *safe, harmonious*…. Open your spiritual gaze to see this and you are well in a moment."[45]

When it came to revising the textbook, she took his advice only when she thought it made her meaning clearer. She wrote to him at one point, "If anything is a muddle and you so see it indicate it on a slip of paper page and par. or make it correct yourself, but never *change* my meaning, only *bring it out.*"[46] She did allow him to insert many literary allusions, as well as chapter headings that quoted from well-known writers (and in one instance from the *Bhagavad-Gita*). But such allusions, probably meant to convey a sense of connection with the insights of the past or of other authors, tended to dilute the integrity of her unique style of presentation. Had they remained in future editions, they would have made the book somewhat less a work for the ages, just as the contemporary references she was already in the process of removing would have. She had a clear sense that she should be preparing a book that would be free of superfluities – that in generations far into the future every page should say something vital and direct to the reader. In the spring of 1886, when the new edition appeared, she said in a letter to a student who had been through her Normal class the previous year, "Six clergymen have applied to enter my next class. The new Book is *reaching* them, they all say it is much clearer, that they see the meaning of Christian Science now. Oh! do they not see it? How little they dream of the awfulness of its heights and depths."[47]

Two years earlier, in the sixth edition of *Science and Health,* she had introduced a "Key to the Scriptures," making the title of the book *Science and Health with Key to the Scriptures.* This section contained a glossary of biblical names and terms, to each of which she had given their spiritual significance. Now she added three more chapters to this section, "Genesis" and "The Apocalypse," dealing with the first and last books of the Bible, and "Prayer And Atonement." Much of the material in

"Genesis" was drawn from a chapter entitled "Creation"; it was subject matter dealing with the two versions of the creation story that she had treated as early as the first edition of the textbook.

Besides feeling that she had made a significant advance with this edition of the book, which had occupied much of her time during 1885, she had taught four Primary classes and a Normal class that year and had continued to teach, reprimand, and encourage via her correspondence. These middle years of the 1880s were pivotal ones in what would become the history of Christian Science. Mrs. Eddy sensed the responsibility to carry through to completion what she believed God had given her to do. And she sensed more than most of her students the animosity of not only the Christian pulpit and the medical profession, but also what she identified as the collective human mentality, toward what Christian Science was accomplishing.

The psychoanalyst C. G. Jung, after 1900, would be writing about the collective unconscious. While this term is most certainly not identical in derivation or meaning with what Mrs. Eddy termed mortal mind, both concepts do represent a collectivity of thought that has to be taken into consideration in dealing with the individual's mental world. The collective unconscious, in Jung's system, could be a unifying force in one's experience, uniting him with the accumulated experience of the entire human race. Mortal mind, in Mrs. Eddy's system, on the other hand, stands for the "sum total of human error," for the commonly shared belief in materiality that is the core of all evil. As Mrs. Eddy grew in sensing the scope of what she had introduced to the world, she felt herself to be the focus of what she identified as mortal mind's attempt to fight back. Thus she expressed herself in increasingly strong and authoritative language to her followers and, sometimes, probably stepped beyond the bounds of what she would have liked to be remembered for. Nevertheless, a few samples from her letters, all in this one year, 1885, when she was accomplishing much in both teaching and preparing a new edition of the textbook, illustrate the peaks of emotion to which she could still rise.

To a Mr. Chase: "I have a letter informing me that you told a patient their case was not treated right, they of the Mass. Met. College were causing her sufferings and you took it up so. I have only to say if that can be proven or if you ever repeat the offence I will prosecute you for the basest slander. You need not reply. I have no time to spend on such as you have proven yourself to be."[48]

To Mary Hinds Philbrick, who would be in a Normal class in 1886: "The spiritual darkness that malicious mesmerism leaves on your mind is all that you are really in danger from. I see this darkness in every one that writes me on this question from Chicago. Now knowing the physical symptoms of disease is no aid spiritually, and you can heal them only by spiritual not material power. Arouse yourself from this spiritual blindness that seeking other Gods occasions and find *Truth* and *Love* the only only power, for they are and you ought to know this."[49]

To Mrs. Swarts, who with her husband had attended a portion of Mrs. Eddy's 1884 Chicago class and then gone her own way: "… you speak in your letter of the naturalness of the birdling to leave the Mother nest and make his own. I admit that is natural, but this is unnatural – for the bird to peck the Mother bird's eyes out, and destroy her nest, if it can before quitting her kind care."[50]

Yet in that same month she wrote to another student: "Only those whose mental action is always induced by love can abide in its light. I am above all human warfare. My sphere is now divine peace."[51]

She also continued to find time for the visitor and the occasional interview. In the summer of this same year, 1885, she granted a young woman journalist, Lilian Whiting, an interview that appeared in the *Ohio Leader.* From it one gets the sense of a person not only very much in control of herself, but also expressing the qualities of love and dominion that she was teaching the students in her classes. Whiting describes how, after being ushered into the reception room of the house on Columbus Avenue, Mrs. Eddy first appeared to her:

> Presently Mrs. Eddy came in and greeted me with a manner that, while cordial and graceful, was also something more, and had in it an indefinable element of harmony; and a peace that was not mere repose, but more like exaltation. It was subtle and indefinable, however, and I did not think of it especially at the time, although I felt it.

The conversation eventually turned to metaphysics. But it was the effect of being in Mrs. Eddy's presence that remained the strongest impression with Miss Whiting:

> I remembered afterwards how extremely tired I was as I walked rather wearily and languidly up the steps to Mrs. Eddy's door. I came away, as a little child friend of mine expressively says, "skipping." I was at least a mile from the Vendome [her hotel] and I walked home feeling as if I were treading on air. My sleep that night was the rest of Elysium.[52]

One might pause for a moment and consider all the elements that comprised Mrs. Eddy's daily life in these mid-1880s – the almost constant teaching, writing monthly for the *Journal,* and the correspondence with her students, with its mixture of encouragement, cajoling, and occasional reprimand. It is evident that she had advanced into a new maturity since returning to Boston in 1882, and that this growing sense of dominion was evident even to a casual visitor such as Whiting.

❖ ❖ ❖ ❖

As the movement began to take on national scope, Mrs. Eddy needed to find students who could, in addition to being healers, take pupils of their own and help organize Christian Science in their areas. The decade is replete with names of those who flowered for an instant and then wilted. Several of the women who came to study with her soon decided that they could combine what they had gotten from Mrs. Eddy with insights of their own and start their own movements. It was this misuse of Christian Science, or borrowing from the textbook without being honest about the source of the ideas, that kept Mrs. Eddy on the alert night and day.

She had hoped that several ministers could help carry the torch as she slowed down her pace. Yet not one of those who came forward in the 1880s stayed with her or proved himself satisfactory to her. Her experience with one of them suffices to illustrate the problem. William Gill had been a Methodist minister in Lawrence, Massachusetts. He became attracted to Christian Science, but never to the point of unqualifiedly accepting Mrs. Eddy's authority on the subject. Somewhat of an intellectual, he had published a book called *Philosophical Realism.* Mrs. Eddy found that when he was teaching a class on Christian Science he had used this book instead of hers as his basis for teaching. He also bemoaned the low intellectual level of many of her students. This was a matter of concern to Mrs. Eddy as well, and at this period she was encouraging some of her students to start Christian Science institutes that included in their curricula the study of English. But she also recognized that grasping the spiritual content of Christianity was not a matter of human intellect, and that for many, human intellect could actually be a barrier to spiritual understanding. Rev. Gill also exhibited some of the characteristics of his sex, as in writing to her, "I do not think there is one other man in all the world so thoroughly prepared to take up this work...."[53] He apparently thought that she needed males to get the proper attention, or even that she needed former ministers. As it was, she appointed him the assistant pastor of her church, which by now was meeting in Chickering Hall in Boston, and for a brief time made him editor of the *Journal.*

Beyond all the attitudes he had that were not in tune with Mrs. Eddy, however, there lay a fundamental theological difference. Gill never fully understood what Mrs. Eddy meant by the unreality of evil. It should be clear to anyone reading this that Christian Science was directed against evil in all its forms, not just human physical illness. Through the differentiation Mrs.

Eddy made between the divine Mind, or God, and the human mind, she felt she was showing her followers the way to adopt the Mind of Christ and put off the sinning, erring, mortal mind, based on a belief in the reality of a material life, which by definition separated man from God, omnipresent Spirit. Gill must have, at some point or in some partial way, understood her. But his theological training proved too great an obstacle for him to accept the simplicity of her metaphysics, namely: God is All; therefore, there is no evil. Mrs. Eddy had told him that he would never fully understand her metaphysics until he healed the sick. But he liked to argue, and he wrote to her after one such confrontation:

> It is clear that God cannot *know* (by experience, impression, acquisition) evil; but He must be able to *understand* it as the logically contrasted opposite of himself, as a falsity, a claim to be what it is not. I have all along thought that this must be what you mean.[54]

But this was *not* what she meant. His preaching had less and less to do with Christian Science, and by the end of 1886, they had parted ways – unfortunately, with acrimony on his part.

The Gill episode, as well as two similar ones with preachers who had had class with Mrs. Eddy, convinced her of the near impossibility of putting new wine into old bottles. The old bottles of theological concepts could not hold the fresh insight that Christian Science had brought to the Bible. One who thinks it unfortunate that Mrs. Eddy did not have an academic training in theology or that, after she discovered Christian Science, did not have the benefit of honing her terminology by rubbing shoulders with the all-male theological school faculties around Boston should ponder the Gill incident.

Mrs. Eddy claimed that she was led to the revelation of Christian Science solely through her study of the Bible. Certainly her articulation of it took place in an atmosphere just beginning to be aware of a new psychological language. Some of her terms seem more modern than biblical, terms such as mortal mind or animal magnetism. Yet she gave to even these terms a unique content, as she did to traditional Christian concepts such as atonement and grace. There may be some merit in the view that Christian Science would, in the beginning, have been taken more seriously by theologians if there had been a more direct line of continuity inside the boundaries and terminology of traditional Christian debate. One can only suggest that what Mrs. Eddy gleaned from the Bible was sufficiently different from what the theologians since Augustine's time had been making of it to require a fresh start. Yet to overemphasize the new start would be to overlook the strands of continuity that were also one of the elements appealing to thoughtful Christians dissatisfied with their own churches.

Nowhere was Mrs. Eddy's theology more radical in terms of its contrast with tradition than in her emphasis on the unreality of evil – the point that caused Rev. Gill so much consternation. She stood in complete agreement with orthodox theology that the man we see in the flesh needed regeneration. But orthodox theology, most Protestant as well as Roman Catholic, had not gone beyond Augustine's concept that man was a sinner who could do nothing to save himself. Mrs. Eddy absolutely refused that concept as a definition of man. Rather, she saw man as the image of God, as the first chapter of Genesis describes him. Whatever blotted out that image in human experience was what was evil. It was that impersonal evil, or devil, including the belief in the reality of matter, that must be progressively overcome in order for the real man to appear – as he already is.

There is a tradition that, in the scenes on the Sistine Chapel at the Vatican, Michelangelo did not paint the creation and then proceed to do scenes that ended in man's fall from paradise. The tradition is that Michelangelo intended the paintings to be read from the opposite end of the chapel. Starting from a fallen sense of himself, man, through the experience of rebirth, gradually comes to see his unfallen, sinless nature, until in the last (first) mural his hand is grasped by the hand of God. Whether this story can be verified or not, it expresses the theological difference that separated Mrs. Eddy from traditional Christianity.

Her experiences in trying to separate Christian Science from thought systems that appeared to have some similarity to it, as well as to maintain the integrity of her teaching from students who went off with little bits of it, led her to undertake some further writing after she had revised *Science and Health.* During the next year she wrote two pamphlets and a small book that illustrate the points she felt had to be clarified at that moment. The first of them, *Christian Science: No and Yes,* was the closest in organization to the topics of orthodox Christianity. It came in part out of her experience with her ministerial critics. She tried to answer the charges that Christian Science was in any way connected with spiritualism or theosophy, or that it was pantheistic. She also addressed such questions as, Is There a Personal Deity, Is There a Personal Devil, Is There any such Thing as Sin, and Is There no Sacrificial Atonement?

In the other two books she made a more open break with the categories of orthodox Christianity and showed that the concepts of God, man, and salvation that had come to her through her study of the Bible were essentially a new explication of Christianity that could not be poured into old wineskins. The short work, of no more than five thousand words, that eventually bore the title of *Rudimental Divine Science,* was organized around a definition of Christian Science, God, a discussion of the nonexistence of matter, and the basis of Mind-healing. Later in 1887 came the third book, *Unity of Good and Unreality of Evil,* eventually shortened to the simple *Unity of Good.* Here, in several short chapters, she discussed from different aspects the basic difference between her theology and traditional Christianity: the absolute allness of God and the consequent nothingness of matter and evil. Completely aware of the radical nature of what she was teaching, she wrote, "The Science of physical harmony, as now presented to the people in divine light, is radical enough to promote as forcible collisions of thought as the age has strength to bear." "No wise mother," she wrote, "though a graduate of Wellesley College, will talk to her babe about the problems of Euclid."[55]

Yet that is just what she did. It was only by rising to a standpoint of consciousness from which one could approximate the way God sees His creation – entirely perfect and of a spiritual nature – that one could experience the kind of healing that occurred with regularity in Christian Science.

This year of 1887 marked a kind of writing climax for Mrs. Eddy. She would later revise *Science and Health* in a major way two more times; she would gather the articles she had written for the *Journal* and have them printed in a book; and several of her major sermons and addresses to her church would later be preserved in printed form.[56] But these three small books that she published in 1887 are her longest separate writings apart from the textbook itself and a short autobiography of her life, *Retrospection and Introspection,* which she finished in 1891. They were written to answer specific needs at the time. But they were significant for another reason. In their tone, they showed the position Mrs. Eddy had been led by circumstance to take – to refuse to undertake a dialogue in terms of the categories of theology that had been the source of disagreement among Christians for almost two thousand years, and, instead, to state the fundamentals of this new appearing of Christianity in the language she felt would make better healers and more thorough Christians out of her followers.

The language of Christian Science often used familiar Christian terminology, but with an entirely new light thrown on the words. "Grace," for instance: Was man saved by faith, by the grace of God, or by works? This question had been a weighty one among theologians ever since Martin Luther had revived Augustine's concept of grace in the Protestant Reformation. Mrs. Eddy did not sidestep the question, but the metaphysics of Christian Science put it in a different light. Man, the perfect selfhood of each individual, is already saved, but it remains for each individual in a human sense to work out that salvation, to find out through experience that he is the image of God. That finding out can be called "works," but what one finds is nothing less than that state of grace as God's beloved child that already exists.

❖ ❖ ❖ ❖

There had been a Christian Scientist Association since 1876, composed of Mrs. Eddy's own students. After 1884, when she began to encourage some of her students to go out and hold classes, they also began to have meetings of their students. In 1886, she decided the time had come to organize a National Christian Scientist Association, and it held its first convention in 1887 in Boston. The group decided at that time to meet the following year in Chicago. As the time for the meeting neared, Mrs. Eddy at first indicated that she would not attend. She had taught a Normal class in February 1888 and one of her largest ever Primary classes (forty-seven students) in March 1888. A long way from the days in 1882 and 1883 when she had written to encourage prospects to apply for a class, she was having difficulty taking all the promising students who were applying to her. At the same time, she had very likely encouraged the National Christian Scientist Association to hold its next meeting in Chicago because of the growth of the movement in the West and particularly the strength of Christian Science in Chicago itself. At almost the last minute, she set out for Chicago with her secretary, Calvin Frye, two other Boston students, Captain and Mrs. Joseph Eastaman, and a homeopathic doctor, Ebenezer Foster, who had recently had class with her.

The Chicago trip marked a turning point in Mrs. Eddy's life in ways she could not have planned. As far as the present moment, it gave her evidence of the growth of Christian Science across the United States and confirmed to her the value of the teaching she had been doing for the past five years, as well as the work of at least some of the teachers she had sent out from Boston. Looking to the future, however, the trip raised questions for her that few of her followers would be thinking about yet: the danger of popularity, either of Christian Science or of her own personality; how to care for the demands of increasing numbers of students; and, through a crisis that arose among her local students while she was away from Boston, whether the forms of organization she had so far devised were the right vehicles for the future.

As for the meeting itself, Mrs. Eddy had not intended to speak. But one of the former ministers who had become a Christian Scientist, Joseph Day, had advertised her as the speaker on the second morning of the convention without telling her. Only during the ride to the Central Music Hall did he so inform her. Some four thousand persons, probably a majority of whom were not Christian Scientists, had come in anticipation of hearing her. She at first demurred, but then went ahead. As she came on to the platform, the entire audience rose out of respect for her. She then delivered an extemporaneous address that she later published in edited form as "Science and the Senses." In it she spoke simply of the unique viewpoint one adopts in Christian Science treatment, of seeing the universe as God sees it – spiritual and perfect – a viewpoint that in every detail contradicts the evidence of our senses. It was much the same theme she had been elaborating in *Unity of Good.* She told someone several years later that she had spoken for an hour and, at the audience's urging, talked another thirty minutes. The published speech does not appear that long, but one does not know exactly what her style of delivery may have been.

At the end of her talk, there was a rush to the stage to greet her, and people were saying they had been healed by her speech. The *Chicago Times* reporter wrote:

> When the speaker concluded the audience arose en masse and made a rush for the platform. There were no steps provided for getting on the rostrum, but that did not deter those who wanted to shake hands with the idolized expounder of their creed. They mounted the reporters' table and vaulted to the rostrum like acrobats. They crowded about the little woman and hugged and kissed her until she was exhausted and a man had to come to her rescue and lead her away.[57]

That night a reception was held for her at the Palmer House, where she was staying. The crowds that came to see her were almost unmanageable, and she stayed at the reception only briefly. The great distance Christian Science had come in just a few years must have held some small gratification for her. But she had grown used to looking ahead, to seeing the cross that still accompanied most promises of a crown, and the entire Chicago experience increased her sense of wariness.

Before she had left for Chicago, one event in Boston had given her reason enough for anxiety. A young woman had died in childbirth, as had her baby. The woman's mother, Abby Corner, who had been attending her, was a student of Mrs. Eddy's. Although Mrs. Eddy had exercised caution in how she had advised students to deal with childbirth cases, this particular student had taken on more than she was prepared to handle. In her appearance before the court, she was exonerated, as a doctor testified that the young mother would have died even if medical help had been available. But several of the students in the Christian Scientist Association, the smaller association composed only of graduates of the Massachusetts Metaphysical College, felt that Mrs. Eddy had not leaped to the defense of Mrs. Corner fast enough. For her part, Mrs. Eddy had been concerned about the reputation of Christian Science practice and was not at all sure that her student had not overstepped herself in taking such a case. But some thirty-six students, out of an association of about two hundred at that time, rebelled and wanted to resign. The rules of the association did not allow for a simple resignation. While Mrs. Eddy was in Chicago, these students managed to get hold of the official books, containing the records of the association, from the wife of the secretary, William B. Johnson. For several months they held onto the books. Failing to bring them back into her fold, Mrs. Eddy gave them all letters of resignation.

The Chicago experience, plus this defection of a fraction of the Christian Scientist Association, made an indelible mark on Mrs. Eddy. Chicago had shown her the potential for growth as well as how far the movement had already come; but it had also raised for her the specter of popularity. Would those who looked at Christian Science because it might be popular study it deeply, or humbly, enough to understand it? The experience with the dissident students back in Boston was a reenactment for her of the partial breakup of her small church in Lynn in 1881. It made her wonder if the organizations she had set up so far were ones that could protect her "child," Christian Science, when she was no longer here. And, even while she was living, could she trust the judgment of her students when she was convinced she was always seeing farther ahead than they?

These were questions that must occupy the thought of the pioneer of any new movement. In Mrs. Eddy's case, she had little precedent to go on. She was establishing a form of religious practice that demanded thoughtful obedience to a metaphysical system she felt had been revealed to her by God. Yet she knew that, in individual practice, obedience to a metaphysical rule was only the beginning; it also required inspiration and individual unfoldment. Had she let her students convince her of the need for organization beyond what was actually necessary? Was her organization developing too much like the orthodox churches from which her students by and large had come?

As she was pondering the answers to these questions, there was another urgency placed upon her. Demand for her teaching had grown to the point that she felt she could not handle all the legitimate requests for her classes. She wrote to one student in late 1888 that she had on hand over three hundred applications for class, that if she taught one class she would still have people waiting for three more classes, and so on. At the end of February 1889, she taught the largest class she was ever to teach, some sixty-eight students. This was considerably more than the number she could effectively reach in the kind of one-on-one mental probing that had made her such an effective communicator of her system. She must have known this ahead of time, yet she bowed to the demand the numbers seemed to be making on her.

Then in May she began to teach another Normal class. Exactly what transpired is not clear from the record, but part of the way through the class she abruptly left her teaching. Three days later she was writing from Vermont that she was safe and well. It is only an assumption, but in the absence of any more definitive correspondence on those days, something within her must have said simply, "This is enough; leave." Although the leave-taking was abrupt, she would explain it to her satisfaction later on. But just as quickly as a thunderstorm and a sudden shift in the wind can herald the end of summer, the Boston years, which had launched Christian Science onto a nationwide stage, had ended.

❖ ❖ ❖ ❖

As the system Mrs. Eddy called Christian Science expanded, and particularly as a permanent organization took shape in the 1890s, the people she drew around her increased in number. There was also a change in the nature of the relationships she had. Most of the people she would be dealing with during the final two decades of her life were persons whom she had taught during the mid to late 1880s in Boston, and a few of them would become permanent figures in her story. Up until this point, most of the other individuals in her life had drifted in and out of it more or less like actors playing cameo roles in a stage play.

Before proceeding to the nearly two decades that Mrs. Eddy spent in her native state of New Hampshire following the Boston years, however, one needs to pick up the threads woven into the tapestry of her life by a few persons who have not yet been mentioned during these Boston years, or in the case of her son, to bring his role in her life up-to-date. As one sits back and tries to tell a story, he moves on from what seems to be one connected point to another, all the time recognizing that there are a few figures in his side vision who have not seemed to fit into the story as it was being told.

Such is the case with two women students who were to figure in the Christian Science movement. Unfortunately, both of them typified traits of character that would prove dangerous to the future of Christian Science. Both of these women, Josephine Woodbury and Augusta Stetson, were taught by Mrs. Eddy during the Boston years. Then there is her son, George, who had last visited her in 1881 during one of her winter stays in Boston. He returned for another visit in the winter of 1887-8 and would turn up a few more times in the following decades. Yet as much as Mrs. Eddy longed for a relationship that resembled some aspect of the normal family that she had felt lacking in her life ever since the group around the hearth in Sanbornton Bridge had begun to break up, George Glover could not supply that need for her. And so, after his 1888 visit, another male entered the picture: a homeopathic doctor who had just learned of Christian Science the year before and whom Mrs. Eddy decided to adopt as her legal son.

These four are definitely not cameo figures, so we must pause here to introduce them or make their stories current.

❖ ❖ ❖ ❖

In the end, Augusta Stetson was one of Mrs. Eddy's bad apples. But in 1884, when Mrs. Eddy persuaded her to have class with her, it appeared she might be a plum. Stetson had grown up in northern New England – in Maine. She had married a Civil War veteran who was in business with his father as a shipbuilder. As a young bride, she traveled with her husband to India. For several years he worked there, in Bombay, and then in Burma. He had been maltreated while in prison during the Civil War, and eventually his health deteriorated. They returned to New England, with Augusta determined to earn the living for the family. She had just been trained as an elocutionist and was getting established in that profession when she was introduced to Mrs. Eddy.

There were remarkable similarities as well as differences between the two women. Both were representatives of the emerging female, undaunted by the still male world about them. Mrs. Eddy must have found something very positive in Mrs. Stetson's determination to earn her own living as well as in the experience she had gained from living abroad for many years. But the differences were, in the end, more substantial. Mrs. Eddy was a more retiring person and had had to overcome her own self-distrust to take many of the early steps she took in Christian Science. She had also had enough trials as a Christian Scientist to know that she absolutely must "rest in God," to go each step of the way convinced that it was God who was leading her. Augusta does not appear to have believed in the necessity of humility. She was at first reluctant to enter into Christian Science as a practitioner because of fear she could not earn enough money to support herself and her husband. Around forty years old when she first met Mrs. Eddy, the latter saw in her, as in Julia Bartlett, the next generation to carry on her work.

She studied with Mrs. Eddy in the fall of 1884, and almost immediately went into the healing practice. Augusta's ability was put to an early test when Mrs. Eddy did not appear in a town outside Boston to give a talk that Augusta had scheduled. Augusta rose to the occasion and gave the talk herself, much to Mrs. Eddy's satisfaction. Augusta also did excellent healing work, if her testimony in the July 1885 *Christian Science Journal* is taken at face value. She recounted in it that she had already healed patients of longstanding menstrual problems, breast cancer, sprained ankles, diphtheria, spinal trouble, and heart problems. A vigorous and intelligent worker such as Mrs. Stetson was the kind Mrs. Eddy was understandably looking for. That she had an uncurbed ambition was not at first apparent. Over the years she would become a growing problem for Mrs. Eddy.

The other woman entering the picture in the 1880s who would represent problems for Mrs. Eddy well into the 1900s was Josephine Woodbury. Woodbury had first become interested in Christian Science in 1880 through Clara Choate. Probably because of the Choate influence, she did not go through a class with Mrs. Eddy until late 1884 (a month after Stetson). Stetson is usually described as having a commanding presence; on the other hand, the striking thing about pictures of Woodbury was her physical beauty. She, like Choate, had social inclinations. These, combined with an interest in hypnotism before coming into Christian Science, and a sensuality that would become more pronounced (just as did Stetson's personal ambitions), were all qualities that did not sit well with an unselfed commitment to the spiritual life. But, as in the case of Stetson, her many positive qualities, which included her ability to speak and mix with other people, seemed an asset at the time.

As for George Glover, little had been heard of him since his visit to Boston in the winter of 1881. Suddenly he wrote to his mother that he and his entire family were coming to Boston to spend the winter of 1887-8. Mrs. Eddy was less than enthralled, although all her life she did her best to see in her son the close relative she would have liked her son to be. (He had not answered her need for compassion when she asked him to come in 1882, at the time of Gilbert's death.) So she wrote to him that she had no place in her own house for him, his wife, and their three children, and that what she actually needed was rest. (She was, at the moment, just getting ready to move her personal residence from the Massachusetts Metaphysical College to a new townhouse at 385 Commonwealth Avenue.) "I want quiet and a Christian life alone with God, when I can find intervals for a little rest," she wrote to him. "When I retire from business and into private life then I can receive you if you are *reformed*, but not otherwise. I say this to *you* not to *any one else.* I would not injure *you* any more than myself."[58]

But George, never too sensitive, did not heed her plea. He came on to Boston with his family. By this time finances were no longer a problem for Mrs. Eddy; she rented a house in Chelsea, just north of Boston, and put up her family there. Proud of her grandchildren, she brought them onto the platform with her at a Sunday service. The family visit lasted for the winter months, but it was clear that they did not belong in the confining atmosphere of Boston or, more particularly, in the environment in which Mrs. Eddy was working. Their presence only brought a new ache to Mrs. Eddy, who bemoaned her grandchildren's lack of education. She wrote to George before he left, "I want your children *educated.* No greater disgrace rests on my family name than the ignorance of the parents of these darling children."[59]

Mrs. Eddy had not wanted George to visit her when he did. But the ultimate futility of his trip, which it was if one were to assess it in terms of building a closer mother-son relationship, turned Mrs. Eddy's thoughts in a novel direction. Undoubtedly having George close by during those winter months of 1888 made her long for the son he simply could never be to her. It was natural, then, that she should happen to think about a man just a bit younger than George, who had been in one of her classes in 1887: Ebenezer J. Foster. A homeopathic doctor, Foster had graduated from the Hahnemann Medical College in Philadelphia. Hahnemann may be recalled as the founder of the branch of medicine known as homeopathy, with which Mrs. Eddy had had considerable personal experience during the 1850s. Foster had gone back to his native Vermont and had established a practice in the town of Waterbury. But he had a friend who was healed of a longstanding illness through Christian Science. This piqued Foster's interest, and while visiting an aunt of his in Boston, he made a call on Mrs. Eddy. As it happened, she was just about to begin a new class, and Foster became one of two doctors whom she taught in that class in November 1887.

He returned to Vermont, but shortly thereafter moved down to Boston to begin work as a Christian Science practitioner. When Mrs. Eddy went to Chicago for the 1888 convention of Christian Scientists, she included him as one of her small party. Under its charter, the Massachusetts Metaphysical College was allowed to give instruction on the medical aspects of obstetrics. One can imagine how the idea gradually came to Mrs. Eddy to have Foster, who could coincidentally fill that part of the curriculum, as a permanent companion. He also appears to have been a more cultured individual than Calvin Frye, her personal secretary. After the Chicago convention, she had Foster come to her house, and it was there that she proposed that he become her adopted son. That fall she petitioned the local court to allow her to adopt the forty-one-year-old Foster, who, she said, "is now associated with your petitioner in business, home life and life work, and she needs such interested care and relationship." He became her adopted son in November 1888.

Foster-Eddy was to play a significant role in her life for the next eight years, but it was largely a sad role. Mrs. Eddy's adoption of Benny, as she usually referred to him, was her last attempt to build a wall of security and love based on something resembling normal family ties. It is noteworthy largely because it indicates how deeply she yearned for the normal accompaniments of home. Yet she had many times indicated that she considered Christian Science her "child," and her attempt to give Benny a role he did not prove capable of fulfilling was destined to lead only to more disappointments.

At first, however, all went smoothly. Benny taught part of the obstetrics course in November 1888. The next spring, when she departed suddenly for Barre, Vermont, he jumped into the gap and taught the rest of the Normal class she had begun teaching. And for the next several years he served as runner between Boston and wherever she was living. But he did not develop as she had anticipated, and when the final break came, it would be one more disappointment for Mrs. Eddy. She did not make a habit of saying she had made mistakes. That she took many risks, she would admit. Foster-Eddy was one of those risks that turned out not to be worth it. But the rest of the Foster-Eddy story takes place in the 1890s – beyond the Boston that Mrs. Eddy had left in May 1889.

Chapter 7

Retirement at Pleasant View
Mrs. Eddy's Work as Founder

While Mary Baker Eddy's departure from Boston in May 1889 was sudden and unannounced, those who had been communicating with her in the prior months, if they had gotten together and compared notes, would have been less surprised. Some of the members of her household had been concerned for some time that she was showing the strain of her work more, particularly the strains caused by disagreements among Christian Scientists. She had written in March 1889 to one student, "I do not *want* to teach, I am *tired tired* of teaching and being the slave of so many minds...."[1] A few weeks later she wrote to John Linscott, telling him she would not attend that year's National Christian Scientist Association convention, "... I cannot do as much as I used to do and do it *well.*"[2] Calvin Frye wrote to an applicant for class in early May that Mrs. Eddy might never teach another primary class and that the applicant might consider having class with Foster-Eddy.[3] Finally, just a week before she left Boston, she wrote to Mary Dillingham:

> Many times I wish I could go to some place where I was not known and find the peace that I long for. How sad life seems to me I mean human life. O how cold and unconscious of others is the human heart. If I had not heaven in view the former would kill me. But I must bear and bear on to the end.[4]

The same week in which she left Boston, part way through a Normal class she was teaching, she wrote to a student by the name of General Erastus Bates, asking if he would take her college for a year or more. "I want to have it open, and I have given up teaching, for time to do the things that God demands."[5]

Whatever the reason, her departure from Boston appeared to

have been unplanned. A few days later she wrote to her adopted son, "Just a few words from me will relieve any anxiety you may feel. I am doing well and three months to be *alone* will be the one thing needed."[6] She formally resigned as pastor of her church on May 28, and the next day sent off another letter to Foster-Eddy that, by its contents, confirmed that her exit had been abrupt:

> My own darling: Your good letter is a treat. Send all the checks and orders to me through the American Express and I will sign and return them. Send them every week. Please take my diamonds and jewelry from the drawer on left-side of my dressing case in Chamber, lock them up in little tin box key on the outside of box... I want a place out of Boston for retirement. Barre is not the one. Concord is better.[7]

❖ ❖ ❖ ❖

Over the years it became clear to Mrs. Eddy and to those around her that she had made the right move, whatever the immediate cause had been. The seven years in Boston had served their purpose well. Through her concentration on teaching, she had prepared enough workers in both the fields of healing and teaching for them to spread Christian Science across the United States. Through the *Journal* she was building a publication that could give unity and direction to what was still a thinly scattered field of followers. There was now other work for her to do, and it quickly began to take shape in the form of another major revision of the textbook.

But beyond that immediate task there lay major questions. How could she protect what she considered the integrity, or wholeness, of the discovery she had made? How could she perpetuate and nourish the fledgling movement of Christian Scientists? As one looks at her long life and all of the events that lay ahead in the two decades after 1889, it is too easy to overlook how her immediate world looked to her at that moment. She was close to seventy years of age. Many of her letters indicate that she did not anticipate an extended old age. Given the mental battles of which she often felt herself to be the target, she did not even have any particular desire to live a long life. Moreover, all of her siblings were already dead, Abigail having passed on in 1886. So, one might keep in mind, in looking at the steps Mrs. Eddy took in these first years in New Hampshire, that she did not know then that two very active decades still lay ahead of her.

The years from 1889 through 1892 were turbulent ones for Mrs. Eddy, but the turbulence is seen less in the outward events than in the steps she took in working out the forms of her organization. These steps were not always in a straight line, but they eventually did lead to a solution satisfactory to her. The solutions that appeared most favorable to her in 1889 all had one word in common – dissolution. First, as mentioned, she had already resigned in May as pastor of her church in Boston. Then, in June, she turned over control of *The Christian Science Journal* to the National Christian Scientist Association. In September she dissolved the Christian Scientist Association, the organization composed of students who had personally studied with her.

But the biggest moves were to come at year's end. In September she had written to General Bates that she was waiting for God's direction about the college. Then, as the year drew toward its close, she felt that her prayerful waiting had provided the answers as to organization: dissolve everything. In October she wrote to Bates again, "This is His command, as I understand it, saying to me: Disorganize all that you have organized materially. Start now on a purely spiritual Christ-like basis."[8]

Accordingly, the board of the Massachusetts Metaphysical College met on October 29 and formally dissolved the corporation. In language that certainly reflected her intent at the time, whether or not she wrote the actual words, the resolution that was adopted read in part:

> WHEREAS, Other institutions for instruction in Christian Science, which are working out their periods

> of organization, will doubtless follow the example of the Alma Mater after having accomplished the worthy purpose for which they were organized, and the hour has come wherein the great need is for more of the spirit instead of the letter, and Science and Health is adapted to work this result, and
>
> WHEREAS, the fundamental principle for growth in Christian Science is spiritual formation first, last, and always, while in human growth material organization is first; and
>
> WHEREAS, Mortals must learn to lose their estimate of the powers that are not ordained of God, and attain the bliss of loving unselfishly, working patiently, and conquering all that is unlike Christ and the example he gave; ... [9]

One month later she reached the same conclusion about the church organization. She wrote to her trusted student, Julia Bartlett:

> This morning has finished my halting between two opinions. This Mother Church must disorganize and now is the time to do it, and form no new organization but the spiritual one. Follow Christ Jesus' example and not that of his disciples. Theirs has come to naught in science ours should establish Science but not material organizations. Will tell you all that leads me to this final decision when I see you. [10]

In a statement written later for the *Journal,* Mrs. Eddy said:

> The dissolution of the visible organization of the Church is the sequence and complement of that of the College Corporation and Association. The College disappeared, "that the spirit of Christ might have freer course among its students and all who come

> into the understanding of Divine Science"; the bonds of organization of the Church were thrown away, so that its members might assemble themselves together and "provoke one another to good works" in the bond only of love. [11]

In the same letter in which she asked her followers in Boston to disband as a church, she offered to provide the land on which to build a church edifice. Thus, her intent was not to end church services, but to put an end to whatever it was about organization that had provoked her to take the extreme measures she had taken in the half year since her retreat from Boston. She appeared worn from the stress of the various moves. She wrote to General Bates in November, "I have had little else this year but loss & cross according to the senses," and to Captain Eastaman (who was apparently treating her) at Christmastime, "Your patient in Concord is better but yet there is room for improvement." [12]

❖ ❖ ❖ ❖

Calvin Frye, her secretary, commented that she could have earned $40,000 just for a week's teaching of all those whose applications she had had on her desk for her Primary class when she stopped teaching. But she had come to the conclusion that her personal teaching had done its job: it had seeded the wider field. Perhaps she would be around for only a few more years, and it was more important to do something that would help greater numbers, even if it did not have the unique, probing force of the encounter with her in the classroom. To this end, she began to revise the textbook as soon as she was more or less settled away from Boston.

The dissolution of the church organization is not as easily comprehended, particularly in light of the fact that she encouraged her students to go on forming their own churches elsewhere and that she would re-form the church in Boston in another three years. She had certainly been troubled by the defection of some of her promising students over the Abbie Corner childbirth case. She wrote to Rev. Easton, whom she asked to come to Boston in the spring of 1889 to take over the pulpit of her church, "You have a great work committed to you in Boston. One year ago we had four wealthy and influential and highly cultured families with us who paid liberally to sustain Church worship, that are not with us this year." [13]

But the defection of some of the Boston members does not alone suffice to explain the radical stand she took toward church organization. She had been troubled more each year by the competition among Christian Scientists as they established churches in other cities, and she believed that unless Christian Science was to be signally identified as a religion of the truly reborn – that is, by selflessness, humility, and love without expectation of reward – it would eventually lose the day. Throughout 1890, as she stepped up the pace of her work on *Science and Health,* she was also busy writing letters of instruction, encouragement, or reprimand to students all over the country. In many of them this same theme recurred.

To Laura Lathrop in New York:

> The Principle of our demonstrations as Christian Scientists is *unity* and our demonstrations depend on *united minds* and their at-one-ment with the one Mind. [14]

To Ellen Linscott, over some brouhaha in the Chicago churches:

> How my heart is grieved at such dissensions and quarreling in the ranks of Christians who claim to be more Christlike than other denominations… for once I ask it show yourself the best Christian of the two by taking the *first* step towards reconciliation. [15]

To Elizabeth Skinner:

> You must meet with them, cheer them, in their

> labors, point the way of love to them and show them it by loving first, and waiting patiently for them to be in this great step by your side, loving each other and walking together. This is what the world must see before we can convince the world of the truths of Christian Science.[16]

> To Ruth Ewing in Chicago:

> Oh may love bind you all in its silken cords. For Truth and Love's dear sake we must be living examples of Unity if that *is* our *Principle* and then the world will acknowledge the power and genuineness of C.[hristian] S.[cience].[17]

As she viewed the status of the movement, the enthusiasm over the phenomenon of physical healing was too often unaccompanied by the kind of growth in Christian character that was needed as armor to prevent the attacks of the human, or carnal, mind, which she had found came to every successful healer. The church organization had been meant as a means of protection and mutual support, but in some instances the churches were engaged in what looked more like intra-Christian Science warfare. Thus she continued to mull over the best way to protect and nurture Christian Science in the future.

She was also not yet physically settled. The stay in Barre, Vermont, had been brief, brought to an end when summer musical bands practicing on the town green close to her house disturbed her peace. As she had noted in a letter in the spring of 1889, she found Concord, New Hampshire, more to her liking. Concord lay between her girlhood homes of Bow and Sanbornton Bridge (now Tilton) and must have seemed a natural spot for retirement. But it was not the only place she considered, even while she rented a house there on North State Street. She again thought briefly of moving to Philadelphia, as she had a decade earlier. Knowing something of the reputed provincialism of Philadelphians, she had Foster-Eddy write to her student, James Ackland:

> Mother [Mrs. Eddy] wished me to write and ask you if a beautiful place for a home could be had in the suburbs of Philadelphia? One with large grounds and plenty of shade in a location that would not be sneered at by Philadelphians. We have heard that some of the people of that city are peculiar about such things. [18]

She also seriously considered going to England, and it would appear from one letter that her intent was to remain there. In the spring of 1890 she had written to Marjorie Colles, one of the early Christian Scientists in England:

> I shall want when I go to England in my house five bedrooms. Now let me say it looks doubtful about my getting away this Spring. The circumstances have changed since I wrote you.... I have so many times been disappointed about going there that sometimes it seems to me that I never shall. [19]

Finally, in the fall of 1890, Foster-Eddy found a house with pleasant grounds right in Roslindale, then a suburb of Boston. Mrs. Eddy's close and trusted student, Ira Knapp, had by then moved from New Hampshire to Boston, and he and Mrs. Knapp lived in Roslindale themselves. In later years, when Mrs. Eddy had trouble selling the house for what she had paid for it, she roundly criticized Knapp for having paid too much and laid the blame on the fact (which he had apparently told her) that he had been drinking beer with the owner at the time of the negotiation. While she criticized him for this, the incident tends to show that Mrs. Eddy was less categorical about such habits than she was about the need to cultivate a basic Christian morality. (She also wrote to John Linscott at one time during the 1890s, asking him to promise her that he would stop drinking. Linscott had been a temperance lecturer before she had entrusted him with assignments in the Middle West.) [20]

When the negotiations for the Roslindale home looked as if they were going nowhere, Mrs. Eddy had written to Foster-Eddy,

"Darling, I am sure that it is best for me to go far away from Boston. Let the [Roslindale] purchase go by, and I will go into a far more humble home somewhere." [21] She did get the house, and she did move into it sometime in the spring of 1891. But it did not please her, and within little more than a month she was back on North State Street in Concord.

Just before Mrs. Eddy left Boston, she had hired Joshua Bailey, who was a Christian Scientist, to be the editor of the *Journal.* The arrangement did not work well, and he was replaced in 1892 by Julia Field-King. (Field-King's own brief editorship lasted only for the spring and summer months of 1892.) While Bailey was editor, however, he had begun to help Mrs. Eddy on the revision of *Science and Health.* That work also did not go well under him, and Mrs. Eddy turned again to Rev. Wiggin, the retired Unitarian minister who had helped her with the revision in 1885 and who had also had his stint at being editor of the *Journal* from 1886 through 1888. In April of 1890, Mrs. Eddy had written to a student that the work was almost finished. "It has been a difficult task to get it straightened out and *right;* but I have done it all and by working a little while each day." [22] As it turned out, a good half year's work still lay ahead of her.

Mrs. Eddy intended this edition to be a major revision, and she must have had in mind that this edition might stand as her last revision, one that would have to substitute for her personal teaching in the future. While she and Wiggin went over some rough terrain together, with his resigning at one point because of a sharp letter she had written to him, they managed to stay together on this project until it was completed. She instructed Wiggin:

> I and my students greatly desire the first chapter of Science and Health to be introductory to the whole work, a chapter that shall convey gently perfectly and systematically my meaning to the minds of the readers. I want you to use your own good judgment how this should be done, and do it. I want you to give it consistency, beauty, strength, and honesty but

> to leave untouched the figures I employ but to shape my ideas as aforenamed and greatly improve the manner of expressing them. [23]

It was in this same letter that she wrote of "the difficulty of stating metaphysics just right." Wiggin was no flatterer. She reminded him, "Your interest in the work you are performing for me and mankind has the rare quality of King Lear's daughter's affection. It never flatters." [24] A few weeks later she told him, "My faith in your criticism continues, but you know faith sometimes needs Mr. Wiggin's notes, and his notes, occasionally, need my metaphysics." [25] A month later she admitted, "In some instances you lose my meaning and again by challenging it cause me to bring it out." [26]

When the textbook did appear early in 1891, it was recognized as a major improvement over previous versions. It came close to being the textbook Christian Scientists study today, although the order of the chapters would be changed in a major way in the one big revision that still lay ahead after the turn of the century. As work on the revision went ahead, Mrs. Eddy felt the strain. She wrote to Hannah Larminie, a student in Chicago, toward the end of summer, "I do desire to depart. At times I feel heavenly-homesick…." [27] But toward the end of November she wrote to her again, "My nights are quiet now. But you cannot know unless here the miracles of His grace." [28] The book was at last finished. She wrote at about the same time to Helen Nixon in Boston, "My *last words for you all in the Book* Science and Health were written yesterday and sent off." [29] One cannot read that sentence and simply chalk it up to the hyperbole that Mrs. Eddy occasionally used. As 1890 came to a close, she saw a major, if not the only, reason for her departure from Boston to have been to find the time to improve *Science and Health.* Moreover, she was aware of her age and her moments of incapacity. At about the same time she began to be leery of George, her son in the West. She had a premonition that he would try to break her will, and she set about finding a way to assign her copyright to the textbook and to *Unity of Good* to someone else. It was yet another example of her alertness to doing all she could to protect what was most important to her after she was no longer here.[30] She was beginning to live with what she considered her legacy to mankind uppermost in her thought.

❖ ❖ ❖ ❖

By the end of 1890 there were nineteen formally organized Christian Science churches listed in *The Christian Science Journal* and another seventy-five groups advertising regular meeting places and times of service. There were also almost three hundred Christian Science practitioners listed in the *Journal.* Christian Science was moving ahead in most parts of the country and even beginning to be heard of in the British Isles. Mrs. Eddy had finally had some time to give more thought to the adequacy of her writings for posterity and to whatever else she could do to provide for the future of Christian Science. Then there was yet another sideshow that, like the defection of some of her students in 1888 over the Abbie Corner case, made for the kind of publicity she would have preferred to do without.

In the summer of 1890 her student, Josephine Woodbury, in whom she had once had high hopes, had an illegitimate child – apparently the result of an affair she had had while visiting in Montreal. Mrs. Woodbury's husband had not been on intimate physical terms with her for some time, and Mrs. Woodbury had in fact pushed her own students in the direction of abstention from sexual relations. Woodbury chose the big lie as a way out of her predicament and announced to the world that her infant son had been conceived spiritually. She had a summer house at Ocean Point, Maine. On the grounds was a pond, which she had named the Pool of Bethesda, and in this pond she proceeded to baptize her son the Prince of Peace.

Mrs. Eddy does not appear to have been as disturbed by Mrs. Woodbury's moral lapse as she was by the attempted cover-up, which made Christian Science appear ridiculous in the eyes of the public. But Mrs. Eddy continued to have at least limited communication with her in spite of her outrageous actions. Woodbury as much as admitted to Mrs. Eddy the facts of her case, when some years later she told her that her son had been "incarnated with the devil."[31] Woodbury wanted to get back into the church organization after Mrs. Eddy reorganized her church, and this accounts for her continued approaches to Mrs. Eddy. The latter's forbearance with her, especially in light of Woodbury's failure to face up to her immorality, worked to turn Woodbury even farther away from the teacher from whom her own actions continued to separate her. Some kind of remorse over her shortcomings can be seen in these lines from a letter she wrote to Mrs. Eddy later in the 1890s:

> I think I never suffered as I suffer now when I am beginning to understand you. Every time I see you it is harder to bear – this great chasm between your life and mine, and only because you are so gentle do I dare try to undo what I have helped to do in the past.[32]

But Woodbury remained unrepentant at heart, and she was to turn against Mrs. Eddy with a vengeance later in the 1890s and set in motion a chain of events that would become one of the major public episodes in Mrs. Eddy's life after 1900. If it were not for what happened later, the "Prince of Peace" himself would not belong to this story.

❖ ❖ ❖ ❖

Mrs. Eddy moved into 1891 well satisfied with the revision of her textbook, which appeared toward the end of January. She wrote innumerable letters pointing out what she considered the important improvements in the book. To Captain Eastaman she wrote:

> The old editions did their work and did it well. But the new has a new task, it takes into its office that of *Teacher* as well as healer; it becomes a living power to uplift the whole human race. I have done for this

> edition what the lapidary does, – brought out the gems and placed them well burnished, in sight.[33]

The thought that the book itself could be the teacher of Christian Science occupied several of her letters. It indicates that she was unsure about the soundness or inspiration of much of the teaching going on. Yet she realized that she would never again personally teach more than a handful of people. In fact, she was to hold only one more class, and it fits into a category all its own. She told Caroline Frame, herself a teacher in New York:

> My last revised *Science and Health* is teacher of itself. The best student that can be made in this period is the one who studies this book by himself and practises it as I have taught them. Students can not interpret *Science and Health* as correctly to another student as God will interpret it to them if they do this. It is doing this that makes them catch *my true meaning.*[34]

The year was filled with a growing volume of correspondence, with letters of both appreciation and reprimand to Augusta Stetson, and with increasing doubts about the spiritual capacity of her adopted son, Benny. Indeed, every one of Mrs. Eddy's so-called years of retirement was a year of intense activity.

In addition to her correspondence with innumerable persons, two activities accounted for much of the year: finishing a short autobiographical work, and thinking about the future of her church organization. The latter was to occupy her thought intensively well into 1892 until she arrived at her solution.

As for the autobiography, she had written a pamphlet in 1885 entitled *Historical Sketch of Metaphysical Healing.* This had been issued partly in defense of some of the misrepresentations of Christian Science by Julius Dresser in Boston in the mid-1880s. She now expanded this pamphlet into a small volume that she named *Retrospection and Introspection,* a title that more aptly describes the book than does the term "autobiography." Although the work was autobiographical up to a point, some of her early family history is not entirely accurate. She was more interested in tracing the mental and spiritual preparation that she felt had led her to the discovery of Christian Science. In the final chapters of the book, "Admonition," "Exemplification," and "Waymarks," she is clearly giving guidance to Christian Scientists about the path she recommends following. In their present form they stand as timeless advice for Christian Scientists; but one can also read them as the final words of instruction from a leader who was unsure how much longer she would be present. Whether or not she meant for these chapters to be viewed that way, this short book coming on the heels of the major revision of *Science and Health* indicates a tidying up of her affairs as Mrs. Eddy entered the eighth decade of her life.

Meanwhile, the move back to North State Street in Concord had not satisfied Mrs. Eddy. It did not provide the peaceful setting for which she was looking. She was accustomed to going on a daily carriage ride, her only pastime. One day, on a ride outside of town, she noticed a modest farmhouse that was for sale. The house was of less interest to her than the grounds and view, sloping off to the south and looking toward the hills of Bow, where she had been born. The surrounding land gave her a sense of privacy, and she had the house remodeled, constructing a tower at one corner and a back veranda from which to survey the landscape. She moved into the house, which she named Pleasant View, in June 1892. This became her home for the next fifteen years.

The other line of thought that preoccupied her during this period was the form of her church. She had dissolved the original organization, but was intensely interested in having a church building erected in Boston. Throughout the preceding few years there had been several transfers of title to the piece of land in Boston's Back Bay, where the original Mother Church edifice now stands. The land had been bought, subject to a mortgage, in 1886. During the period in 1888, when a group of her Boston students was in revolt, she purchased the mortgage. When the mortgage came due, she was able to take title to the land and thereby control the steps leading toward its development. Some of the transactions between then and 1892 may sound unnecessarily involved to someone not familiar with the intricacies of real estate law, but in tracing them, one can discern Mrs. Eddy's simple purpose: to maintain control of the land for the benefit of Christian Scientists who would eventually build a church on it, and to prevent its becoming entangled in any future controversy. While the land was steadily rising in value during these years, she had no interest in making any financial gain from it.

This does not settle the question of how Mrs. Eddy looked on the institution of church, however. She had written rather explicitly in 1889 about church organization no longer being necessary. Yet she lived in a society in which the church was a major institution, and a unique one in the sense of being the only institution exclusively devoted to promoting moral, ethical, and spiritual values. She seems to have decided as early as mid-1891 that the church must be reorganized, but the means or manner of reorganizing was still a question. In July 1891, she wrote two letters that show how far her thought had evolved:

> To William G. Nixon, her publisher: I should have asked you to put your name with your wife's down for a charter member of the Church, but I heard you once object to joining a church, saying, when she asked you if you had sent in her name, it is easier to get in than to get out of a church, which is true.[35]

> To Mr. and Mrs. Gale: Our Church needs organization to uphold it from the degrading interpretation that sects give it as much as you need a name to distinguish you from someone not as good as you.[36]

She was also trying to determine the best method of preaching for the church service. Even though the Boston church had been formally dissolved, Christian Science churches were springing up in many cities by the early 1890s. Mrs. Eddy had had only equivocal success in finding preachers in Boston, Chicago, and New York. Most of the former ministers who came into Christian Science in the last half of the 1880s turned out to disappoint her, either because they had not completely shed their old theological beliefs that conflicted with Christian Science or because their manner was too personal and therefore apt to stand in the way of the simple spirituality underlying the message of Christian Science. Yet she was only beginning to see that the future of her movement could not be built on a foundation of personal preaching, for she wrote to Laura Lathrop in New York in July 1891:

> If I name the best mode of worship it will be a Pastor, a church, and this Pastor one who uses no notes but lives so near the heart of God he speaks from inspiration.... I have named beginning with the Bible and Science and Health only for those who are not feeling fully equipped at first.[37]

Later that year she edged nearer to the ultimate solution of reading only from the Bible and *Science and Health.* She recognized, however, that the reading from the textbook must be directly relevant to what was read from the Bible. She instructed Caroline Noyes in New York, presumably for her church only, to have four of her (Mrs. Eddy's) students selected to arrange paragraphs from *Science and Health* to be read along with the Bible. She wrote essentially the same instructions to Mary Adams in Chicago, but introduced her letter by saying, "I want you to carry out the following directions for your Sunday service in the pulpit until you get a good pastor."[38] And at the very end of 1891, she wrote to LeNoir White, "When you get tired of reading my book in the pulpit and get any arrangement outside of this, I for one shall be pleased. A church should have a Pastor and I would never suggest the one."[39] She was still three years away from ordaining her textbook, along with the Bible, as pastor of her church. If she had found enough good preachers, maybe that day would never have come. But Christian Science was beginning to flourish, and there would soon be hundreds of churches needing pastors.

If the answer to her questioning about the proper pastor for the church service had to wait, the answer as to the form of her church itself was close at hand. During the course of the next year (1892) Mrs. Eddy reorganized the church and, in so doing, established a pattern that prepared it to become a global organization. That goal, however, does not seem to be what was on her mind in 1892, even if the end result was a church that was organizationally set for the next century.

The problem that forced Mrs. Eddy's hand in the reorganization was the ownership of the land in the Back Bay. She wanted the church to own the land on which it was to build, but she did not want an organization that could again be broken up by fratricidal disagreements. In March 1892, she wrote a memo asking the directors of the disorganized church to take out a new charter for a church to be called the First Church of Christ, Scientist. They were blocked in this attempt, as the original charter granted in 1879 had never been canceled. In April, William B. Johnson, clerk of the church, wrote to Alfred Lang, one of the trustees then holding title to the land:

> In regard to organization it is my firm conviction that our Teacher does not want us to return to organization, and I find that others are of the same mind on this point. Therefore I feel that whatever steps are taken they should not imply the thought, or be such as can be construed to mean that the Church is to return to organization.[40]

Sometime over the summer months she resolved the matter. Not wanting to return to the organization that had been in place under the still existing charter from the state, and preferring not to have a corporate form of organization at all, she asked her attorneys to find some vehicle in the law that would allow her to deed the land. They found an article in the Public Acts of Massachusetts that provided for "deacons, church wardens, or other similar officers" to be "deemed bodies corporate for the purpose of taking and holding in succession all grants and donations, whether of real or personal estate...." This settled the matter as to how she could vest the property in a church body without involving the church members themselves in corporate decisions.

Early in September Mrs. Eddy wrote with evident satisfaction to Helen Nixon:

> I have settled the legal question for the Church, rather, God has. I tried to incorporate anew, but the *legal arm* said no. "We could not be chartered by our former name." I would not quarrel, but took the pacific step and God has done great things for us in giving us a church independent of religious or civil oppression.[41]

Whether Mrs. Eddy at first realized the full import of what she had managed to accomplish is not entirely evident. Her immediate aim had been to get the title to the land in some hands besides her own, in order to get on with building a church edifice, but also to avoid the possibility of the kinds of clashes within the organization that had already set it back twice, in 1881 and 1888. However, in giving the body of four directors the authority to run the church organization, she was also erecting an institution in which membership would represent a spiritual commitment rather than an active role in setting the policies of that institution. In the year 1892, the directors of this new organization had but one goal, to build a church on the land to which they had been given title. But as the church grew in membership, their duties would also expand. Yet in her one act of deeding the land to the directors and their successors in perpetuity, she had set in motion the entire framework of her new church. That she did have some sense of what this might bring forth is to be noted in a letter she wrote to the Linscotts in Chicago a month later:

> God has given me the travail of my soul (sense) in the form of this church government. It is unity in bonds of love divine not human law.... It is to be a

> church set upon a *hill, universal,* God guided, having the liberty of God's children.[42]

❖ ❖ ❖ ❖

Having settled the question of the ownership of the land in Boston that was intended for a building, Mrs. Eddy moved forward to work, through her new four-member board of directors, to erect a suitable house of worship. The deed of trust had been signed in the fall of 1892. Christian Scientists would worship in their own church in Boston's Back Bay on the last Sunday of December 1894.

During those two years, the building of The Mother Church was Mrs. Eddy's first priority. But it was not her only concern. The years 1893 and 1894 were filled with her growing correspondence with practitioners and teachers of Christian Science around the country. Two other episodes in 1893 involved a considerable amount of her attention: the writing and illustration of her poem, "Christ and Christmas," and the presentation of Christian Science at the World's Parliament of Religions, a part of the 1893 Columbian Exhibition (World's Fair) in Chicago. Throughout these two years she was also increasingly involved in thinking and praying about the form of church service that would be appropriate for her growing movement. She must have felt some inner compulsion to have this matter settled by the time the church in Boston, built as a testimonial to her, held its first service.

"Christ and Christmas," an illustrated poem issued for the 1893 Christmas season, is only a small episode; but the turmoil that attended its production and subsequent withdrawal are illustrative of something larger. Mrs. Eddy was continually looking for new ways in which to engage the public's interest in her discovery. Apparently impressed by the illustrations for Phillips Brooks's still famous Christmas carol, "O Little Town of Bethlehem," she engaged the services of a traveling artist to do something similar for the poem she was working on. At the same time, some of the conversations she had with the artist, James Gilman, as he recorded them some years later in his memoirs, show Mrs. Eddy grappling with a challenge that was to engage her attention for many years – portraying to the public what she increasingly believed was her unique role in religious history without letting her be turned into an icon or, in a phrase she repudiated, a "second Christ."

James Gilman was an art teacher who earned extra money during vacations by doing portraits, as well as paintings-to-order of family homesteads, in rural New England. He had become interested in Christian Science sometime in the 1880s, and in December 1892 he came, apparently on his own initiative, to Concord. A local photographer, who was doing a book of photos of Mrs. Eddy's home at Pleasant View, arranged with him to do a painting to be included as a picture in the book. He came to Mrs. Eddy's attention when he was spending some time on her grounds in preparation for painting her house. His first view of her had been of a woman walking back and forth on her balcony, apparently deep in thought. The figure he watched was dressed in black, wearing a large black bonnet, and Gilman had been impressed by the blackness of the figure. When he formally met Mrs. Eddy a few days later, she commented on the dress he had seen her in from a distance. His reply was that he had looked on it "as a type of the darkness of materiality which she was contending with."[43] This answer obviously ignited her interest in him, and she may have felt that his sensitivity as an artist was an outward expression of an inner spirituality. During most of 1893, he worked for her, trying to produce the pictures that would properly illustrate "Christ and Christmas."

Their relationship seems to have been unique in the long list of people Mrs. Eddy worked with. They had frequent contact during 1893 and little reason for any contact thereafter. (He did revise one picture some years later.) The assignment Mrs. Eddy gave him was a difficult one. He was to do the drawing, but the inspiration came largely from her own sense of the meaning she wanted each picture in the little book to convey. Beyond that, she seemed for most of the year to be testing Gilman, to be attempting to see how fast someone of his sensitive artistic temperament could grow into an appreciation of where her thought was leading her.

Given the other things on Mrs. Eddy's mind, one wonders at the amount of time she appears to have given this project. She also appears to have been somewhat hard on Gilman more than once, and entries in his journal leave the impression that she was testing her capacity to force growth in a fledgling Christian Scientist. Early in 1893 he had taken class instruction with Benny. Foster-Eddy had taught the class without Mrs. Eddy's permission, and it was her conclusion, arrived at partly from questioning Gilman about his experiences in the class, that Benny was unfit for teaching. As a result, she may have been trying to impart more of her own understanding of Christian Science to Gilman as they proceeded with the drawings. He was undoubtedly of a different mentality than Foster-Eddy, whom she was beginning to find incorrigible, or Calvin Frye, faithful to her wishes but ever a plodder.

A few of the incidents Gilman recorded help to show Mrs. Eddy's attitude at the time. In the illustration of Christian Science healing, he wanted the healer to have "an attitude of peaceful composure and calmness born of perfect faith in omnipotent Spirit… the likeness of the Infinite would realize the perfect reality of all things, hence could have no agitation of mind as to the outcome of the healing thought." But Mrs. Eddy's reply suggested yet another quality: "Yes, *but Love yearns.*" [44]

In another picture, he wanted to show *Science and Health* bound together with the Bible. Mrs. Eddy rejected the idea, but apparently for practical reasons more than philosophical. She said that "such a suggestion now was not in accord with wisdom and was very far from acceptance by the general thought of mankind. In non-essentials we have always to consider what the general public can accept." [45] In another instance, which might have confused Mrs. Eddy personally with her revelation, she rejected his idea of having the central figure in a representation of the ascension be a woman. "It was decided that the time had not quite come for the woman to be represented in such a picture. To be too fast in such a case with even one illustration would be to spoil the good effect of the whole work, Mrs. Eddy said." [46]

On one occasion when he was visiting her in midsummer, he commented on the beauty of a single flower in her house. "It looks beautifully sweet and courageous in its loneliness I think," he told her. His diary continued:

> Doesn't it?, she replied with much feeling. She added, "That is the way it is in spiritual living - in Christian Science, often... How much I would have given sometimes if I only could have had some one to talk with, some one who knew more than I did. But that could not be to the pioneer." [47]

Confidences such as these indicate that the tender Gilman met a need Mrs. Eddy had for someone who could mentally respond, at least part of the time, to her own yearning for companionship. But she remained ever the teacher and the pioneer with whom no one could keep pace. She had hoped that "Christ and Christmas" would be ready for the Columbian Exposition in Chicago. When it was not, she was unhappy with the delays, which she blamed partly on Gilman, but more on Foster-Eddy, who was to have overseen the production in Gardner, Massachusetts. An almost impish side of her is revealed in this reprimand Gilman describes. He had come up to Pleasant View "prepared for stormy times."

> [She] began to talk to me severely, telling me I had deserted my post at Gardner, asking me sternly why I could not understand, and then looking away as if disgusted with me, but I thought I saw her smiling twice on the sly, and it has seemed to me as if she thought a scolding would do the most good of anything, if I was only faithful enough to bear it patiently.... [48]

When "Christ and Christmas" did appear, for the Christmas season, it was an immediate success among Christian Scientists. But Mrs. Eddy soon heard too many stories of people supposedly healed by merely looking at the pictures, or of the pictures being misunderstood. While she had written about the "poem cum pictures" very positively in *The Christian Science Journal,* in January 1894 she withdrew the book from circulation. It was reissued in 1897, with one picture changed, but there was never again the same kind of publicity that had accompanied it the first time.

The episode may have convinced Mrs. Eddy that combining words and pictures was more trouble than it was worth, or that the pictures were an inevitable distraction from the kind of regeneration of thought that must precede healing. She was also experimenting during these same years with appropriate hymns and music for her church. While she had her reservations even about music and its tendency to be sensual, she found an accommodation with music that she apparently did not find with visual art, as far as illustrating the lessons of Christian Science.

One more experiment she engaged in during 1893 was giving her students permission to present Christian Science at the World's Parliament of Religions, which was to be held in conjunction with the Columbian Exposition in Chicago. Mrs. Eddy had been encouraged by Augusta Stetson, her ambitious student in New York, to have Christian Science represented there.

Representing Mrs. Eddy, as it were, were two gentlemen who would figure prominently in her growing movement for most of the next two decades: Edward Kimball and Judge Septimus Hanna. Kimball and his wife had taken class with Mrs. Eddy in the late 1880s. Formerly a successful businessman in Chicago, Kimball quickly entered the public practice of Christian Science, and it was to him that she turned for most of her assistance with the World's Fair. Judge Hanna had been a lawyer and judge in Leadville, Colorado, when he became interested in Christian Science. After attending the National Christian Scientist

Association's convention in New York in 1890, the Hannas had moved to Pennsylvania, and Judge Hanna became a Christian Science practitioner. Following a series of *Journal* editors who had not worked out well, Hanna had been appointed editor by Mrs. Eddy in 1892.

Mrs. Eddy wrote to Stetson at the end of March 1893, "Mr. Kimball is my favorite student with whom to do business. He and I always chime in time and purpose just as you and I. My son, you, or Judge Hanna, must be the genius to preside over the space we have in the Publishers Section at the World's Fair."[49] There was a Christian Science booth, at which all of Mrs. Eddy's writings were exhibited. But more importantly, Christian Science was represented at the Parliament by a speech delivered by Judge Hanna. The speech had been prepared by Mrs. Eddy and consisted of selections from her writings that she felt explained the main points of Christian Science as well as possible in such a public forum.

The address itself went well enough. Many of the Christian Scientists felt it was a great victory for their religion to have such major representation. When Hanna read the address, none other than the Rev. Joseph Cook, who had given Mrs. Eddy just ten minutes to defend her views in Boston back in 1885, was on the platform and was observed to be highly uncomfortable. Mrs. Eddy was happy with its success, as far as it went. The day before the speech was read, she wrote to Kimball, "Through tears of joy I thank you and our God for the dawn of a new day. The night is far spent."[50] And a few days after the event, James Gilman was trying to take a photo of Mrs. Eddy's balcony and had to move a banner that was flying on the porch. Laura Sargent, one of Mrs. Eddy's personal household helpers, came and told him, "[The banner] had been put out in honor of the triumph of Christian Science at Chicago at the Religious Congress at which the Christian Science address had been read the day before and highly commended by leading officials there as one of the most notable contributions to the success of the Parliament of Religions."[51]

The display of the banner, however, must have represented the high point of Mrs. Eddy's satisfaction with the Chicago events. First came the news that Judge Hanna had given her address to the newspapers to be printed, in violation of her orders. Hanna had done this, he said in his defense, because the reporters would have printed garbled versions of the address if they had not been given the full text. In the process, the fact that Mrs. Eddy had written the address was omitted.

But far more significantly, Mrs. Eddy quickly came to feel that the so-called success of the Christian Scientists at the Parliament was creating a new, more organized kind of opposition to Christian Science from clergymen such as Cook. It was also a kind of mental opposition that, she felt, Christian Scientists as a group were not yet mature enough to handle. As sensitive as she had become to the turning of even one individual's thought to her, it is entirely credible that she felt a sense of renewed opposition to Christian Science within just a few days of the event. She wrote to Charles Bonney, who had introduced Judge Hanna at the Congress, "Christian Science inculcates spiritual love for all men but no worldliness. I fear the ambition of my students was touched."[52]

A short time later, it also became more apparent than it had been earlier that the fair's significance would be in the introduction to America of Oriental religions on a level of consideration approaching that given to Christianity. So far, Mrs. Eddy had gone to great lengths to separate Christian Science from the Oriental tinges of thought in Theosophy. Now that the Oriental teachings themselves were gaining serious attention, as they were at about the same time in England, she did not want Christian Science to become confused with them, even though she was not entirely negative regarding what she did know of them. In that same summer she had written to Margaret Easton:

> In answer to Rev. Mr. Easton's questions relative to the Hindus will say, the true sense they entertain of humanity is the best part of Buddhism. And the

> sense of taking no thought for what we shall eat or drink, is Christ-like, for Jesus taught it. This therefore is far from self-mesmerism, rather is it a native Christianity which presages science – a denial of personal life and sensation that admits the existence of Being where it is, namely, in God not man, in Spirit not matter, in Soul not sense.[53]

Although her references to Buddhism were not entirely correct, they do show some knowledge of the general tone of Buddhism as well as her appreciation for the validity and elements of commonality that might inhere in any of the world's great religions. Her concern throughout her work in establishing Christian Science, however, was to keep Christian Science separate in thought from any of the systems that either imitated it or paralleled it in some details, but not in its entirety. Thus, for Christian Science to become in any way connected with the introduction of Oriental philosophy or religion into America represented a setback for her. She wrote to Kimball, who along with Judge Hanna was severely reprimanded for what she felt went wrong in Chicago, "...you should not blame me for my fear and reminders of the danger.... I have suffered from the fear that God's cause would be dishonored, not that I was in danger for nothing can exceed the insult I have quietly borne for the sake of this Cause 27 years...."[54] Whatever mistakes were made in bringing so much public attention to Christian Science in Chicago in 1893, though, some slight aroma of exaltation that Christian Science had reached a new plateau of public attention must have remained, even though Mrs. Eddy was seeing new dangers at the same time her best students were seeing only successes.

❖ ❖ ❖ ❖

The Christian Science address at Chicago had been given on September 22. The Kimball letter just quoted was written sometime in October. But as this narrative has shown many times already, there was no time for idleness in Mrs. Eddy's schedule. Nothing illustrates this more than the fact that during the weeks she became so concerned over the outcome of the Chicago address she was also deeply involved in the beginning of the construction of The Mother Church in Boston. On September 29, she had written to her directors in Boston:

> Do not delay one other day to lay the foundation of our Church, the season will shut in upon you perhaps, and the *frost* hinder the work. God is with you, thrust in the spade, Oct. 1st 1893. And advertise in next No. of Journal that you have begun to build His temple a temple for the worship and service of Divine Love the living God.[55]

The four men, Ira Knapp, William Johnson, Joseph Eastaman, and Stephen Chase, whom Mrs. Eddy has appointed as the first Board of Directors, had not been inactive. In the spring of 1893, looking for more business expertise on the Board, Mrs. Eddy had replaced Eastaman, the faithful old ship captain, with Joseph Armstrong. Sometime during 1892, the City of Boston had enacted a tougher building code, including a requirement that public buildings be fireproof. The directors had had several architects submit plans for a building in brick, the usual building material in Boston. After a plan had been selected that made full use of the triangular plot of land at the corner of Falmouth and Norway Streets, the directors decided to build with granite instead, so the plans had to be submitted once again.

Mrs. Eddy watched from afar – that is, from her Pleasant View home in Concord, New Hampshire. For her, the execution of any task consisted primarily of its mental elements. In this case, she was, in a very real sense, testing her new Board of Directors as to their wisdom and vigilance in seeing their first major task to completion. Already, in March 1893, she had told the directors that the church building must be completed during 1894. Now, as the end of 1893 approached and another New England winter was about to set in, she was concerned that no actual construction had yet begun – hence her admonition at the end of September about getting the foundation laid before winter.

When one considers the inexperience of the directors in carrying through a major construction project, or the fact that they had not worked together as a team before this, or the fact that Mrs. Eddy was not always informed about technical details that they were trying to work out, it seems amazing that the work went ahead as quickly as it did and that, in the end, the church was finished by the end of 1894.

The directors were not allowed to go into debt. After the reorganization of the church, Mrs. Eddy wrote to Johnson, reminding him, "Be more than ever careful who you let into our church. And do not get in *debt.* Remember these two points *steadfastly.*"[56] The fact that they needed cash on hand for every step of the project was one element that slowed them down at first, since they did not feel free to sign a contract for the whole job. When Mrs. Eddy learned of this difficulty, she suggested that they get an agreement from the contractor that they could halt the work at any point if they needed to. This was somewhat unusual, but the contractor agreed – possibly because the country was going through one of its most severe financial crises in 1893.

Mrs. Eddy used the building project as a means of letting key practitioners and teachers demonstrate their devotion to the Cause. She wrote letters asking forty of them to send $1,000 each for the church. The edifice eventually cost about a quarter of a million dollars, but this $40,000, which was quickly subscribed, acted as a pump primer, and funds began to flow in from the wider field of Christian Scientists as well.

One incident in connection with her personal solicitation from these forty people indicates the care she took to maintain the purity of her teaching, even in connection with what might have seemed the more mundane business of raising money for a construction project. One of her teachers, Julia Field-King, had briefly been editor of the *Journal* in 1892. Her editorship had not been successful, and she had been relieved of the post. But Mrs. Eddy was to turn to her for other assignments later in the 1890s. She was one of the forty from whom Mrs. Eddy requested a check for $1,000. Mrs. Eddy heard rumors, however, that Field-King, a medical doctor for many years before coming into Christian Science, was teaching that Jesus could not have been conceived by other than the usual human means. Upon hearing this, Mrs. Eddy rescinded her request. She wrote to Field-King, "My students, two of them, told me that you certainly do teach that Jesus was an illegitimate child of Mary, and not conceived of the Holy Ghost." [57] Whether the story had some basis in fact or was concocted out of jealousy of Field-King one cannot be certain. Field-King did convince Mrs. Eddy, however, that she had no such reservations about Jesus' conception, and Field-King's name stands as one of the forty who contributed $1,000 for The Mother Church.

Besides the delay in laying the foundation of the church, there were more obstacles in the summer of 1894 when the iron work for the church, ordered from a mill in Pennsylvania, was delayed. For an entire month, no construction took place because of waiting for the iron delivery. Mrs. Eddy complained in many of her letters to others about the directors. To Benny, whose discernment she also doubted, she wrote, "As it is I have to do most of the thinking, remembering, and all the guiding and then speak to blanks almost, or have to listen to a long jabber of why they did forget." [58] In a moment of exasperation she wrote to Field-King, "I shall withdraw now from doing any thing more or even advising them if the Church is never built.... They are not fit to own a church, I am *done with* it all." [59] She wrote to Julia Bartlett that she had never had any male students who knew how to hold their ground and that she could not do all the watching from Concord. But she added, "What will we be if not *watchers.*" [60] On the other hand, she wrote to Ira Knapp just a few days later in an apologetic tone. "Am sorry I did not get the understanding of your business. The spiritual intent I never lose but the material matter you cannot leave to me. I am not familiar with that now. God has great lessons for me." [61]

It was a testing time for the directors and also for Mrs. Eddy. At one point she addressed the directors as the "Sleepers in

Boston" and asked them to get six students to do specific mental work to finish the church. [62] As the autumn of 1894 approached, it became obvious to most Christian Scientists who stopped in to see the work that it could not be done by year end. In November the contractor estimated there would be another six months' work. But during October Mr. and Mrs. Edward Bates, students of Mrs. Eddy's from Syracuse, New York, had virtually taken over the job, with Mrs. Eddy's approval. Bates had a heating and ventilating business and was well-to-do. No doubt stepping on some toes, he and Mrs. Bates took nine rooms in a Boston hotel and set up a virtual operations center to see that the job got done. From the start, Bates said he had never doubted that the work could be done by December since Mrs. Eddy had determined it would be. In the little book he wrote later, *The Mother Church,* Joseph Armstrong tells how all the craftsmen worked together in the final weeks, something most of them were not only unused to doing but generally would have refused to do. On Saturday night, December 29, many local Christian Scientists appeared to help clean up the church, and services were held in it on Sunday, December 30. Mrs. Eddy's goal had been met.

The church itself is not large, seating about one thousand persons. It is a version of Romanesque architecture, with some of the detail work reminiscent on a smaller scale of Boston's famous Trinity Church, built in 1877. The auditorium has a feeling of intimacy and warmth. One enters and has a sense of coming home amid the stained-glass windows depicting Bible personages and events, and the warm curly birch pews (with rose velvet cushions) set in a crescent centered around the platform and surrounded by the deep rose-colored plaster walls.

Mrs. Eddy did not attend the dedicatory services early in January 1895, but she sent an address to be read. At least one reason for her not coming was to deflect attention from her own person. But later, in the spring, eager to see the building that she had shepherded through the construction phase from New Hampshire, she made a private journey down to Boston just for that purpose. On this occasion, she walked down one of the aisles and stepped up onto the platform. Then she recited aloud the ninety-first Psalm, after which she repeated the words of a familiar hymn, whose first lines were a recital of her own life experience:

> Guide me, O Thou great Jehovah!
> Pilgrim through this barren land:
> I am weak, but Thou art mighty,
> Hold me with Thy powerful hand.

Standing in that auditorium, she must have been thinking not only of the two years of work that had gone into this church building, but also of all the experiences stretching back almost thirty years that had brought her to this moment.

❖ ❖ ❖ ❖

Even while Mrs. Eddy was keeping track of the building of The Mother Church, she had time for her usual correspondence with practitioners and for many everyday details. She took time to have Camilla Hanna's salary raised. Mrs. Hanna was the de facto assistant editor of the *Journal,* and Mrs. Eddy felt she was being underpaid because of her gender. And one note in particular (to her gardener) indicates not only her attention to detail, but also her desire to have her new home in harmony with its surroundings. It is also interesting to note her knowledge of the plant materials that many people enjoy looking at but never come to know by name:

> Could you today take up the Boston ivy at the wall on my back piazza and have it placed nearer the wall, and start the tendrils in the proper direction?... Get *vines started* on my front piazza and remove the bittersweet vines. I want on that piazza a *woodbine,* the same on the rear piazza, and on the rock walls the Boston ivy. I want the trailing roses on the summer house and the porch specially cared for.[63]

As the construction of The Mother Church had neared completion, Mrs. Eddy felt compelled to come to a decision about one item that was much more than a detail. This concerned the form of preaching she would have in The Mother Church. Her ultimate decision was the opposite of the direction in which she had appeared to be moving during the preceding several years. As her movement began to grow and to spread out across the United States, it became increasingly harder to find speakers or preachers who could say something both accurate and inspiring about Christian Science every Sunday.

She had been particularly concerned about adequate preaching in New York and Chicago, the two main cities outside of Boston where Christian Science was thriving. When no preacher was available, she had allowed her students to read from *Science and Health.* She did not want the book read indiscriminately from the pulpit, however. In 1893 she wrote to Martha Bogue in Chicago, "I have not requested you to give up the present mode of reading from my stores of Truth. But this I do say that the time has come when you certainly, at least, some of my students - ought to be prepared and feel it a privilege to stop *reading* Sunday services and out of the abundance of the heart declare the Truth."[64]

When she obtained the services of Rev. Easton early in 1893 for The Mother Church, she seems still to have had in mind to continue with personal preaching. She wrote to him about a "special need" of The Mother Church:

> It is in short a *revival.* An outpouring of love, of the *spirit* that beareth witness. I found it essential, when the pastor of this church, to lead them by my own state of love and spirituality. By fervor in speaking the Word, by tenderness in searching into their needs – and specially by *feeling myself* and uttering the *spirit* of Christian Science – together with the letter.[65]

In the same month she also wrote to students in Chicago to be prepared to give up their church reading and "to find a service that is your *own* whence the streams of grace shall flow. Jesus and his followers have done more than read the Word."[66] And to another student in Chicago, "I have not yet said stop reading from S[cience] & H[ealth] for your public service. But I do think the time has come when it would be better for my students to preach from the heart than the head and prepare from the heart and not the pen the offerings they lay on the altar of worship."[67]

What happened between early 1893 and the end of 1894 is not entirely clear. Rev. Easton passed on suddenly, and Mrs. Eddy called on Judge Hanna, who had been editor of the *Journal* since 1892, to assume the additional duties of preacher. She was undoubtedly aware of the extra burden this placed on him, but in time she could have found a replacement. It must have become increasingly apparent that, as the movement grew, it would be next to impossible to find enough preachers "from the heart" as she had envisioned they should ideally be. As The Mother Church neared completion, it must have also occurred to her that this would be an ideal time for a change to be made. When it did come, it was at first for The Mother Church only, as if she was saying that from the pulpit of "her" church no mistaken metaphysics should ever be heard.

Just two weeks before the first service in The Mother Church, she wrote to Judge Hanna, "I received last night a certain sound on the direction that I named to one of you sometime since, namely. That no sermons are to be preached by mortals in the Mother Church as pastors appointed or placed over this Church. That the Bible and Science & Health are to be the preachers."[68] A day later, apparently sure of her vision, she gave the same word to the directors:

> The Bible and Science and Health with Key to the Scriptures shall henceforth be the Pastor of the Mother Church. This will tend to spiritualize thought. Personal preaching has more or less of human views grafted into it. Whereas the pure Word contains only the living health-giving Truth.[69]

❖ ❖ ❖ ❖

Just after the new year of 1895 began, Mrs. Eddy moved to have the directors appoint Judge Hanna as reader in The Mother Church. (In the form of church service that she evolved, two readers read alternately from the Bible and *Science and Health.*) So, saved from having to preach a sermon each week, he continued to hold forth from the podium for the next seven years. In her request to the directors, whom she was preparing more and more to be the active agents in her church, she said, "He is morally fit... I am *sensibly* aware of the wire pulling by the croaking mental messages pouring in on me. But God's voice I hear above it all and shall obey Him."[70]

The wire-pulling Mrs. Eddy was referring to was probably the continuing effort of Benny, her adopted son, to gain a position for himself in the church. He wanted to be the reader. But Mrs. Eddy had another outcome in mind for Benny. With the building of The Mother Church now behind her, she moved on to deal with the problem Benny had become. Before the year was out, she had effectively, but with considerable agony to herself, cut him out of her life. After she had returned to live in New Hampshire, she had made him the publisher of her works. In this capacity, he often had meetings with William Dana Orcutt at the University Press. As Orcutt describes him in *Mary Baker Eddy and Her Books,* he sounds out of place in Mrs. Eddy's world. He came to his meetings in Cambridge, not by horse car, as his predecessor had done, but by a private hansom. In wintertime he would wear a fur coat and display a prominent diamond stickpin. In their professional relationship, Orcutt says that he was better at promises than at delivering on them.[71]

Foster-Eddy also seems to have had continuing problems with the people with whom he worked. Some of this may be counted as jealousy on their part because of his familial relationship with Mrs. Eddy, but certainly the greater part stemmed from his incapacity. As for his relationship with Mrs. Eddy, the others may have assumed that Mrs. Eddy hoped to groom him as a kind of successor or, at the very least, as her most trusted confidant in her later years. But if that was the case, Mrs. Eddy would have been testing him for his present capacity and his ability to grow even more than she was testing her Board of Directors. It could not have been an easy relationship.

When she learned in 1893 that Benny had taught a class with James Gilman as a pupil and, after questioning Gilman, decided that Benny did not have the inspiration to impart a true understanding of Christian Science, her worst fears were confirmed. Yet in the same year she was still defending him to others. She wrote to Mr. and Mrs. Greene (he was later to teach one Normal class) some months after Benny had taught a class:

> It almost surprises me sometimes when I survey what he with God's dear help has accomplished for himself within the past 5 years. He seems almost the master of the "three measures of meal" into which the woman put her leaven. This makes him far, far in advance of what he could have been had not he had war, Theology, and Medicine to have crossed swords with.[72]

Yet she blamed Benny, along with Gilman, for not handling the print production of her poem, "Christ and Christmas," correctly and for thus not having it ready for sale at the Columbian Exposition. She also blamed Benny for not being alert in allowing the press to obtain copies of her speech that Hanna had delivered in Chicago. Toward the end of the year (1893) she seems to have felt that he was a positive hindrance. Writing to Joseph Armstrong in Boston, she said:

> He will *ruin you* unless you defend yourself mentally against his influence. Take it up daily that he cannot govern your *conclusions* or *actions* and keep aloof from him.... He knows no more than an *insane* man the nature of his actions and thinks it is all right till I struggle hours with him to get his eyes open and

> then he repents acknowledges. But in a few days does it right over again.[73]

Throughout 1894, when the church was under construction, she found Benny unreliable. Toward the end of the year, when Mr. and Mrs. Bates had taken effective charge of the project, she wrote to Caroline Bates, "Three months of the best time for work was thrown away, money *squandered,* and the Dr. [Benny] bearing false reports to me. So that between his talk and the Directors sloth and disobedience the mesmerists have had it their own way."[74] Finally, her tone hardened as the year came to a close. In the first of two letters to Benny, written in late November, she said:

> The last twice you were here I felt most emphatically your unspiritual condition but I love you and had not the *grace* to take up my cross and tell you of it. Also I cannot now bear this cross *(carry it)* as in times past. I do not feel equal to it or that it is my duty. I have done this and you must now do your work.[75]

But she still signed herself, "Your loving Mother." In the second letter, two weeks later, she signed off formally as "Mary Baker Eddy." This much sterner letter read:

> When learning you are so even again in the full service of sin – falsifying to me, and *spending* your time as you did last Summer, and as the mesmerists bid you – trampling on my requests and all your promises, my hopes, and God's demands, and again going to *speak under this spell* only to make a fool of yourself – I felt it was beneath me to again waken you.
>
> Don't come to Concord till you have some character, some conscious, and proper sense of your conduct.[76]

Early in the new year (1895) she confided in her notebook, "He does nothing whatever for me but works against me in every subtle way.... Every student of mine who he is intimate with he demoralizes. All the way he has done this starting from the first to the last.... All this has gone on and been covered up for six long years. Oh see the change in my health from six years ago to now and the trouble and anguish and labor he has made me has been the belief in the case causing it all."[77] She went even further and told the directors, "I have an awful revelation of him that I must make to you but I confess I am afraid of him & can only do it when he will not know what I am doing." She concluded, "Absalom was not half to David what Dr. is to me. He is so treacherous, so sly and untruthful. I do *fear* him."[78]

Mrs. Eddy's anxieties were not imaginary. Three months later it was uncovered that a woman whom Benny had employed in his office as his private secretary had left her husband to come and work there. Although there were intimations of personal intimacy, Mrs. Eddy accepted Benny's word that no physical improprieties had ever occurred. Nevertheless, the entire situation proved her right in that Benny had never told her more than what he cared to have her know. On finding this out, she wrote to the directors that God was "uncovering rapidly some of these hidden works that have laid me on the altar for the last six years."[79]

These admissions on Mrs. Eddy's part that she had had a sense of heaviness as well as challenges to her physical condition add further credence to the position taken earlier in this chapter that Mrs. Eddy, in the first few years of her so-called retirement, was actually working under the belief that she must set her affairs in order for what seemed her approaching demise. She even wrote to Julia Field-King, half apologizing for the unsuccessful editorship the latter had had in Boston:

> I now see clearer than ever the Absalom. The cause of the action in Washington, the cause of what took place in your history in Boston, the cause of my quitting my field in Boston and the change in my health and what God means in establishing the inheritance and heritage of His in the worthy line of succession.[80]

Mrs. Eddy had the First Members of The Mother Church convene in October and adopt a new by-law that limited the term of one's presidency of the church to one year. Benny was president at the time. She then arranged for him to be called to Philadelphia as a "missionary" to the church there. But it was not until some time in 1896 that Benny actually left Boston, and his stay in Philadelphia could have been predicted to be the failure it turned out to be. With Benny removed from Boston, even if he had known how to conduct himself, rumors must have prepared the way for his ruin.

It would appear that he never had a deep understanding of the mental forces that Mrs. Eddy felt were doing battle because of her discovery. He enjoyed a few vacation trips with his brother's family after he left Philadelphia, and from the letters he sent back to Mrs. Eddy, it would also appear that there was little mutual comprehension between mother and adopted son. He continued to address her as "Dearest Sweetest Mother" or "Most Blessed of Earth," neither of which appellations were sentiments apt to receive a positive response from Mrs. Eddy. In one letter, written in 1897 about a trip to Yellowstone, he wrote, "Do try and have one summer to yourself." Mrs. Eddy wrote across the envelope, "Dr. F-E and pleasure seeking."[81] In the end, he turned out to be even less appropriate as a son than George, the uneducated, rough-hewn miner. But if Benny had failed to rise to her expectations, her hopes had been based on an unrealistic assessment of the material she had chosen to work with. Once again, Mrs. Eddy's sense of human family had been frustrated – even while the household of working Christian Scientists continued to grow.

❖ ❖ ❖ ❖

When Mrs. Eddy reorganized her church in 1892, she could not have seen in advance exactly how one step would lead to another. But she felt certain of the divine guidance, or spiritual intuition, that had resulted in finding the means of placing the power to act in a Board of Directors and not in the whole church body. This led in a short time to invitations being extended to Christian Scientists everywhere to become members of The Mother Church in Boston, even while they maintained their memberships in what came to be known as branch churches. Thus the growth and support of The Mother Church was no longer dependent on the number of Christian Scientists in the Boston area. While she may not have seen the entire future of this step in 1892, she did speak even then of a church universal. And as the 1890s progressed, Christian Science began to have some students in the British Isles, France, and Germany.

When she had appointed four directors to run her church, the new church at that moment actually had no members. Shortly thereafter she appointed twenty First Members, and these members selected other members by approving the applications of other Christian Scientists to join The Mother Church. She wrote to the Linscotts in Chicago just after the church had been reorganized, "I will send you the few church Rules for business and form of membership as soon as they are printed." [82] The first rules were adopted in February 1893, most of them having to do with the conduct of business meetings. The various rules that Mrs. Eddy sent down from Concord for adoption grew in number, and by 1895 she decided it was time to put them together in some order. This was the genesis of the *Manual of The Mother Church.* She explained its purpose to Judge Hanna in these words:

> The Rules and By-laws in the Manual of The First Church of Christ, Scientist, Boston, originated not in solemn conclave as in ancient Sanhedrim. They were not arbitrary opinions or dictatorial demands, such as one person might impose on another. They were impelled by a power not one's own, were written at different dates, and as the occasion required. [83]

The *Manual,* with revisions she continued to make in it up until her passing in 1910, remains the governing document of The Mother Church. The codification of the *Manual* represents, in one sense, a change in Mrs. Eddy's attitude toward church organization. Even as late as 1893, after she had constituted the Board of Directors in Boston, one can see both attitudes at work in various bits of her correspondence. She wrote to a Mary Purple in March, "Churches, at present, and institutes of learning are indispensable for my students as means of unfoldment, and may continue to be for another half century. But I long to have this necessity over for there is such flagrant misuse of these means by some students." [84] Yet a few months later she wrote to another student in the tone that would dominate for the rest of her life:

> I have suffered enough from Associations and organizations to know their susceptibility of being wrong. But we must forget self and do the most good for the largest number.
>
> To do this organizations are at present indispensable, Churches especially. For if we conform all that we can to present religious modes we shall catch more fish, and our Master made his students *fishers of men.* [85]

The issue for Mrs. Eddy was that she saw Christian Science not primarily as another religious denomination but as an entire way of life comprised of demonstration – demonstration not of things, but of Christian character, regeneration, and the physical healing that witnesses to the presence of the Christ in each man and woman. What she was teaching had not been accepted by the established churches, so in the end she had to conform to human usage to some extent. But to the degree that organization was needed, it was there primarily to assist the individual in his or her own spiritual progress. On the other hand, having decided that Christian Science was going to be accepted only as it came via the avenue of a separate religious denomination, she wanted that denomination to succeed in the largest possible way. Regardless of any opinions she had expressed earlier about organization, there was no ambivalence about her position from this time forward.

Retirement at Pleasant View

These years succeeding the exposure Christian Science had had in Chicago and after the building of The Mother Church saw major growth in the movement. Although she remained skeptical about a kind of popularity that was unaccompanied by a deeper understanding of Christian Science, this did not prevent her from savoring each sign of progress. In the spring of 1895, just a few months after the opening of The Mother Church, she told Laura Sargent, who had been a member of her household but was now in Boston, "All over our land the holy influence of this church is felt. A millionaire merchant in Boston has left his church and he and his family attend ours. It is rumored every Sunday."[86] And she wrote to Ira Knapp's wife, Flavia, "The *times* are *changed* – C[hristian] S[cience] is taking the place that I knew it would when our church was built, hence my labor and efforts in that direction."[87] In July she noted that The Mother Church had 5,391 members.

Later that year she wrote to Carol Norton in New York:

> Commence in earnest and at once to get the funds for a church edifice in N. York City and build it as soon as possible – Mrs. Ewing and others in Chicago must do the same. Our largest cities are without church edifices of our denomination. This must not be. It is conceding to the side of error a point of great value viz. the influence that a house of your own in which to worship would give to our Cause.[88]

It was just a few weeks later that she paid her third and last visit to The Mother Church and preached in it for the second time. (She had also spoken extemporaneously on one earlier, unannounced occasion.) The visit disappointed her. She wrote to Judge Hanna and his wife that "the general atmosphere of my church [is] as cold and still as the marble floors."[89] And to the Armstrongs:

> My students are doing a great, good work and the meeting and the way it was conducted rejoiced my

heart. But O I did feel a coldness a lack of *inspiration* all through the dear hearts…"[90]

❖ ❖ ❖ ❖

By late 1897, Mrs. Eddy was expressing herself quite positively about the growth of Christian Science. She told Edward Kimball in Chicago that there were now nearly one million Scientists, surely somewhat of an exaggeration. The Mother Church had grown in two years from 5,000 members to just over 8,000. In the same spirit of exuberance she wrote to the Marchioness of Bath, "My heart goes out to you in gratitude for your deep appreciation of the great Truth that opens the door to the captive,– and at no very distant day will be the religion of the whole world."[91] And to Julia Field-King, who was working in the new field in London, she said, "Our dear Cause is hastening apace in America. Men women and children of the wiser and better kind are flocking to it like doves to their windows."[92] She expressed similar sentiments in other correspondence during this period.

Yet at the same time, she continued to be skeptical of any kind of attention for Christian Science that was only the result of internal attempts to seek publicity. When First Church in Chicago was dedicated in 1897, she advised Kimball that it was "not Christlike to act in any worldly way to promote anything… . The press should act spontaneously then we will know the true status of public opinion and not one gotten up. It spoke for the Mother Church spontaneously."[93] After both the Chicago and London churches had been dedicated, she said she hoped the "church shows" were now over.

The seeming inconsistencies in some of these comments are easily reconciled. She knew that the life of a Christian Scientist is not an easy one, and she was continuing to learn difficult lessons herself. But with the memory of her early years of poverty when just starting out in Christian Science, to say nothing of the memory of the scorn she had received from both pulpit and press in the 1880s in Boston, it was only human to embrace the moment and from the tangible signs of progress to hope that all mankind would someday come to love and practice Christian Science. It was in this mood of expectancy that she told the Board of Directors at the end of 1898, "I want to encourage the building of all the church edifices that can be built; and the organization of as many churches as do not interfere with each other's interests but rather promote it."[94]

Amid the many signs of growth in the movement of which she increasingly referred to herself as its Leader, Mrs. Eddy's thought was never far from her role as the teacher of her flock. It was with this in mind that she carried out two further tasks in the second half of the decade: in 1897, publishing most of her writings that had appeared in *The Christian Science Journal*, and teaching what came to be known as her last class in 1898. Sometime in the second half of 1895, after most of the work in getting the *Manual* published was behind her – as well as the turbulence she experienced in getting Benny out of her life and out of Boston – she began to compile all the articles she had written since the early 1880s.

She had originally planned to call the book *Repaid Pages*, but by the time it was ready for the printer, she had settled on *Miscellaneous Writings.* The compilation contained some of her most important sermons. In the early years of the *Journal*, she had written many, if not most, of the articles for some of its issues. She went back through the fourteen years and picked from the *Journal* the most important articles she had written. The textbook was to remain as the authoritative source or statement of the metaphysics of Christian Science, but *Miscellaneous Writings* gave a sense of that portion of the journey this small movement had already completed. Mrs. Eddy showed herself, in some of the articles and letters included in the book, in a more personal manner, or, at least, more connected to the events of the moment, than she allowed in the textbook.

During the last four months of 1896 she worked on the project constantly. As was usual with her, when she was giving all her attention to a particular project, she expected the same degree of dedication from those who were helping her. She instructed Laura Sargent to tell the woman assisting with the compilation:

> Read this and tell it to Jessie. She must read proofs next Sunday. I have worked Sundays 30 years for you all. Tell her also to use her eye-glasses till she is done reading my proofs. I have *reasons* for this request. The proof-reading must include 40 pages *per day.* It must go on *faster.*[95]

In January 1897, Mrs. Eddy wrote a short preface for the work. Besides indicating that the book showed some of the waymarks of Christian Science until that time, the preface showed her belief, or at least her hope, that the future progress of her movement would meet with less outright opposition:

> … In compiling this work, I have tried to remove the pioneer signs and ensigns of war, and to retain at this date the privileged armaments of peace.
>
> With armor on, I continue the march, command and countermand; meantime interluding with loving thought this afterpiece of battle. Supported, cheered, I take my pen and pruning-hook, to "learn war no more," and with strong wing to lift my readers above the smoke of conflict into light and liberty.[96]

❖ ❖ ❖ ❖

One episode of these mid-nineties years seems almost like a comedy, at least when compared to some of the more serious challenges Mrs. Eddy faced. It is worth mentioning, however, because it throws some light on the ways in which Mrs. Eddy was willing to experiment – if the experiment would aid the establishment of her cause. In this sense, it is reminiscent of the poem, "Christ and Christmas," which belongs to 1893. In this case, she sent Julia Field-King to England to help establish Christian Science there. Field-King has been mentioned as the medical doctor who became a Christian Science teacher in St. Louis and for a brief period edited *The Christian Science Journal.* Mrs. Eddy had more than a small degree of trust in her at this point, even though Field-King seems from the start to have had an uneasy relationship with Mrs. Eddy. From her correspondence, it appears that she did not know how to approach Mrs. Eddy other than to idolize her somewhat. Her intent was probably honest, but she exhibited a kind of adulation toward Mrs. Eddy that the latter abhorred.

While Field-King had still been in this country, she had interested Mrs. Eddy in the possibility that Mrs. Eddy's genealogy could be traced back to King David. As preposterous as this sounds today, one must recollect the various theories of American destiny that reigned a century ago and, in this case, the curious theory of Anglo-Israel. According to this pseudo-historical doctrine, the various tribes that eventually made up the British Isles were none other than descendants of the ten lost tribes of Israel. The main carrier of this doctrine in America was a Yale professor by the name of Charles Totten, who wrote in his book, *Our Race: Its Origin and Destiny*, "… these Ten Tribes are now in existence, somewhere, as a nation, and as one notably under divine favor."[97] Totten engaged in questionable biblical exegesis, as well as in a manipulation of recent comparative demographic statistics, to show that the Anglo-Saxons would eventually rule the world by the sheer weight of their numbers. (One might wish that all those who make a living extrapolating from current trends could be confronted with their conclusions a century hence!)

Field-King had interested Mrs. Eddy in proving her descent from David even before she went to London, but the genealogies she had traced contained at least one missing link. All this assumed, of course, that the British themselves were the descendants of David. Had this been the case, Mrs. Eddy's lineage would presumably have been shared by multitudes of other people of British descent and would have been next to meaningless. What apparently attracted Mrs. Eddy to the theory was that, if proven in her case, it might serve to further authenticate

Christian Science. That it was being authenticated daily in the lives of a growing number of students was the most important proof of its validity, she would have agreed. But just as she was, to some extent, enamored by the growth of branch churches in major cities of the United States, this proof by lineage must have, at the time, seemed to hold the promise of further authenticity for her discovery.

Mrs. Eddy did not send Field-King to London to research her lineage. She sent her to establish Christian Science, and Field-King did good work. Mrs. Eddy's instructions in early 1896 were, "Go in the name of no one but as God-directed… Build up a church there as you have at St. Louis and establish there genuine Christian Science."[98] But Field-King was soon sending back new information about Mrs. Eddy's line of descent. To one letter Mrs. Eddy responded:

> Oh the joy the bliss your lines brought me saying the descent from David can be traced on my mother's side… It might be the means of cleansing the White House at our Capitol of Mind cure pestilence…. Mrs. Cleveland, I am told, accepts Christian Science as my disloyal students in Washington D.C. teach it. Now I see how I could get the axe laid at the root of that error if only you can *establish* my lineage from the Hebrew King coming from the line maternal.[99]

Mrs. Eddy told Kimball almost two years later that when he next visited her at Pleasant View she would "give you a peep into my genealogy of both father and mother from Adam to David and thence to Mary Baker Eddy."[100] Thus, judging from the length of time that had elapsed, it seems evident that Mrs. Eddy remained interested in the project. Fortunately, she was careful not to say anything about it publicly until she was convinced the genealogy could be verified. And just as fortunately, there always remained one missing link. For, if that link had been found and the claim made public, it would have been humiliating later on when the entire Anglo-Israel doctrine was discredited.

The episode illustrates well the need to understand the era in which any figure lives out her life. In her published writings, most particularly in the textbook, Mrs. Eddy appears almost outside of time, because she made every attempt humanly possible to write in a simple, direct way that would reach far into the future. Her writings are not devoid of illustration and metaphor, but there is, even one hundred years later, relatively little in them that has lost its meaning with the passage of time. The Anglo-Israel theory was a kind of respectable speculation coming just at the moment before the British Empire began its long, slow decline. But in the 1890s the Empire seemed to confirm the greatness of the Anglo-Saxons. Even in 1898, when she was writing to Miss Marie Schoen about her unsuccessful attempt to find someone who could successfully translate *Science and Health* into German and French, Mrs. Eddy concluded, "The English language will no doubt become universal and the Anglo- Saxon Israel will be restored according to His promise."[101]

❖ ❖ ❖ ❖

Field-King eventually became too independent for Mrs. Eddy to fully trust her, and she disobeyed several of Mrs. Eddy's explicit instructions to her. She disappears from Mrs. Eddy's story, but she disappears quietly. Augusta Stetson, on the other hand, was a major figure in Mrs. Eddy's life almost from the time Mrs. Eddy taught her in 1884. She went to New York at Mrs. Eddy's direction to establish Christian Science there. She was an immensely successful healer and teacher, although from the start there was an element of what Christian Scientists call "personal sense" mixed with her spirituality. Reading between the lines of the specific instances for which Mrs. Eddy had to rebuke her over the course of almost twenty-five years, it seems clear that Stetson basically regarded the Christian Science field in New York as her "territory" and Boston as belonging to Mrs. Eddy.

Mrs. Eddy's relationship with Stetson was remarkably frank, but Stetson simply did not "hear" her. By the time Mrs. Eddy had become established in her so-called retirement in Concord, she expected her main helpers in the movement – and Mrs. Stetson would certainly have to be classed as belonging to that small group that she looked on as being important in spreading Christian Science – to look upon her directions as commands. Judge Hanna, by contrast, worked well with Mrs. Eddy, partly because, as he once commented, he looked on her as a general commanding his troops. As long as he worked for her, he felt it his duty to obey.

Mrs. Stetson, on the other hand, had a commanding way about her, and she must, from the beginning, have had some mental reservations about accepting Mrs. Eddy's leadership without question. Once in 1894 Mrs. Eddy wrote to her:

> Twice before when you were nearing a fatal plunge I have saved you.... I have helped you with steady hand to a place in the field that I have seen others whom I have lifted to the same, dash themselves down from it. *Watch,* you know that God is not mocked and I *cannot be* deceived. [102]

Three years later she told Laura Lathrop, a teacher in New York who had had to deal with Stetson's aim to dominate that field, "Almost all of my rules in the Manual have been made to prevent her injuring my students and causing me trouble in my church.... She does not trample on my students as she used to, for she dare not owing to my church bylaws." [103]

A few months later she reminded Stetson that she had "always been the most troublesome student that I call loyal," the kind of reprimand that would have made most of her followers sit up and take notice. [104] A year later she wrote to her in the veiled tone that a more sensitive ear might have picked up as being meant for her, "May you, my *faithful dear one* be strengthened and uplifted by the cross of others – by seeing sin and so avoiding it in your own dear self." [105] But she could also tell her at almost the same time, "I cannot sufficiently thank you for what you are doing. Oh what a child you are to watch and work so faithfully for mother."[106] Mrs. Eddy remarked to Irving Tomlinson, a former minister who came to live and work at Pleasant View in 1898, that she had "rebuked her more severely than almost any other student and *am still trying to save her.*"[107] Such was the material with which Mrs. Eddy had to work, and almost until the end, she hoped to bring forth more selflessness in Augusta Stetson and, at the same time, use her undisputed talents to forward Christian Science in the nation's biggest city. Stetson was one of the long-term risks that Mrs. Eddy took.

What of Mrs. Eddy herself during this first decade in New Hampshire? Physically she had undergone change. Before the move, she tinted her hair. In New Hampshire, she had let it go entirely white, and at least by the later part of the decade, she was using a hairpiece on occasion. She has never been described as being anything other than extremely attractive in her Boston years; yet she told Flavia Knapp in 1894 that since coming to Pleasant View she had gone from being 164 pounds to less than 100.[108] She apparently regarded this loss of weight as temporary, as she ordered a dress frame that could be adjusted when she "fattened out" again. She adhered to an extremely orderly day, rising at six in the summer and seven in winter, having her meals at regular hours, and saving long periods each day for prayer and meditation.

Her daily routine, with definite times set aside for handling correspondence, for giving instructions to Calvin Frye, her secretary, or for reading and prayer was a large factor in explaining how she could be so productive. But even the orderliness of her schedule, or perhaps the larger demands she felt were being made on her thought, did not allow her to see to every detail during these years. She complained many times in the early years at Pleasant View that she could not find important papers because she had had no time to put her desk in order. And in 1898, six years after she had moved into the old house and renovated it, she wrote to Judge Hanna one morning at 4 a.m. and included these lines: "I have not yet in six years had time to look over the contents of my desk that I brought from Boston so long ago."[109]

She remained an indefatigable worker. The schedule she followed is one that few who consider themselves workaholics a century later could equal. The important thing for her was to keep thinking about ways to advance her cause, to improve her written exposition of Christian Science, or to sense some coming challenge before any of her students comprehended what she was even warning them about. And in the midst of all her church work, she made time for such details as scanning the legal papers concerning a piece of land she had purchased near The Mother Church. On seeing that there was an unrecorded lease in effect, she questioned her lawyers about its effect on her title. She wrote to the Metcalf family, who had donated the organ for The Mother Church, somewhat self-deprecatingly (but also in the vein of the sarcastic wit she sometimes employed):

> Between the C. S. Publishing office, the Editor's chair, the Board of Directors, the work of our church, and the open field I ply like a shuttle putting in the filling that weaves the web for time and eternity.
>
> I am busy. Not an hour of vacation, although much that I do may be vacant.[110]

She never stopped her yearning for human family and the normal human touches. Although she had written in *Science and Health,* "Never record ages," this did not prohibit the celebration of birthdays. On the eve of her seventy-fifth birthday in 1896, she wrote to Joseph Armstrong, "Tomorrow is my birthday. So saith mortal mind."[111] And when five of the teachers in Chicago remembered her birthday with a silver pitcher, she was pleased.

❖ ❖ ❖ ❖

The year 1898 saw the culmination of Mrs. Eddy's work of organizing The Mother Church. It also coincidentally marks roughly the halfway point of the years of her absence from Boston, to which she was to return in 1908. By 1898, The Mother Church had been in existence as an organization for a full five years, although the first two of those years had been occupied largely by the building of the original church edifice in Boston. Experience had helped provide Mrs. Eddy with the answers to her constant prayers and thoughts as to how she could protect the practice and teaching of Christian Science and, at the same time, help promote her teachings to a wider world.

During the course of 1898, and spilling over into January 1899, she augmented the monthly *Journal* with a new weekly religious magazine; established a more formal system under the *Church Manual* for providing for teachers of Christian Science; established a Board of Lectureship and a Committee on Publication, both of which were meant to deal in a unique manner with the wider public; and reorganized the publishing operations of the church under a separate entity with its own Board of Trustees – The Christian Science Publishing Society. And at the end of the year that saw this amazing burst of new modes of activity established within the movement, she called together her most trusted students for two days of instructions and questioning in Concord – in what has become known as "Mrs. Eddy's last class."

Two of these moves involved the publishing activities of her church. In January 1898, Mrs. Eddy set up a Board of Trustees, three in number, under a deed of trust. They became the publishers of *The Christian Science Journal.* In setting up The Christian Science Publishing Society as a separate legal entity within her church, she provided the means by which its activities could expand in future years without involving the directors of the church in all their details. The trustees appointed each other, but the directors had the power of removal. This clearly made the trustees subordinate to the Board of Directors, a principle that was tested in the courts when a major disagreement arose about ten years after her death.

By setting up this trusteeship to oversee the publishing, however, she put into motion an organization that could evolve a business management suitable to the times and to whatever its activities might be in future generations. (It seems most likely that Mrs. Eddy did not foresee the directors becoming deeply involved in business operations. She was concerned about legal limitations on the earnings of a church. As much as one could foresee the future, the larger sums of money that might pass through her church would have to do with its publishing operations. The Christian Science Publishing Society, while under the ultimate control of the church's Board of Directors, would be free to evolve and make use of the business methods and practices that would be most appropriate for its business operations in future generations.)

Some of the events of 1898 may have precipitated her second action regarding publishing that year: in September, the start of a weekly religious magazine, the *Christian Science Weekly* (by 1899, renamed *Christian Science Sentinel*). That spring and summer, the nation had been involved in the Spanish-American War, of which Mrs. Eddy disapproved. A monthly journal did not give her the opportunity to reach the Christian Science field in a timely enough way when there was something she wanted transmitted to it. The early years of the *Sentinel* included items of news, so in one way the *Sentinel* can be seen as a precursor in her thought of *The Christian Science Monitor,* still ten years in the future at that time.

These were also the same years in which Christian Science was taking hold in a modest way in Great Britain and Germany and in which Mrs. Eddy's attention was turning outward. There is no way of knowing exactly how or when she began thinking as a world citizen. Nevertheless, both the spread of Christian Science abroad and the emergence of the United States as a major force on the world's diplomatic scene at the end of the 1890s worked in the direction of applying the metaphysics of Christian Science to the wider problems of mankind.

The other notable organizational moves in 1898 were her establishment of the Christian Science Board of Lectureship and the Board of Education. The concept of lecturing itself was not a new one; before the advent of radio, lectures were a major means of communication, education, or entertainment. They also proved to be a splendid way to interest those who had barely heard of Christian Science in coming to the door of the tent, so to speak.

Mrs. Eddy may also have been influenced by the fact that the branch churches had gone over to the method of impersonal preaching used in The Mother Church since 1895 – the reading of the Lesson-Sermon from the Bible and *Science and Health.* The Lesson-Sermon consisted of alternate readings from the two books together, which became the impersonal pastor of the church. A Bible Lesson Committee developed a sermon around twenty-six different subjects chosen by Mrs. Eddy in 1898. Although the subjects were repeated twice annually, the scope of the Bible and *Science and Health* offered the opportunity for virtually infinite development of the subjects.

While this use of an impersonal pastor solved the problem of a lack of preachers who were adequate in education, rhetoric, and inspiration – a problem common to all churches, but even more to Christian Science, which had no clergy trained as such – it left no room for the articulate Christian Scientist who could effectively reach a public audience. The lecture format opened this door. The first Board of Lectureship was composed of the modest number of five men, but Mrs. Eddy soon added women to the list.

In a challenging letter (written a few years after 1898) setting out the goals of the lecturer, Mrs. Eddy said:

> … You soar only as uplifted by God's power, or you fall for lack of the divine impetus. You know that to conceive God aright you must be good.
>
> … You go forth to face the foe with loving look and with the religion and philosophy of labor, duty, liberty, and love, to challenge universal indifference, chance, and creeds. Your highest inspiration is found nearest the divine Principle and nearest the scientific expression of Truth.[112]

The establishment of the Board of Education, under the *Manual,* in September of the same year, was her means of institutionalizing the future procedure for providing new teachers in the movement. Although Mrs. Eddy had closed the Massachusetts Metaphysical College in 1889, she had not surrendered its charter. The Board of Education, described as an auxiliary of the college, now became the institution for certifying teachers. In this way, she provided for the continuity of the teaching function. But one final class of her own remained – a two-day meeting of her most promising students in Concord later that fall.

Before considering that class, however, one other organizational step belonging to the same burst of foundational activity remains. In January 1899, Mrs. Eddy set up a Publication Committee, which shortly was renamed the Committee on Publication. Unlike the lecturing work, which went out to seek those who might like to hear about Christian Science, the work of this committee was to correct false impressions about Christian Science that had been implanted in the public's mind by either the pulpit or the press. Unfortunately, the growing popularity of Christian Science during the 1890s led to a reaction against both it and Mrs. Eddy. The work of the committee did not really get started on an ongoing basis until Mrs. Eddy invited a Christian Scientist by the name of Alfred Farlow to come to Boston from Kansas City later in 1899. But its starting point, as a kind of defense, and corrective arm of the church, belongs to the unusually active formative year, 1898, in which these other church activities were established.

❖ ❖ ❖ ❖

With these steps initiated, even though their usefulness was still to be proved through actual experience over the next decade, Mrs. Eddy had largely finished the organizational work that made her the Founder of Christian Science as well as its Discoverer – two terms that she used from the early 1890s to define what she felt was her unique role as a religious leader. But while the outline of the organization was complete, two elements continued to engage her thought. Mrs. Eddy's concern was unflagging that the message in the textbook be stated as accurately and plainly as human language could achieve and that the quality of the teaching be maintained. When *Miscellaneous Writings* came out in 1897, she had asked all the teachers to hold no classes for one year. She felt that the study of her various instructions given over the years and now compiled in one volume would be better than most of the teaching then going on. After that year was finished, in March 1898, she authorized each teacher to hold as many as two classes per year with a limit of thirty pupils per class.

Several times during the nineties she had written to students about the possibility of holding another class and promised some of them a place in it. What she now decided on, and what was later referred to as her "last class," was less a class than an examination of the state of thought of those, many of whom were then young men and women, who would be carrying the responsibility for the movement in the decades after she was gone. Something of her intent is seen in this letter she wrote to George Moses, publisher of the *Concord Monitor* and not a Christian Scientist:

> I herewith send you a *hint* of what will come off in Concord the first of next week and will say. It is to be the examination by me of about 50 Christian Scientists preparatory to receiving the degree of the Massachusetts Metaphysical College.
>
> I invite you complimentary. If you want to see Judges, D.D.'s, M.D.s, professors, the local M.D. of Wellesley Col. - Lawyers and Christians I say in the words of the Revelator "Come and see" for they will be at 4 p.m. Nov. 20 at the little C.S. Hall in this city and mother also. [113]

In meetings over two days, Mrs. Eddy talked to them about the allness of God and gave many illustrations from her own healing work. The accounts left by many of the men and women there each pick up a different thread. All were of course impressed by Mrs. Eddy herself – not so much by a sense of her personality as by her dignity, dominion, love, and insight into the thoughts of her students. According to one account, she asked each one what God meant to him or her, learning from their answers what their states of thought were. Many, if not most, of the sixty-seven who were there had not seen her in several years and were impressed by her youthful manner and obvious vigor (she was at this time in her seventy-eighth year). George Wendell Adams, who was to become a director of The Mother Church in later years, said of the experience:

> She was vigorous and vivid and appeared much younger than her years, but there was also great meekness and holiness in her bearing. One never could forget her heavenly expression as she looked searchingly into the face of each one as he stood in response to the roll call. Well we knew that this experience would indeed impart a fresh impetus to higher spiritual attainments. [114]

While the experience undoubtedly had lasting significance in the lives of everyone who answered the invitation to come to Concord, it was for Mrs. Eddy largely a means of assessing the strength of the movement at a given point in time. She told the Metcalfs in Boston a few days later, "Why I closed my class on the 2nd day was this. I saw they had gotten all they could digest and not lose the strong impression (to some extent) already made on their minds." [115]

Earlier that year, Mrs. Eddy had written an intimate letter to her son in South Dakota. After telling him of some of the famous people now wanting to meet her, she wrote:

> Now what of my circumstances?
>
> I name first my home which of all places on earth is the one in which to find peace and enjoyment. But

> my home is simply a house and a beautiful landscape. There is not one in it that I love only as I love everybody. I have no congeniality with my help inside of my house, they are no companions and scarcely fit to be *my* help.[116]

She also complained to him about Foster-Eddy's disappointing her, and her disappointment that George's own children were not getting a good education. "I would gladly give every dollar I possess to have one or two and three that are nearest to me on earth possess a thorough education." In the midst of her success at founding a movement to promulgate Christian Science, she still found time to think of human family. In fact, the yearning for a real human family seems never to have left her, although she was admitting, as in this letter, that it was to remain a frustrated hope.

Mrs. Eddy realized, as very few of her followers did, that the very success of Christian Science would engage the human mind in battle against it. She saw the battle not in terms of persons, but of malicious animal magnetism – what older theologians simply called the devil – against the power of God, which would eventually root out all evil. Twice the year before she had referred to the weight she felt of the human mind's resistance to the healing that was taking place through Christian Science. She had written to Marjorie Colles, one of the early Scientists in England, "... darling, when will my hour come. The students' seem to have come already. They have less and less to combat while I seem to have more and more because of their prosperity. Evil would revenge on me for the prosperity of our Cause."[117] Also with foreboding, she told John Linscott in Chicago that "you all sit peacefully in the security of knowing the worst is over with all but me."[118]

Thus, while 1898 was a year of triumph in terms of her foundational work for the church, Mrs. Eddy saw the problems that still lay ahead of her. The year 1898 is the watershed of the New Hampshire "retirement" years. She had successfully exercised her authority to lead her movement, and the number of persons seriously interested in Christian Science was growing. But that success led to new challenges, and the critical moments of several of her remaining years at Pleasant View were to be shaped largely by these challenges.

Entr'acte 3

The Terminology of Christian Science

Simple Words; Precise Meanings

Two short essays earlier in this book, one on Puritanism in New England, the other on the precursors of mesmerism, explained some of the background needed to put the development of Mrs. Eddy's life into context. One final essay is in order at this point. Christian Science has necessarily been explained in rather broad terms, because the development of its metaphysical system, its practice in physical and mental healing, and its organization as a movement form the focal point of Mrs. Eddy's life.

It would also be helpful to understand (before proceeding to the next chapter) the reason for some of the terminology common to the practice of Christian Science. It is not a particularly difficult terminology to comprehend, but it is perhaps confusing at first because of the juxtaposition of two classes of terms. It is a language full of biblical reference points, but also one that, because its practice deals with states of consciousness, superficially resembles some of the developing language of psychology.

Mrs. Eddy presented Christian Science in the then much more familiar environment of biblical language, even though she endowed many familiar biblical concepts, such as salvation, atonement, and grace, with meanings that set them apart from their orthodox usage. Clearly the most important word for Mrs. Eddy was God, and it was from her concept of God as the very basis and center of all being that she could argue that, metaphysically speaking, both matter and evil must be nothing. In answer to a question once put to her, "Does the theology of Christian Science aid its healing?" she answered:

> Without its theology there is no mental science, no order that proceeds from God. All Science is divine, not human, in origin and demonstration. If God does

> not govern the action of man, it is inharmonious: if He does govern it, the action is Science.[1]

As a Christian Scientist would explain it, the recognition of God's allness is the starting point for all Christian Science prayer, or treatment, as it is called. And the language of Christian Science employs a rather precise vocabulary in speaking of this process of treatment. In particular, if the real man is perfect and spiritual, who or what is the physical being doing the praying and needing the healing? Mrs. Eddy came to speak of man mainly as the spiritual idea of God, as a perfect spiritual identity. She used other words to denote the human being. She was not always consistent in this, but it is almost always clear from the context of a sentence whether she is speaking of the perfect, spiritual man or of the human being, who is not yet living in the full consciousness of his or her perfection.

As for the whole human situation, the misrepresentation of what really is, she referred to the opposite of God, the divine Mind, as mortal mind, even while making it clear that by using that term she was not bestowing reality on it:

> Mortal mind is a solecism in language, and involves an improper use of the word *mind.* As Mind is immortal, the phrase *mortal mind* implies something untrue and therefore unreal; and as the phrase is used in teaching Christian Science, it is meant to designate that which has no real existence. Indeed, if a better word or phrase could be suggested, it would be used; but in expressing the new tongue we must sometimes recur to the old and imperfect, and the new wine of the Spirit has to be poured into the old bottles of the letter.[2]

If mortal mind stands for the generalized belief in life and intelligence apart from God, the individualized manifestation of that belief – you and me – can be referred to as "mortal man." The mental activity of this mortal man takes place in the "human mind" or "human consciousness." Where Mrs. Eddy uses the term "human mind," she almost always means a mind that is unregenerate, unevangelized – a human consciousness that dwells only on the level of what the material senses report about life.

On the other hand, when she uses the term "human consciousness," she means a consciousness that has been touched by the Christ, by some knowledge of the real man and his inseparable relationship with God. An example from her writing may make the distinction clearer. In speaking of St. John's vision of a new heaven and a new earth in the Book of Revelation, she writes, "This testimony of Holy Writ sustains the fact in Science, that the heavens and earth to one human consciousness, that consciousness which God bestows, are spiritual, while to another, the unillumined human mind, the vision is material."[3]

The process of healing in its broadest sense consists in departing from a sense of reality based on limited physical sense testimony and adopting a spiritual model of reality, a model that in terms of Mrs. Eddy's interpretation of the Bible is preexistent. This, one might say, is the grace of God we all must learn to accept. She referred to this process in her message to her church in 1902, and in this particular instance she used the term "human mind" in a more positive manner:

> When the human mind is advancing above itself towards the Divine, it is subjugating the body, subduing matter, taking steps outward and upwards. This upward tendency of humanity will finally gain the scope of Jacob's vision, and rise from sense to Soul, from earth to heaven.[4]

The terms "mortal mind," "human mind," and "human consciousness" thus have a specific meaning in Mrs. Eddy's lexicon. We progress from a human mind whose outlook is based solely on the evidence of the material senses – and is therefore a kind of specific "instance" of mortal mind – to the human consciousness that has some knowledge of the Christ, or real man. This human consciousness is not entirely free from the limitations of the belief in mortal existence and a sense of life apart from God, but it has experienced some evidence of the Christ-power to redeem human existence.

What remains to be discussed is some terminology that Mrs. Eddy made use of that is less clear – and also that is virtually absent from her published works. But these are phrases of which she made use in the first decade of the 1900s: Christian psychology and malicious animal magnetism. Christian psychology comes toward the end of her years and is of less importance, as it was a movement within the Protestant churches that, at least under that name, did not survive. Malicious animal magnetism is another matter, for her letters are sprinkled with warnings against it, usually abbreviated to m.a.m. At the time of a lawsuit against Mrs. Eddy, discussed in the next chapter, an attempt was made to ridicule the phrase and, with it, Mrs. Eddy.

Malicious animal magnetism would today be called mental malpractice. If that phrase is equally obtuse to the modern reader, one can substitute for it the biblical word "curse." Mental malpractice denotes the attempt of one person to control or influence another from either selfish or malicious motives. Not everyone will believe that such a thought could have its intended effect; but everyone reading this has had experience with advertising that tries to convince him he needs something he never thought of buying. And through repeated suggestion, he may have come to believe it – indeed, to have taken hold of the thought as if it were his very own idea. The difference is that we see the ad that tries to persuade, while it is more difficult to concede, unless one has had some experience of it, the effect of a silent, malicious thought. Mrs. Eddy's use of the term "malicious animal magnetism" stemmed from her acquaintance with the early stages of psychological vocabulary. In her day, the Boston Public Library had numerous volumes on animal magnetism, and a court-appointed psychiatrist who interviewed her in 1907 was not at all put off by the phrase.

In the past decade, numerous books on spiritual healing have appeared; most admit the power of thought to influence the body, although such a practice is usually combined with orthodox medicine. One recent book, *Healing Words,* by a well-known American surgeon, Larry Dossey, includes a chapter on "negative prayer." Examining the evidence from many more primitive cultures, he notes that the belief that one person's thoughts can harm another is widespread. He writes that most people who believe in the efficacy of prayer do not want to think that prayer can ever be harmful to someone else. "But after examining the ethnographic and experimental evidence, I believe we must come to grips with the possibility that negative prayer is real."[5]

Entr'acte 2 indicated the origins of the phrase "animal magnetism" and also indicated that even Mesmer quickly went beyond the literal belief in magnetism as a curative agent. Mrs. Eddy found the term aptly descriptive of the nature of error. Unlike the field of psychology, which was just burgeoning in the United States, Christian Science adhered to the biblical distinction between good and evil. Because Mrs. Eddy defined evil as anything that would make one believe that life could be severed from God, or lived independently of God, she felt that the attempt of one person to influence another's thoughts, even with good intentions, was inherently evil. Animal magnetism correctly described the only way in which mental malpractice could ever seem to be effective: if the intended victim was to continue believing in individual physical personalities, separated from God, then he could be susceptible to influence by another person. Alfred Farlow, the effective spokesman for the Christian Science movement as head of the Committee on Publication in Boston during the first decade of the century, wrote in an article in the *Boston Post* later in the decade:

> The meaning of the term "animal magnetism" has gradually broadened, and now applies to any and all supposed action of the human mind, and is similar if not identical in meaning with the term mesmerism or the more modern term hypnotism. From this

> description it may be noted that from the very introduction of the term to the present time the word has been applied to that particular power, influence, or force which is supposed to be possessed by the creature in contradistinction to the creator.

As Mrs. Eddy saw it, malpractice could seem to be effective only if one did not consciously guard himself against such false mental influence, however its *modus operandi* might be described. Farlow ended his article by saying:

> In the light of Christian Science we recognize that the effects of the black curse and all other means of frightening folks, are the outgrowth of delusion, of suggestion or auto-suggestion, which becomes powerless in the presence of Christian Science, the apprehension of the Truth of being. The manifestations of human will are silenced by an understanding of the omnipotence and omnipresence of divine Mind.[6]

By the year 1900, Mrs. Eddy had seen enough of setbacks, along with successes, to know that one must be continually alert to what would otherwise be the effect on one of false mental influences. This precaution did not constitute the reintroduction of the devil into a metaphysical system that recognizes only unlimited good as reality; it was the modern equivalent of the biblical injunction to guard one's own thinking from whatever would make one deviate from that heritage of good. In the language of the First Epistle of Peter, "Be sober, be vigilant; because your adversary the devil, as a roaring lion, walketh about, seeking whom he may devour."[7]

She was well aware that novices in the practice of Christian Science found a large measure of freedom in the concept of God and His creation as entirely good, but that until their practice became deeper, they were often not able to understand her warnings against the influence of one human will on another. In *Science and Health* she wrote, "Many are willing to open the eyes of the people to the power of good resident in divine Mind, but they are not so willing to point out the evil in human thought, and expose evil's hidden mental ways of accomplishing iniquity."[8] And in "A Rule for Motives and Acts" in her *Church Manual,* which she asked to be read at the Sunday church service once each month, she admonished:

> The members of this Church should daily watch and pray to be delivered from all evil, from prophesying, judging, condemning, counseling, influencing or being influenced erroneously.[9]

Finally, in 1908, she added a simple injunctive sentence to the textbook: "Christian Scientists, be a law to yourselves that mental malpractice cannot harm you either when asleep or when awake."[10]

Had Christian Science been a form of psychology, instead of being founded on the moral absolutes of the Ten Commandments and the Sermon on the Mount, it might be more difficult to understand Mrs. Eddy's concern with malpractice. But because everything in her system of metaphysics emanated from the concept of God as the one infinite Mind, it was essential that mental practice, or prayer, conform to her concept of God as the source of all true thought and not become mixed with any kind of belief in a mental influence passing from one human consciousness to another.

❖ ❖ ❖ ❖

As for the matter of "Christian psychology," current religious histories do not even use the phrase. But in the first decade of this century, a movement combining religion with the psychological techniques of the day developed at Emmanuel Church in Boston, at least partly in response to the then phenomenal growth of the Christian Science movement. Although careful not to appear to be criticizing other religions, Mrs. Eddy felt that the words "Christian" and "psychology" were incapable of being combined. In an article she asked to be written for the *Christian Science Sentinel,* it was stated that "Christian psychology is equivalent to Christian phrenology, physiology, and mythology, whereas Jesus predicated and demonstrated Christian healing on the basis of Spirit, God." The article further showed her desire to reach out to her fellow Christians in the new century, but concluded with the reason she could not condone the use of these two words together:

> Mrs. Eddy has shown that she loves all that tends towards Christianity; she loves Catholics and Protestants, – Methodists, Congregationalists, Baptists, Quakers, Shakers, – she loves all save that which stands still or has no part in Christianity. Her teachings further show that she cannot consistently endorse as Christianity the two distinctly contradictory statements and points of view contained in the term "Christian psychology" – otherwise Christian materialism... [11]

The particular movement that called forth these comments lasted for some decades, but at least under that name it did not become a major force in American religion. Many of the liberal Protestant denominations, at the close of this century, do, however, make use of the insights of psychology and see no apparent conflict with Christian doctrine. But these branches of Protestantism do not draw the same metaphysical insights from Jesus' life and healing work that Mrs. Eddy did. Somewhat like Mrs. Eddy's warnings to be on guard against mental malpractice, while not fearing it, her concern about "Christian psychology" was not to start a war with the field of psychology, nor to be uncharitable toward others, but to point out the gulf that separates a mental practice founded on the human psyche, whether body or mind, from a wholly spiritual concept of individuality.

Today, a century later, psychology pervades our society and linguistic structures. Useful psychological approaches seem to help in everything from child rearing to successful salesmanship.

Psychologists and psychiatrists fill the role in some people's lives formerly filled by one's minister or religious counselor. Mrs. Eddy would presumably still be warning that, however useful, these approaches do not mix with a spiritual definition of man, in which all men are controlled by one divine source. And that, in dealing with what were originally the more fundamental uses of psychology, the repair of the damaged human psyche, there is no room for a mixture of the two approaches, predicated as they are on two diametrically opposite views of the nature of man.

Chapter 8

Pleasant View – Retirement Postponed

Challenges to a Growing Movement

As the decade of the 1890s drew toward its close, Mrs. Eddy had laid the foundations for the institutional structure of her church. Her work as described in broad brush strokes during the nineties had been substantially different from the eighties. In the earlier decade she had concentrated on teaching the fundamentals of Christian Science and its healing practice to several hundred students. Not all of them remained faithful to Christian Science as she had presented it. Many tried to mix it with strands of harmonial religion, for instance, which did not require the radical change in direction of thought or the continual attention to individual regeneration. Yet enough of them understood what was required to be a consistent healer and were supported in their work in the field by her publication of the monthly magazine, *The Christian Science Journal,* that by the end of the eighties Christian Science was becoming known in most of the larger population centers of the United States.

With the establishment of The Mother Church in 1892, and the publication of her *Church Manual* a few years later, Mrs. Eddy set the pattern for her work at Pleasant View. She had hoped that Christian Science would be taken up by the main Protestant churches of her era. Instead, it continued to meet opposition, sometimes even more organized opposition as the numbers of Christian Scientists grew. So, while the unique organization of The Mother Church allowed it to grow into a worldwide movement, the church organization was also a tacit recognition that Christian Science was going to reach the public through the channel of yet another religious denomination.

With the burst of organizational activities in 1898 behind her, what remained for Mrs. Eddy to do but to have a real retirement and live in quiet for the rest of her years? This was certainly the wish she had expressed in much of her correspondence in the preceding years. Had she been the archetypal grandmother, such might have been the end of her life story. But although she was, biologically speaking, a grandmother, since her son George had four children, she still thought of herself as nursing her "real" child, Christian Science, through its infancy and early maturity. The Board of Directors of The Mother Church had the legal authority to conduct the business of the church, but the actual authority continued to reside in Mrs. Eddy until the end of her life. She continued to test the perspicacity of the directors and, on some occasions, was dissatisfied with their performance. Yet a gradual change did occur, as they became more accustomed to their responsibilities and as her advancing years affected her ability to be as directly involved in all the affairs of a rapidly expanding movement.

The main area in which Mrs. Eddy continued to find weaknesses in the directors or in other people she relied on to carry out assignments for the church was in their lack of insight into the challenges or forms of opposition confronting them – at least a lack of insight relative to her own. Mrs. Eddy had an uncommon ability to feel the thoughts of others. Someone who has had no experience of another person's superior intuition might doubt this statement, but it is made and accepted here on pragmatic grounds alone. There are too many instances in which Mrs. Eddy's concerns about future events or the motives of particular people were borne out to dismiss her ability in this regard. So, while the general history of the progress of Christian Science in the final twelve years of her life is one of growth and even gradual acceptance as a major presence on the American religious landscape, these were not years of equanimity for Mrs. Eddy. She continued to feel the opposition against Christian Science. And even though it appeared in the form of particular persons doing specific things, she identified these challenges as the inevitable rising up of more general thought forces that were being challenged by the demonstrated presence in human thought of the Christ.

When she was dissatisfied with those around her, it was their lack of spiritual discernment that most discouraged her. She had to wonder what the future of her movement would be after her passing, if they did not see the challenges that were being laid down in the same way she saw them. The words that she used in *Science and Health* to describe Jesus' experience at Gethsemane are relevant to what Mrs. Eddy herself was to experience in the last years of her life: "Remembering the sweat of agony which fell in holy benediction on the grass of Gethsemane, shall the humblest or mightiest disciple murmur when he drinks from the same cup, and think, or even wish, to escape the exalting ordeal of sin's revenge on its destroyer?"[1]

The nine years after 1898, which she was still going to spend at Pleasant View, and the three years after that, at Chestnut Hill, close to Boston, were not to be years of outward peace for Mrs. Eddy. The turn-of-the-century years were preoccupied with the Woodbury Trial. Then, after a few years of relative peace, Mrs. Eddy had the ordeal of what is known as the Next Friends Suit. This occupied her attention for more than a year in 1906-07. Although both suits involved Mrs. Eddy personally, the aim of each was to discredit Christian Science. Finally, after her move to Chestnut Hill, she had to face the challenge represented by the activities of Augusta Stetson.

These were also years of turning outward, of learning how Christian Science could be applied to the larger challenges of society. In Mrs. Eddy's reactions to the Spanish-American War and, later, to the Russo-Japanese War, one sees a further extension of the practice of healing to the ills of human society. This kind of outreach culminated in her last piece of foundational work: the founding of the church's daily newspaper, *The Christian Science Monitor,* in 1908.

❖ ❖ ❖ ❖

The turn-of-the-century years saw Mrs. Eddy making her last major revision of *Science and Health.* She also made a serious effort to take her grandchildren's education in hand, even though she was frustrated by the results. But the main undercurrent in her life from the spring of 1899 until mid-1901 was Josephine Woodbury, whose personal ambitions had finally overcome her moments of contrition. After the episode of her illegitimate son, whom she had tried to pass off as the result of a virgin birth, she experimented increasingly with the dark side of mental practice. She wanted to rule others and, at one point, even said that she was out to wrest control of the Christian Science movement from Mrs. Eddy.[2] The record of her relationships with others, which was gathered in preparation for the defense in her libel trial against Mrs. Eddy in 1901, revealed a longstanding pattern of mental manipulation that was the very reverse of Christian Science practice.

After The Mother Church had been reorganized, Mrs. Woodbury wanted to be admitted. At Mrs. Eddy's urging, she was eventually accepted for membership in April 1895. But she was in trouble almost immediately and was dropped in November of the same year. Again at Mrs. Eddy's urging, she was readmitted in early 1896, only to be excommunicated (a final dismissal under the Church's By-laws) a month later. At that time, Mrs. Eddy wrote to her:

> How dare you in the sight of God and with your character behind the curtain and your own students ready to lift it on you – pursue a path perilous?[3]

Woodbury now turned resolutely against Mrs. Eddy and sought to destroy both her and Christian Science. Her activities in this direction crescendoed until, in 1899, she contributed one of two articles to the May issue of the *Arena* magazine attempting to debunk Christian Science. (The other was written by Horatio Dresser, son of Julius. Horatio had become an assistant to the famous philosophy professor, William James, at Harvard, and was eventually to become a Swedenborgian minister. Horatio continued the line of argument started by his parents, namely, that Mrs. Eddy had gotten Christian Science from Phineas Quimby.)

Obviously in reply to the viciousness of Woodbury's attack, Mrs. Eddy intended to handle the threat this woman represented by warning her congregation about it in her annual communion message a few weeks later. The message contained these sentences:

> The doom of the Babylonish woman, referred to in Revelation, is being fulfilled. This woman, "drunken with the blood of the saints, and with the blood of the martyrs of Jesus," "drunk with the wine of her fornication," would enter even the Church, – the body of Christ, Truth; ....[4]

The shoe fit too neatly for Woodbury to ignore it. As a matter of fact, she may have welcomed the opportunity she thought it gave her to even the score with Mrs. Eddy. Within a few weeks she brought a libel suit against Mrs. Eddy, the directors, the trustees, and Hanna (as editor of the periodicals). She was able to keep the suit in suspense for close to two years, during which period Mrs. Eddy became increasingly agitated over it and the threat it represented.

Mrs. Eddy knew enough about Woodbury's specialty of mental malpractice, or manipulation, to be concerned about more than the $150,000 in damages she was seeking. She recognized that Woodbury was out to discredit Christian Science. And given her past experiences, which had led her to feel that most of her subordinates were not alert enough to the normal challenges around them, she was apprehensive that Woodbury would, through devious means, exert a destructive mental influence on some of them.

The preparations for the trial revealed Mrs. Eddy as both an inspired leader and a human being who could momentarily be laid low by the attacks on her and at times lose her patience with those around her. As for her inspiration, she overruled the legal strategy of her lawyers at several points, at first to their discomfort, but ultimately to their amazement at her discernment. As for her moments of despair, young William McKenzie, a relatively new worker in her household, wrote to his fiancee, "My love is tenderer for the Leader today while I see her in wild tumult raging with Elizabethan frankness against those who are serving her with their lives…"[5]

Mrs. Eddy became less positive in her assessment of the judgment of Judge Hanna and his wife as a result of the Woodbury trial. At the start of the suit, Hanna had advised her to try to have the case handled in Massachusetts, where she did not own property, instead of in New Hampshire. Instead, Woodbury's lawyer, Frederick Peabody, filed against her in both states. To make matters worse for Hanna, Mrs. Eddy regarded some of the material he published in the *Journal* during the pretrial period to be detrimental to her defense.

More important, Hanna had indicated as early as 1898 that he regarded Mrs. Eddy literally as the woman portrayed in the twelfth chapter of Revelation. A part of the suit alleged not only that Mrs. Eddy had been talking about Mrs. Woodbury as the "Babylonish woman" in her communion address, but also that she considered herself to be the personification of the woman in the Apocalypse. The Hannas had served her well as editors of the periodicals for almost a decade; like the general Hanna had earlier recognized her to be, however, she felt free to change her subordinates when they did not measure up. And one result of the trial would be her decision to make some changes in Hanna's assignments in the church organization.

Early in 1901, she brought Edward Kimball to Boston to take charge of the mental defense (the prayers of a small group of practitioners) for the case. She had been close to Kimball for more than a decade, even though she had not been entirely satisfied with his performance for her at the time of the World's Parliament of Religions in 1893. But he, more than anyone else, had built the movement in Chicago and kept the field there on a stable basis. The work he did for her at the time of the Woodbury trial made him her closest confidant for the next several years.

As the spring of 1901 progressed, it appeared as if the case still might not be brought to trial in that court season. Calvin Frye wrote to Kimball in early April, "She is literally living in agony from day to day waiting to have this case called up and disposed of and W[oodbury] is pouring in her hot shot declaring she cannot live through the ordeal."[6] Mrs. Eddy wrote almost daily instructions to Kimball or to her attorneys. In early May she told the latter, "I regard the immediate trial and disposition of this case as being of the utmost importance to me and our denominational interests."[7] The case was finally called on May 29, and a day later she wrote to Kimball, "I have no fear of losing the case."[8] By June 5 it was won.

Woodbury's lawyer, who was about to embark on his own "career" of trying to demolish Christian Science via the lecture circuit and the writing of pamphlets, had included many extraneous items in the suit, such as Mrs. Eddy's alleged claim to be the woman in the Apocalypse. The judge threw out all the items except for the alleged libel against Woodbury. Only two persons could be found to testify that they thought Mrs. Eddy had been referring to Woodbury personally, and the jury found Mrs. Eddy innocent.

❖ ❖ ❖ ❖

Besides the unfriendly newspaper publicity the suit had evoked and the toll it took on Mrs. Eddy's regular work for her church, it highlighted the issue of how Mrs. Eddy thought of herself. There were certainly some of her followers who did think of her as the woman in the Apocalypse, and the evidence at this point indicates that she did not explicitly correct that false impression. Ira Knapp and his wife had class instruction from Mrs. Eddy in Boston in 1884. When she discussed the twelfth chapter of Revelation, Knapp exclaimed to her, "Thou art the woman." Appreciating his recognition of the significance of her discovery, she may not have felt a need to correct the statement.[9]

The weight of her writings on the matter, however, shows not only her extreme reluctance, but also her actual refusal, to personalize the twelfth chapter of Revelation. In fact, her own exegesis of biblical passages in general tended to spiritualize them, to find the universal message that each story held for mankind in general. Thus, while Woodbury was correct in one sense in applying the "Babylonish woman" to her own mental condition, characterized as one of both physical lust and the desire to manipulate others mentally, Mrs. Eddy could honestly tell her attorneys that she meant the phrase as "only a symbol *of lust,* but Mrs. Woodbury has applied this symbol to herself." [10] Over the last two decades of her life, Mrs. Eddy had many occasions to speak about herself. Every single recorded statement, in conversation or letter form, does not always accord with every other one. Yet there is a consistency to them if one tries to understand them in context. Mrs. Eddy was convinced that she had discovered the science of being, the method by which Jesus healed. In this sense she felt that she had fulfilled a unique mission, which no one else would ever duplicate. This was one reason she could be outraged at the insensitivity of a Josephine Woodbury or, later, of an Augusta Stetson, who in one way or another assumed they could take her place in the movement. Mrs. Eddy did write to Ira Knapp in 1899, "There is but one Christ but there is more than one appearing of Christ." [11] This might seem to apply to her, but she did not apply such a phrase exclusively to herself, since all men and women in their spiritual selfhood are understood in Christian Science to be individual representations of Christ. She also referred in one letter to being crucified for "repeating the Revelation of St. John." [12] But even in this obvious reference to the woman in the Apocalypse, she was not leaving out the possibility that others would have a similar experience. In fact, one is losing the main thrust of her Scriptural interpretation in paying attention to only such statements and ignoring others. At the time of the Woodbury trial, she wrote:

> I never taught or thought that I was the Woman referred to in the dim distance of St. John's period nor that the Babylonish woman can be identified or individualized in our time. I have rebuked such a thought and written of this [latter] woman not as an individual but as *lust.* [13]

She also wrote, "What St. John saw in prophetic vision and depicted as 'a woman clothed with the sun and the moon under her feet' prefigured no specialty or individuality. His vision foretold a type and this type applied to man as well as to woman…. The character or type seen in his vision illustrated purity."[14]

She was convinced that her work had established the science of Christianity, but it was Christian Science, not Mrs. Eddy, that was the "second witness" (a reference to a verse in Revelation 11) along with Jesus. She also explicitly defined the woman in the Apocalypse as symbolizing "generic man, the spiritual idea of God." The appearing of this spiritual idea to human consciousness is today, as in Mrs. Eddy's own time, an individual experience and is accompanied by the attempt of error (as Mrs. Eddy would explain it) to prevent its full development. That the experiences related in the twelfth chapter of Revelation seem to coincide so closely with Mrs. Eddy's own revelation and subsequent trials does not make her the woman; indeed, many Christian Scientists who have persevered in their practice of this religion have found themselves at times identifying with the same Scripture. And there are untold other Christians who, taking at least a similar meaning from the passage, would find it significant in some of their life experiences.

Alfred Farlow, the first person to head the Committee on Publication that Mrs. Eddy established in 1899, said much the same thing in an interview with Dorothy Dix, then a young columnist for the *New York Journal.* On May 31, 1901, the third day of the Woodbury trial, Dix's interview appeared. As for the woman in Revelation 12, Farlow said, "The metaphorical figure of the woman clothed in the sun could not according to Christian Science apply to any mortal, but what it inculcates can be incorporated in the life of every individual."[15]

❖ ❖ ❖ ❖

Mrs. Eddy had long ago given up any thought of influencing the education or other development of her son, George, who was now in his late fifties. She had been generous to his family, had sent him money at times, and in 1900 presented him with a house in Lead, South Dakota. The house she had built for him was probably a better one than her own remodeled farmhouse in New Hampshire and certainly more presumptive of his accomplishments than he deserved. And she still had a normal grandmother's concern over his children's education; she did not want another generation of her progeny to grow up as uneducated and ill-bred as she considered George to be. But the chances of her preventing that, as long as they lived in the mining towns of South Dakota, were slim.

With this in her thought, she launched a plan in 1900 to have Charles Howe, a teacher of Christian Science in St. Joseph, Missouri, oversee the education of at least some of George's four children. St. Joseph was not an unlikely candidate as a medium-sized city in those days; once larger than Kansas City, it had close to 100,000 people living in it at the turn of the century. It was situated on the Missouri River, south of South Dakota.

The project seemed to begin well. Mrs. Eddy wrote to Howe in early 1900, "Words are weak to tell my gratitude to you for taking my dear grandson. . .under your care till he is thoroughly prepared to enter Harvard College. . . .What I am most grateful for is the moral teaching and training that I know *you* will give him." [16] Before long, all four of the Glover children were in St. Joseph. Mrs. Eddy hoped that at least one of her grandchildren would become sufficiently interested in Christian Science for him or her to have class instruction. She wrote to Howe, "The children must make their home in St. Joseph and they must keep the best of company or have none. I shall never allow them to study in a class Christian Science till they give up their `worthless' associates and graduate at the high school.... Tell them if they will do as abovenamed then I will put them in the Mass. Met[aphysical] Col[lege] and pay all their expenses...." [17] It was also evident that she felt their mother was a bad influence on them.

Then one of the daughters, apparently unhappy over the situation there, wrote home implying that Mr. Howe had proposed marriage to her. Whatever the misunderstanding was that led to this impression in Lead, South Dakota, the triangle of Pleasant View, Lead, and St. Joseph proved too difficult to negotiate. It appears that Mrs. Eddy briefly believed some of the things that were reported to her about Mr. Howe via South Dakota, but upon sorting it out in her own thought she decided it was George's jealous wife who was causing the trouble. In any case, she put an end to the arrangement and wrote to Howe in August:

> Do not let this great disappoint[ment] trouble you.... You was [sic] so kind and so was I in this thought. The uncouth mother does not understand us.... I have suffered, so have you; now let us remember they that suffer with me shall reign with me. [18]

The children stayed on in St. Joseph for some time. Early in 1901 Mrs. Eddy wrote to Howe, thanking him for a Christmas present he had sent to her. She inquired of all the children, adding, "This information is *closed* to me *now*." [19] Once more, the door had closed for her on any hope of human fulfillment or satisfaction from ties of the flesh. How much human family did mean to her can at least be glimpsed, though, by considering the amount of time and thought she gave to this small episode with Howe and St. Joseph in the context of the same busy period of preparation for the Woodbury trial and of her last revision of *Science and Health.* She told Kimball, whom she had called to Boston for help on the Woodbury case, "I have lost the education of my grandchildren and my most cherished earthly plans for them." [20] It was at about this same time, during the Christmas season of 1901, that Irving Tomlinson recorded a remark Mrs. Eddy made at the supper table one evening: "In all my long years everything that I have loved dearly has been taken from me." [21]

❖ ❖ ❖ ❖

The revision of *Science and Health* belongs largely to the years

1901 and 1902. After the Woodbury verdict in June 1901, Mrs. Eddy was somewhat freer to pursue this project. Her continual concern about the Christian Science textbook needs to be appreciated in the context of what she expected that book to accomplish. One of her organizational steps in 1898 had been to reinstitute a procedure for certifying teachers in Christian Science. Each of them was at first allowed to teach two classes of not more than thirty pupils a year. This was changed in 1904 to only one class per year. It must have been clear to her from the simple arithmetic of the matter that, if Christian Science continued to grow, class instruction would not be readily available to large numbers of students. Moreover, she remained concerned about the quality of some of the teaching. Now, as she began her ninth decade, she was aware once more that her years on earth were limited and that she herself would probably never teach a class of future teachers again, as she had done in 1898. Thus, it seems obvious that, in looking ahead many generations, she saw *Science and Health* itself assuming an important teaching function.

To help her with the new edition, she enlisted the support of Edward Kimball, whose understanding of Christian Science was as much in tune with her own as anyone she knew, and a young man named William McKenzie. The latter had briefly been a Presbyterian minister and then a college professor of English at Rochester University. Kimball and McKenzie went over the text of *Science and Health* line by line to look for the utmost clarity of expression. Their changes were minimal. At one point Mrs. Eddy sent them this message:

> While praying this morning there came to me as consciously as a voice could come this, "Neither add nor diminish to the textbook of Christian Science say this to the dear brethren." [22]

Any suggestions for changes to be made were sent to Mrs. Eddy with an explanation, and she would either approve them or not. She specifically asked them to correct, when necessary, the marginal headings. These had been added by Mr. Wiggin, and she felt that many of them were incorrect. But the two most important changes in the book were a rearrangement of the order of the chapters and the addition of one hundred pages of testimonies from people who had been healed solely by reading the textbook. She wrote to Kimball, "The book will be much improved no doubt. The *700* pages signify wholeness." [23] The testimonies made it come out at an even seven hundred; the somewhat mystical remark, probably harking back to a belief that the number seven stands for wholeness, or perfection, would have found greater receptivity with an Ira Knapp or Judge Hanna than with Kimball.

Inclusion of the testimonies was Mrs. Eddy's manner of saying, You can learn what you need to know to be healed from reading this book. She had known from the beginning that reading it could bring healing. As her own thought became clearer, she was able to improve the exposition of the metaphysics of Christian Science. But beyond the matter of exposition, which might be considered as an almost intellectual exercise (albeit a vital matter in setting out metaphysics), the language of the textbook, on almost every page, combined a sense of the demand for that change of thought required by scientific Christianity with the assurance of God's grace, the knowledge that the understanding of God's presence and power was, in the last analysis, the gift of an already present spiritual reality. She had been constantly reminded of this capacity of the book to both teach and heal by letters she received from Christian Scientists in the field. Early in 1900, Kimball had written to her about the experience of a student of his:

> A lady who came to study with me said, "My father was for 30 years a physician in Texas. Five years ago his sight began to fail. The oculists said that the retina in each eye was being absorbed and that total blindness would ensue. In four years he was blind and the last oculist said, 'He is eternally blind. It is useless for you to hope.' [His daughter began to read to him from *Science and Health.*] We did not know enough to

> discuss it. We just read it. I used to assist him, and one day as I took him to the washstand he said, 'Oh, how I wish that I could see you.' Then he turned to wash his face, and as he did so he said, 'But I can see that God is All - There is nothing but God.' Then he turned and looked towards me and instantly I knew that he saw me. At that moment his sight was restored and he can now see better than I can. The oculist afterwards examined his eyes and said the retina in each eye was perfect. Every thought about this unspeakable blessing fills me with such holy awe and humility that I have as yet been unable to tell it in public but Oh! how I wish that the world might know what it means."[24]

The rearrangement of chapters gave an orderly progression to the book, which even many Christian Scientists may not have taken time to think about. Reading it from week to week in small segments that correlate with the Bible passages in the Lesson-Sermon, they may not be aware of this progression. The arrangement was suggested by McKenzie. The subjects of the first two chapters in the book became "Prayer" and "Atonement and Eucharist." Since all Christians pray and have some theological beliefs regarding the significance of Jesus' life, these chapters are about familiar material; yet they help orient one's thought to the difference between Christian Science and what was then orthodoxy. The same can perhaps be said of the third chapter, "Marriage." Then follow two chapters that deal, on the surface, with thought-forms that were the talk of the day a century ago: spiritualism and animal magnetism. In each case, Mrs. Eddy goes beyond the more limited uses those terms had in everyday jargon, but their inclusion is one indication that even a book meant to be written for the ages has some reference points that denote its place in time. With these five chapters lifted out of their order in the 1891 revision, the remainder of the original chapters had a logical development, and their order was left untouched. They lead progressively into an explication of the metaphysics of Christian Science and then to a discussion of its practice.

❖ ❖ ❖ ❖

The period immediately after the Woodbury trial (June 1901) did not feature any such dramatic event. By the turn of the century, Christian Science had become one of the most viable forces on the American religious scene. Mrs. Eddy, as the Leader of the movement and because of her longevity, was increasingly big news herself, however much she might try to recede into the background. Newspapers in Boston and New York frequently asked for her comment on major public issues.

After the revision of *Science and Health,* Mrs. Eddy made several personnel changes in the growing church organization in Boston. She also had to deal with the problems associated with growth, such as whether to allow a foreign translation of the textbook or how to deal with the negative publicity that came as a backlash to the growth. During the same period, she was not in what could be described as failing health, but she spoke frequently with her closest associates about the challenges associated with aging and, on several occasions, felt severely tested physically due to her sensitivity to attacks on her teaching.

As the Christian Science movement grew, she remained alert to the need for spiritual growth among its adherents. Yet she combined this *sine qua non* with a practical Yankee insistence on getting the right people to fill the posts in Boston. A major reason for her reliance on Edward Kimball for so many years lay in her feeling that he combined the spirituality that was a prerequisite with valuable business experience. She had written to him in 1900, "I have no words to thank God for you, your wisdom and business ability are just what I have prayed to find in a student, and my prayer is answered in you."[25]

She had grown somewhat dissatisfied with Judge Hanna, as already mentioned, in spite of the decade-long service he and his wife had performed as editors of *The Christian Science Journal.* He had disappointed her during the Woodbury proceedings, and she now decided to replace him as both editor and First

Reader (he had filled the latter post for seven years, since its establishment in 1895). Kimball had told her about a fellow Chicagoan, Archibald McLellan, who was an attorney. Mrs. Eddy now thought of him as Hanna's replacement as editor. She wrote to Kimball:

> The editor of our issues should be in touch with me he should do as you did carry things against the enemy and not through cowardice yield to it as Hanna does in direct opposition to all his agreements or rather promises to me. I must have an advocate, the cause must have an advocate, in those at the head of our periodicals and not *dodge* when they should fire and not fire when it is unwise… Also learn if his wife will influence him rightly on these matters. Mrs. Hanna does not.[26]

McLellan left Chicago and began his work as editor in Boston in 1902. During the same year Mrs. Eddy expressed some impatience with the work of her own student, Ira Knapp. She was grateful for his faithfulness and had a warm personal relationship with the Knapps. But on two occasions she wrote to William Johnson, the Clerk of The Mother Church and one of its directors, that she wished he or the other directors could get Knapp to resign. Beyond the matter of the close personal relationship, she was thinking of the particular talents and experience she felt the Board of Directors would need in the immediate future. She wrote, "We need a *strong* and a *business* man to help you on the pull through getting a new church."[27] This referred to the decision made in June 1902, at the time of the annual meeting of The Mother Church, to build a large extension to The Mother Church building in Boston.

Mrs. Eddy hoped that Kimball would stay in Boston after the Woodbury trial. Kimball, at various periods during his years as a Christian Scientist, had recurring physical difficulties, however, and the two years after the Woodbury case were especially hard ones for him. He continued to come to Boston to teach classes for the Board of Education. Mrs. Eddy would have liked to have had him as one of her directors. In fact, of the correspondence that has been preserved, she seems at times to come close to talking with him on a collegial basis, something that, as the Leader she saw herself to be, she did not or could not easily allow herself to do. In one letter to Kimball in 1902, she hoped that he would stay on in Boston even while working out his problem:

> I know you can master it, the lie, there as well as elsewhere. To run before a lie is to accept its terms. This works like running before the enemy in battle. You will be followed pursued till you face about *trust* in *God* and stand on *Spirit* denying and facing and fighting all claims of matter, and mortal mind both *one.* I and you have *grown* to be honored by God with entrance into this department of learning. [28]

During 1902, she had ample opportunity to test McLellan's sensitivity in the editor's chair. She wrote to him several times to correct metaphysical points, but on the whole was pleased with the way he assumed his tasks. So, apparently deciding that Kimball would not come to Boston to stay, in early 1903, she asked the directors to make McLellan a fellow director. "I have watched him and so far he has been right on all important subjects. You will have *three* in unity that leaves a majority when they are right." [29] Her reference to a majority refers to the fact that at the same time she added McLellan to the Board she changed the *Manual,* making a Board of Directors of five instead of four. This prepared the way for an effective working board after Mrs. Eddy's time, since an even number could have created problems in case of a tie vote. It has been at least generally believed over the years that, as a matter of practice, the Board of Directors has made important decisions by consensus. But the fifth member does prevent a deadlock if an immediate decision must be made.

The other major change Mrs. Eddy carried through in this same period was to end the tenure of Kimball as the teacher in the Board of Education. After his undoubted closeness to her through the Woodbury trial, as the Normal class teacher from 1899 through 1903, and as the holder of the copyright on *Science and Health* since 1899, it came as a shock to Kimball to begin hearing rumors that Mrs. Eddy was dissatisfied with him. He was spending several months of the winter of 1903-4 in Santa Barbara, California, and upon hearing disturbing stories about himself, wrote to Mrs. Eddy:

> [After the Hanna experience] I resolved that if I ever got the slightest hint of the kind concerning myself I would make short work of it by speedily getting out of the way.... Knowing as I do that many other teachers regard the College as a rival and competitor and that they have no flowers for the pathway of the teacher, I would not for a moment be willing to be that teacher if your confidence in me could be impaired by falsehood and misrepresentation.[30]

That Mrs. Eddy had heard rumors about Kimball's teaching there can be little doubt. Sitting in her hillside retreat in Concord, she was buffeted almost daily by rumor. In a small but rapidly expanding movement such as Christian Science had become, there would naturally, but unfortunately, be some jockeying for position. Among the strong, loyal men she had used in the key positions in the movement since 1892, there was no question of any one of them trying to usurp her place as Leader. That kind of competition was left to Woodbury and, later, to Stetson. But it was clear to Mrs. Eddy that other kinds of competition could be equally as harmful to the movement, and one such example would be if a group of teachers were to claim that the teaching they had had was superior. Kimball himself had warned her of this in reporting on a Normal class he had taught in 1903:

> The entrance of this new corps of teachers upon the scene of class teaching was unwelcome to very many if not most of the old teachers.

> They were regarded as intruders and rivals and there speedily ensued a constantly growing antagonism to the College which was putting forth these new teachers. This antagonism is waxing more virulent every day and must be stopped.
>
> There is no doubt that the College teaching has been a rebuke to, and in repudiation of a good deal that has been taught, and of bad practices which have prevailed....[31]

Some of the rumors that reached Mrs. Eddy did purport that Kimball's students were claiming to be better taught than other students. If Mrs. Eddy had not moved when she did to rotate teachers, this kind of exclusivism might have grown worse. In removing Kimball as the sole teacher in the Board of Education, she was moving to prevent such a development.

She was probably also making the change for other, very practical reasons: Kimball had taught four Normal classes since 1899, as well as several Primary classes. The teaching, which had been less regulated in the 1890s, was now well established, and even with a growing membership, there was no lack of authorized teachers of Christian Science. Thus, Mrs. Eddy appointed Eugene Greene from Providence, Rhode Island, to teach the next Normal class, and she later changed the *Manual* to provide for only one Normal class every three years. This change took effect in 1907. Probably in order to show that she had trust in both of her stalwarts, she appointed Judge Hanna to teach the class in 1907 and Kimball to teach again in 1910. (When Kimball passed on in 1909, she appointed one of his students, Bicknell Young, to take the 1910 class.) Thus the evidence is clear that she did not in any way repudiate Kimball's teaching, only the exclusivism that was being attached to it by some of his pupils.

Mrs. Eddy had again demonstrated her capacity to lead in an uncomfortable situation. Because she could be confident of the dedication of both Hanna and Kimball, she could take the steps she did. But at least in Kimball's case, there was some evidence of hurt on his part. In answer to his letter expressing his hurt in April 1904, she showed no excessive sympathy. Referring to the rough time Frederick Peabody, Woodbury's lawyer, continued to stir up for Christian Science, Mrs. Eddy said:

> What have you passed by of absolute falsehoods about me in P's pamphlet, and let it go unnoticed and now trouble me about yourself on hearsays of no special character. Have you faith in your Teacher and Leader? Then show it in dignity and love and by resting on the assurance that I gave you, of my satisfaction with your teaching. [32]

This was indeed straight talk from the woman he acknowledged as Teacher and Leader, and there was no question that he would accept it. But neither was it an easy task for Mrs. Eddy to talk at times to even her most trusted students and helpers as if they were mere children. More than once she half apologized for her tendency – and, indeed, need – to correct; at times she jumped to conclusions or may have temporarily gotten a false impression. But she was usually right, and her most trusted students recognized that fact. Without that kind of acceptance on their part, she could not have continued to lead the movement. That they would someday have to make it on their own, without her personal guidance, cajoling, and correction, they had barely begun to consider. For the moment, events were moving too swiftly.

❖ ❖ ❖ ❖

One mark of the growing recognition being given to both Mrs. Eddy and Christian Science was her inclusion in the publication in 1905 of a volume called "The Book of the Presidents and Representative Americans." It contained the biographies of the Presidents and other Americans distinguished as being at the head of their professions. Although several other women of Mrs. Eddy's generation had achieved renown by 1900 and were still living, Mrs. Eddy was the only woman represented in the volume. An article in the *Boston Herald* said, "The distinguished place accorded to Mrs. Eddy is another of the many evidences of the widening sphere of her spiritual ministry, and emphasizes the patent fact of her growing influence among the intelligent and cultured classes of this and foreign lands." [33]

But popularity exacted its toll, as Mrs. Eddy had long ago learned. Ever since Josephine Woodbury had lost her libel suit against Mrs. Eddy, her attorney, Frederick Peabody, had been on the lecture platform trying to discredit both Mrs. Eddy and Christian Science. In 1902, Judge Hanna consulted with Mrs. Eddy's lawyer from the year before, Samuel Elder, regarding a suit against Peabody. Elder strongly advised against it and went on to say:

> It is inevitable that a great movement like the one Mrs. Eddy has inaugurated, which departs from the tenets held by a great majority of the public and which is spreading to most unexpected proportions, should be the subject of a great deal of public discussion. In spite of it Christian Science has grown vigorously and powerfully. It is an open question whether the violence of the attack upon it and upon its founder have not aided rather than retarded its growth. No such movement as this can possibly protect itself in the Courts. Its success has been, and will be, in a different form. [34]

Elder closed by deploring "the distress which these attacks have caused Mrs. Eddy."

If the Peabody campaign against Christian Science was difficult to counter on legal grounds, the publicity given the religion and its founder by Mark Twain caused another kind of distress to Mrs. Eddy over a period of several years. Twain, whose legal name was Samuel Clemens, was a nationally known humorist and satirist, although today he is remembered chiefly for his novels, *Tom Sawyer* and *Huckleberry Finn.* The mere fact that he ridiculed Christian Science showed the important place it had come to occupy in public thought. Ironically, the ridicule acted only to make Christian Science even more widely known.

Twain had started taking jibes at Christian Science in 1899. But it was the publication of a series of articles by Twain in the *North American Review* in 1902 and 1903 that caused the consternation in Mrs. Eddy's household. Her initial response to the Committee on Publication, Alfred Farlow, was to leave Twain alone. She advised him to "take no notice of Mark Twain's effusion of folly and falsehoods. Time tells all stories true."[35] But the attacks continued. William McCrackan, a fairly new Christian Scientist, had been made the Committee on Publication for New York. McCrackan was a respected author, having written a history of the Swiss Federation. In time, he developed a civil talking relationship with Twain.

Twain was a complicated fellow. His earlier career as a storyteller and humorist was overshadowed by financial missteps in the 1890s, which left him deeply in debt, and by the deaths of two of his daughters and of his wife, Olivia, in 1904, after a long illness. His later writing was bitter and sardonic, and it is to that phase of his life that his attacks on Christian Science belong. At one point before 1900, he had briefly had Christian Science treatment for himself, and over the years before his death in 1910, he made many positive statements regarding Christian Science. He claimed, apparently seriously, that within fifty years Christian Science would be a dominant force in American life. But at the same time, he maintained that Mrs. Eddy was a fraud and that someone else had written *Science and Health.*

Twain was aided and abetted in his attacks by Frederick Peabody. He also fell into a habit, inexplicable even to himself, of composing disagreeable letters to Mrs. Eddy at night, then tearing them up before mailing them. He did the same thing to McCrackan, but made the mistake of mailing at least one of them. He called McCrackan to apologize; his apology was answered by McCrackan's magnanimously returning the letter to Twain so he could destroy it himself. McCrackan thought that the tendency resulted from a kind of hypnotic influence over Twain on the part of Woodbury; but he felt it would be impossible to explain this convincingly to Twain.[36]

There was one interesting and positive outcome of Mark Twain's attacks on Mrs. Eddy. For most of the period that she had been residing in New Hampshire, she had allowed her students to address her as "Mother." Given the formality of the age, this was an innocent enough compromise between continually addressing someone they felt close to as "Mrs. Eddy" and the socially unacceptable practice in that age (particularly with an older person) of using her first name. "Mother" had its counterpart in the use of familial appellations in Roman Catholic orders. While Mrs. Eddy was not consciously duplicating that use, there was certainly a combined sense of recognizing her spiritual authority as well as her human motherliness by those close to her. Twain's ridicule ended the habit, however, and Mrs. Eddy wrote to McCrackan early in 1903, "I shall stop the students calling me mother if I can. God never was in that line of action. I never thought it were wise in the beginning and now it is proven unwise."[37]

If the Twain publicity could not be directly countered, it at least served to illustrate the popularity of Christian Science. At the same time that this new religious movement was "big news" in America, it was also beginning to spread in Europe. In early 1900, Mrs. Eddy wrote to Frau Bertha Günther-Peterson in Hannover, Germany, asking if the laws of Germany allowed her to accept a small bequest from Mrs. Eddy in America. A few months later, she sent a check for one thousand dollars to be used by the fledgling church in Hannover (she had earlier done the same thing in London). In the meantime, an American woman, Frances Seal, who had begun healing in Dresden without even knowing the German language, moved to Berlin and was having good results introducing Christian Science in the German capital (albeit with substantial Prussian bureaucratic resistance dogging her first steps).[38]

Mrs. Eddy remained skeptical about the possibility of having a German translation of the textbook. Her earlier experiments with translation had left her unconvinced that the metaphysics could be accurately translated. In 1904, she wrote to the Countess von Moltke:

> ... I would joy to be a German to the Germans in language as I now am in spirit. When first I wrote *Science and Health* I deeply desired to have that book translated properly and sent to Germany. The idealism of the Germans seemed to me quite in accord with the realism of Christian Science in other words it seemed to be more spiritual than that of most languages. But I have learned at length that neither the German nor French language is capable of expressing the absolute Science of Christian Science. [39]

She did, however, authorize in 1903 a monthly periodical, *Der Herold der Christian Science,* in German. This was the forerunner of what were eventually many other foreign language editions of the *Herald.* One side note about the times appears in a letter written by William McKenzie, recommending the start of a German periodical. McKenzie noted that there were some 300,000 Jews in New York City whose native language was German. A German periodical would be a good way of reaching out to them, he claimed. [40]

❖ ❖ ❖ ❖

The events of the early 1900s left their mark on Mrs. Eddy. Until her passing at the end of the decade, she did not lose her capacity to inspire others or to be their Leader. Given the various attacks on her and her movement during the decade – the same decade that she was in her eighties – her continuing capacity to lead and to command the obedience of her directors and editors in Boston, as well as the lecturers she sent out to the field, is the most important point to bear in mind. She had largely succeeded by this time in separating Christian Science in the public mind from the various mind-cure systems still extant, and the largely successful healing practice of her followers was steadily gaining adherents to the movement.

None of these accomplishments was carried out without personal cost, however. Nor did she hide that cost in her conversations with her household or in her correspondence. She wrote to Marjorie Colles, one of her early followers in England, at the end of 1902, "Words cannot tell you in a letter all that I have accomplished for our cause since you were here, nor what I have experienced because of it."[41] What Mrs. Eddy suffered from physically was partly the aging process; but more important in her case was the hostility she felt directed against her. The two elements were combined, of course, and one must remember, in judging any of Mrs. Eddy's comments about her physical well-being, the extreme demands she placed on herself and the fact that she did not change her manner of living very noticeably even in her ninth decade. She still had her breakfast at six, dinner at noon, supper at six. (It was still considered normal to take one's main meal at midday.) The days were filled with reading mail, interviews with church officials or her secretaries, writing letters, and several hours of individual Bible study and prayer. Her only relaxation appears to have been her daily carriage drive through the streets and environs of Concord. All the days of the week appear to have been treated equally, and she took no vacations. She wrote many times at intervals of how many years it had been since she had taken a vacation. Given the task she had set for herself of watching over her movement, however, it is perhaps unrealistic to imagine her ever mentally taking any time off for herself.

Periodically she agreed to be interviewed by the press. In 1900, she granted a short interview to a reporter from the *Boston Post*. At that time there had been rumors that she had cancer and/or was being visited regularly by a medical doctor. When the reporter wrote his story, he was obviously impressed by Mrs. Eddy's presence:

> Mrs. Eddy impressed one as singularly graceful and winning in bearing. Her figure is tall, slender, and flexible in movement as a Delsarte disciple. Her face is oval in shape, the features regular yet indicative of strong character. Her eyes are a luminous blue, a bright contrast to the mass of wavy white hair that falls over her temples.
>
> Mrs. Eddy is a striking picture of health in old age. Her step is firm and she walks with an easy grace, strongly conveying the impression of health and strength.[42]

Yet even to this outsider, Mrs. Eddy was not reluctant to mention her human years. After assuring him that she was not ill, she continued, according to his article: "'I am an old lady,' she added more softly, and then smiling, added 'That is, in years but not in my own sight.'" Earlier she had written to Carol Norton, a young male practitioner in New York who showed much promise for the future, "But who can sympathize with the twilight of age and starless nights?"[43]

The turmoil of the Woodbury case seemed to have some continuing effect on her. She had periodic metaphysical help during 1901 from Dr. Alfred Baker, a former homeopathic physician and distant relative who had become a Christian Scientist. The next year, she wrote to Kimball, who was still struggling with his own physical problem, "Do not neglect this as I have neglected myself and now regret it."[44]

In May 1903, Mrs. Eddy suffered such severe pain that a doctor, Ezekiel Morrill, who also happened to be her cousin, was sent for by her household. He determined that she was suffering from kidney stones, and he gave her a shot of morphine to deaden the pain. The same problem recurred a few times during that same year, and again three times during the last two years of her life. Morphine was the only known painkiller at that time. Although she had to be persuaded to have an injection by those around her who saw the extent of her physical anguish, she did not take the matter lightly. This event, plus the fact that one of her helpers in the building project for the expansion of The Mother Church passed on in 1905 in severe pain, caused her to insert a new paragraph in the textbook to make it clear to all that Christian Scientists were free to consider the use of such expedients.[45] She felt, in the case of the worker in Boston, that if he had been free of the pain he was suffering, he could have prayed more effectively and been healed.

Mrs. Eddy must have been aware that she was doing far more than almost anyone else of her age was capable of accomplishing. As the Discoverer of Christian Science, she also felt an individual responsibility to make as substantial a demonstration as humanly possible over the beliefs of debility and deterioration in old age. The demonstration of eternal Life must be a continuous process, even though she did not expect to escape what she referred to in her textbook as "the transitional stage in human experience called death."[46] In 1905, she wrote to Annie Knott, who had come to help edit the periodicals, "After forty years in your service I need more of my time to watch individually. I have neglected myself for others; now help your Leader by helping yourself."[47] That the years were taking some toll on her can be seen by this note from Lewis Strang, one of her personal secretaries, to Professor Hermann Hering, who was then the First Reader of The Mother Church:

> It is indeed a great privilege to help our Leader in any capacity whatsoever. The more he sees of her, and the better he comes to comprehend something of the magnitude of her work and of herself, the greater becomes the desire to aid – the greater also the appreciation of the necessity of help. The pity is that we cannot – or do not – give more.[48]

Yet in the immediate aftermath of Mrs. Eddy's resort to the injection of morphine came one of the brightest events of the decade for her. Groups of Christian Scientists had visited Concord on at least three other occasions, but she had something special in mind in 1903. In March, she told Joseph Mann, who ran the outside part of her household, to have the "florist engaged in time to have our place beautiful by the first of June. I think a large attendance at our Communion may be expected this summer." [49] Then she proceeded to tell the directors to invite church members from all over the world to come to that year's communion. Afterwards, she invited them all to come to Concord; some ten thousand persons came.

In one of her last public appearances, and certainly before the largest crowd, she could see firsthand something of the strength of what she had been building. When the crowd had assembled on the sloping lawn outside her house, she came out on a balcony to greet them. She followed her greeting with a short talk, which began with the quip, "Welcome to Pleasant View, but not to varying views." But the thrust of her comments was a Bible passage from Proverbs, which begins, "Trust in the Lord, and do good; so shalt thou dwell in the land, and verily thou shalt be fed. Delight thyself also in the Lord; and He shall give thee the desires of thine heart." [50] Turning thought to God had been the basis of all that she did, and she could give no more sincere advice to her followers.

According to one account of the meeting, she retired from the balcony after addressing the group and, in the presence of some of her household helpers, opened her Bible at random. She opened to this verse from Isaiah: "And the ransomed of the Lord shall return, and come to Zion with songs and everlasting joy upon their heads: they shall obtain joy and gladness, and sorrow and sighing shall flee away." [51] She was not one who very often looked back, but somewhere lay the memory of the destitute years when she was writing *Science and Health,* or of the first small classes she had taught, or of the short shrift originally given to Christian Science by some orthodox preachers. There must have been gratification at seeing this gathering, the living evidence of how far Christian Science had already come.

❖ ❖ ❖ ❖

Almost from the time the original Mother Church edifice was completed, it had been too small for the Boston congregation. Two Sunday services were held beginning in April 1896. When members came from across the country for annual meeting and communion, which was still celebrated at The Mother Church, there was no way of accommodating them all. Even before 1900, Mrs. Eddy saw that the church would have to be expanded. At one time she asked the directors if they could not find an existing building that would accommodate five thousand people. She also considered expanding the original church, although this would have been almost impossible from the standpoint of preserving its architectural integrity.

Sometime in 1901, a few of her most trusted members in Boston, who had substantial independent means, began acquiring the buildings then standing on the space now occupied by what is called the Extension of The Mother Church – an entirely new building erected between 1904 and 1906. The accumulation of property was done quietly for several reasons. Most obviously, it kept down the total purchase price: some ten separate pieces had to be acquired before the entire tract of three-quarters of an acre was whole again. Mrs. Eddy had also not given the go-ahead for the project at that point. When the directors were considering purchasing some of the property in the church's name, Calvin Frye wrote at her direction:

> Mrs. Eddy requests me to say that upon learning the enormous cost of the running expenses of the Mother Church she does not advise you individually or as a Church to purchase the Hotel or any other real estate until you have sufficient money in the treasury with which to pay for it.[52]

Given her background, it is quite easy to understand her reluctance to spend lavishly. She remarked at about the same time, "I consider it silly expenditure to build a church that costs what ours does to run it."[53] Christian Science had also reinforced this tendency in her, since a vulgar display of wealth was nothing but materialism. But she had a deeper reason for going slowly: she did not want her church to go into debt. Her aversion to debt might be credited superficially to her Yankee upbringing, but it had a more substantial reason behind it. Her church was growing quickly, and she had no reason to doubt that the members would respond to a request for funds at the right time. But taking on debt added a mental burden that she wanted her directors to avoid. She wrote to them in September 1902, after the membership had enthusiastically voted to support the building of a new church edifice:

> We cannot prosper on a wrong premise. We take the *Bible* for *our guide* and find in it this scripture: "owe no man." A slight sum of indebtedness with a speedy prospect of payment would not break the spirit of that scripture, but so large a debt does. Why? Because it involves a material thinking and acting and taking thought that is not advantageous to spiritual growth. The scripture saith "Take no thought for the morrow."[54]

The land that was assembled for the Extension had a peculiar shape, having more width than length. It also had several angles and was bounded by three streets and the back wall of the original Mother Church. This presented the architects with some major challenges. They studied the plans of many of the great cathedrals of the world. The design they eventually used can be described as being Byzantine in some fundamental ways, such as the use of the dome structure and half circle arches within the church edifice. But it remains a unique piece of architecture, unlike any other church in the world, and also relatively timeless in the sense of not belonging to any single architectural style. Many of the building materials – marble, Bedford stone, the brass trim – remind one of the houses of the wealthy that were being built in Newport, Rhode Island, at about the same time.

Mrs. Eddy did not become as personally involved in the construction of the Extension as she had been in that of the original Mother Church. She was consulted on many of the details, approved the floor plan of the building, and selected quotations from the Bible and *Science and Health* to be placed on the walls. From the time the members approved the building at the Annual Meeting in 1902 until its completion and dedication in 1906, the number of Mother Church members grew from about twenty-four thousand to forty thousand.[55] The periodicals occasionally noted that funds were still needed for the building, but the Building Fund was officially closed just before the dedication in June 1906. At that time, thousands of Christian Scientists poured into Boston, and six identical services (one solely for children) were held on Sunday, June 10.

Mrs. Eddy did not come down from Concord for the dedication, a fact that some used as evidence of incapacity on her part. She very likely did not relish the prospect of facing the adulation of several thousand people in an unfamiliar auditorium, after what would have been a strenuous journey by train. But at least as important in her thinking was her desire to turn thought away from her personality. She wrote a brief dedicatory message, "Choose Ye," which emphasized living close to the Golden Rule. In part, she said:

> The First Commandment of the Hebrew Decalogue, "Thou shalt have no other gods before me," and the Golden Rule are the all-in-all of Christian Science. They are the spiritual idealism and realism which, when realized, constitute a Christian Scientist, heal the sick, reform the sinner, and rob the grave of its victory. The spiritual understanding which demonstrates Christian Science, enables the devout Scientist to worship, not an unknown God, but Him whom, understanding even in part, he continues to love more and to serve better.[56]

Referring to the church building, she ended by saying that "Its crowning ultimate rises to a mental monument, a superstructure high above the work of men's hands, even the outcome of their hearts, giving to the material a spiritual significance…."[57]

While the press did not generally give unqualified praise to Christian Science, it did give tribute to Mrs. Eddy's leadership, to the sincerity of Christian Scientists, and to the phenomenal growth of this movement. The church edifice itself was difficult to describe, since it fitted no prior model. The *Boston Globe* wrote:

> When these people enter this new cathedral or temple which has been in process of construction, they will find themselves in one of the most imposing church edifices in the country – yes, in the world. For in its interior architecture it is different from any other church in the world. In fact, nearly all the traditions of church interior architecture have been set aside in this temple, for here are neither nave, aisles, nor transept – just one vast auditorium which will seat exactly five thousand and twelve people on floor and galleries, and seat them comfortably.[58]

The Norfolk, Nebraska, *Tribune* said:

> To those who see no good in Christian Science, it must stagger their faith not a little to read the account of the dedication of the vast temple located in the heart of the city of Boston, the supposed fountain of knowledge and seat of learning of America….[59]

The *Boston Herald* wrote:

> To hear prosperous, contented men and women, people of substance and of standing, earnestly assure thousands of auditors that they had been cured of blindness, of consumption in its advanced stages, of heart disease, of cancer; that they had felt no pain when having broken bones set; that when wasted

> unto death they had been made whole, constituted a severe tax upon frail human credulity, yet they were believed.[60]

One paper after another commented on the fact that the church had been paid for before it was finished, that approximately two million dollars had been raised from its members simply by making the need known. The *Boston Post* gave particular tribute to the growth of Christian Science and to its Founder:

> The growth of this cult is the marvel of the age. Thirty years ago it was comparatively unknown; one church and a mere handful of members measured its vogue. To-day its adherents number probably a million, its churches have risen by hundreds, and its congregations meet in Europe and in the antipodes, and from the Atlantic to the Pacific on this continent.
>
> One does not need to accept the doctrines of Mrs. Eddy to recognize the fact that this wonderful woman is a world power. This is conclusive; it is conspicuously manifest.[61]

Less given to the exaggerations of the moment, the *Denver News* summed it up:

> The growth of this form of religious faith has been one of the marvels of the last quarter century. It is, in some respects, the greatest religious phenomenon of all history. That a woman should found a religious movement of international sway; that its followers should number many thousands during her lifetime; that hundreds of great buildings should be filled at every meeting Sundays or on week-days with devout worshippers, wooed by no eloquence of orator or magnetic ritual, — all these things are new, utterly new, in the history of religious expression.[62]

❖ ❖ ❖ ❖

The public acclaim received by Christian Science at the time of the dedication of the Extension of The Mother Church exacted its price. That price might have been exacted even without the building of one of the largest and most original church edifices in the world. But it was not accidental that Mrs. Eddy had included a line such as, "So, when day grows dark and cold, Tear or triumph harms," in her poem, "Feed My Sheep." She had learned again and again that tears often accompanied or followed her triumphs, as in the death of her husband shortly after her warm welcome back to Boston in 1882 or the dogged attacks on her and on Christian Science that continued after her victory in the Woodbury case.

This phenomenon may be viewed by some as a mere succession of chance occurrences. Mrs. Eddy, however, saw the matter differently. To her, it meant that a false kind of mentality, which she had designated as *mortal mind* in her terminology, felt itself under attack, and was reacting against mankind's gradual acceptance of the concept of God as All-in-all. She herself had written in *Science and Health,* "This material world is even now becoming the arena for conflicting forces.... Mortal error will vanish in a moral chemicalization. This mental fermentation has begun, and will continue until all errors of belief yield to understanding."[63] So, whether it was the building of a new church edifice, which highlighted the amazing growth of Christian Science across the country, or the accumulation of testimonies of spiritual healing that was the proximate cause, it did not surprise her that at each forward step new challenges arose.

Since Mrs. Eddy had not attended the dedicatory services in Boston in June, her absence from an event that was so widely reported in the press set in motion new rumors about the state of her health. During this 1900-era of muckraking and fierce competition among the major metropolitan newspapers, Joseph Pulitzer, owner of the *New York World,* was looking for new targets that would help boost circulation. Whatever his personal motivation may have been, he became convinced that Mrs. Eddy and Christian Science were good targets. He set two of his reporters at work to build a story that would sell. What transpired comprises one of the shabbiest stories in the history of American journalism.

At the same time that the *New York World* reporters began their siege of Pleasant View in October 1906, *McClure's Magazine* was also at work on a series of negative articles about Mrs. Eddy. Thus it became a race between two elements of the media to see who would be the first to attract the public's attention.

The action in what looked like melodrama on the outside, but had to be seen far differently by the intended victims, began on October 14, 1906, when two reporters from the *New York World* appeared unannounced at Mrs. Eddy's house and insisted on seeing her. Claiming that they were merely acting on many rumors reaching the *World* that Mrs. Eddy was dead, they said they would be satisfied if they could see her and have a local Concord resident, a schoolteacher by the name of John Kent, identify her.

Mrs. Eddy had in fact been increasingly sparing of the time she felt she could give for personal interviews, even to serious students of Christian Science. Calvin Frye, her taciturn personal secretary, did not inform her of this request or, actually, demand until the next day, when he had promised the two men, Slaght and Lithchild, he would give them an answer. Mrs. Eddy agreed to see them. Professor Kent, who lived in the neighborhood, was sent for, and she had a short meeting with the three of them. One of her secretaries, Lewis Strang, reporting on the meeting in a letter, noted nothing extraordinary about the interview:

> She explained in a few words that her duties made it impossible for her to receive visitors and that this accounted for her seclusion… Mrs. Eddy remained standing during the entire visit, and as the men left, turned and walked back to her desk in the bay window.

> When we were going down the stairs, Mr. Lithchild said to me with apparent conviction, "She is certainly a well-preserved woman for her years."[64]

The story that appeared in the *World* on Sunday, October 28, however, sounded as if the reporters had seen someone else. It appeared under a headline reading:

> MRS. MARY BAKER G. EDDY DYING;
> FOOTMAN AND "DUMMY" CONTROL HER

The other headlines in the piece claimed that she was suffering from cancer, that someone impersonated her on her daily carriage ride, and that she had a $15 million fortune that was being squandered by those around her.

Concord was outraged. For several years it had recognized Mrs. Eddy as its most distinguished citizen. She was seen by people daily on her drive through town, and whatever their views of Christian Science, most of the town's citizens resented the *New York World*'s attack. In the weeks that followed, many strong statements of support for her were given by Concord's leading citizens, several of whom came to call on her the day after the story appeared. The mayor of Concord came to visit her, whereupon her private attorney, General Streeter, remarked, "You have a cozy corner here, I see, Mrs. Eddy." She replied quickly and with the blend of satire she frequently used, "Yes, and some people would like to see me in a closer corner."[65] She even agreed to a short meeting with several members of the press. Given the strongly negative reaction to the *World*'s story, especially the sense that the privacy of an elderly woman had been violated, the *World* felt compelled to justify its original mistake by going a step further.

Whether what followed was part of Joseph Pulitzer's original plan or was intended to be a cover-up of the yellow journalism he had encouraged, a plan was evolved to embarrass Mrs. Eddy, ridicule Christian Science, and, in the process, take control of her estate out of her hands. This was to be accomplished, ironically enough, by introducing a lawsuit in which Mrs. Eddy, through so-called "next friends," sued her main assistants at Pleasant View and her church officials in Boston.

To this end, James Slaght, one of the *World*'s reporters, was sent out to Lead, South Dakota, to persuade Mrs. Eddy's son, George, to participate in the suit as one of these "next friends." Without her son's participation, it is doubtful that the suit could have gone as far as it did. And it is just possible that the whole episode could have been avoided. According to Irving Tomlinson, who at the time was serving as First Reader in the Concord church, a Christian Scientist from Omaha, Nebraska, by the name of Eva Thompson had visited the Glovers sometime in 1905.[66] Glover complained to her at the time that his mother didn't love him anymore, and that she lavished her affection on Calvin Frye instead. He was not able to get through to his mother, he alleged, because Frye intercepted all his mail. Glover was almost constantly in need of money for his mining ventures and felt that Mrs. Eddy should continue to provide him with funds. Whether or not the lack of good communication between the two can alone explain his going along with the suit, he was persuaded to do so by Slaght. The latter came armed with a letter of explanation, written by former New Hampshire Senator William Chandler, urging Glover to cooperate. Chandler had already agreed with Pulitzer to be the attorney for the suit. Chandler then arranged for Glover and his daughter, Mary, to come to Washington; there he prepared them for an unannounced visit to George's mother in Concord.

When Mrs. Eddy had first heard that George wanted to visit her, she did not realize he was already well along with his private mission. She replied, on Christmas Day, 1906, "I am at present so full of what I must attend to although it is of a very unpleasant sort that I have no moments for anything else. I should love to see you and will let you know when I can have this pleasure, just so soon as I know myself; and I hope it will be in less than two months – the time set for abusing me through a New York magazine."[67] But the next day George and Mary arrived in Concord.

Senator Chandler had implanted the suggestions in Glover's thought that his mother might be "detained in the custody of strangers against her will," that she might be so infirm in body and mind as to be "incapable of managing her business and property affairs," and that those around her "either have already sought or may hereafter seek to wrongfully possess themselves of her large property...."[68] For a son who needed some extra cash, these were heavy inducements to protect his present and future interest in her estate.

If George Glover had had any comprehension of the amount of work his mother was still transacting every day, he would never have entered into the Next Friends Suit. That he was more easily motivated to do so by his need of money and his partial belief (influenced by the suggestiveness of Chandler's letter) after his visit in Concord that his mother was gradually coming under the influence of others is as far as one can go; he was not by nature malicious. In fact, during these same months, Mrs. Eddy was hard at work on what would be her last major editing of *Science and Health.* At the end of November 1906, Lewis Strang wrote to Armstrong in Boston, "If all goes well, I shall finish my reading of *Science and Health* next Sunday, and Mr. Tomlinson, who is reading it after me, should finish by Tuesday. Mrs. Eddy has already completed her examination of the proofs."[69]

Mrs. Eddy was also contemplating a move back to Boston. Although the move has been interpreted as being at least a partial reaction to the stress of the legal procedure she was about to undergo in the year 1907, the evidence points to her anticipating a return to Boston as early as 1906 and actually postponing it because of the Next Friends Suit. In the fall of that year, she asked the directors to see if they could purchase other property near her house on Commonwealth Avenue, so that she could conveniently turn her carriage around in back of it without curious neighbors watching her every move. Early in 1907, she also approved plans for enlarging the Publishing House. The directors planned to build it on St. Paul Street, just opposite the Extension of The Mother Church, and to have it completed by October 1908. She approved of their plan, and that is where they did build it; but at the same time she said she wished it could be built nearer her house on Commonwealth Ave. Thus the Next Friends Suit appears to have acted, not as a catalyst to her move, but as an impediment to it. For, as soon as the suit was over in late summer, she had her agents in Boston begin a serious search for a house in either Newton or Brookline, suburbs just to the west of Boston.

George did not know of all the activity she was engaged in, though, nor the extent to which he was being used by others whose real intentions were not to protect his interests in his mother's property, but to discredit both her and Christian Science. As the winter progressed, it became obvious that something was going on, although Mrs. Eddy could not know its exact shape. During February, she began making plans to put her assets into a trust, so as to relieve herself of decisions regarding their management. Then, on March 1, Senator Chandler filed the Next Friends Suit in Concord. The *New York World* reported the filing of the suit with headlines that read, "RELATIVES SUE TO WREST MOTHER EDDY'S FORTUNE FROM CONTROL OF CLIQUE." The suing relatives were George Glover, his daughter, Mary, a nephew, and, a few days later, Foster-Eddy (Benny), who had been enticed into joining the suit.

Stripped of all its details, the petition filed by the so-called next friends claimed that Mrs. Eddy was unable to manage her property; in its conclusion it stated that "while she has been incapable of any complete volition concerning her property or business affairs, there is abundant reason to believe the defendants and their associates have wrongfully converted to their own private uses… large amounts of property… " It asked that the court appoint a receiver to "take possession of all [her] property…."[70]

As the suit progressed during the summer months, it became evident that its purpose was neither to protect Mrs. Eddy nor her property, but to take her property from her and, at the same time, ridicule Christian Science. Looking at it on a superficial level, one might say that only someone as plucky as Mrs. Eddy could have surmounted this particular challenge. But neither she nor a sensitive observer today would want to consider it on that level. She was immediately alert to this attempt to condemn Christian Science in the public eye. She said to one Christian Scientist, "This hour is going to test Christian Scientists and the fate of our Cause and they must not be found wanting.... I see this clearly that the prosperity of our Cause hangs in this balance."[71]

Looking at Mrs. Eddy's other activities and her correspondence during this period, one is struck by a remarkable growth in her individual equanimity since the 1899-1901 period of the Woodbury suit. She was aware that she was being tested yet again and that there would be an attempt to put the validity of her discovery on trial. There was a grandeur about her demeanor during this summer of 1907, which in one sense makes the Next Friends Suit the capstone in her demonstration of the individual growth in character and accomplishment that Christian Science makes possible. One of the reminiscences about her during this period was written by Calvin Hill, a young worker in the movement at the time. He was frequently her courier between Pleasant View and the directors in Boston, and during the court proceedings, he reported to her on each day's hearings. He wrote later about coming out to the house to tell her about each day's events: "I have a vivid picture of her, sitting quietly and listening to what I had to report. She seemed to me like a gray gull riding calmly, serenely on a storm-tossed sea."[72]

She had absolutely no illusions as to the motives of Chandler, of Pulitzer behind him, or even of the combined mental forces that might be using him as their decoy. She wrote to her church in April, in answer to a communication from it:

> Your love and fidelity cheer my advancing years. As Christian Scientists you understand the scripture, "Fret not thyself because of evil doers;" also you

> spiritually and scientifically understand that God is divine Love, omnipotent, omnipresent, infinite, hence it is enough for you and I to know "that our Redeemer liveth and intercedeth for us."
>
> At this period my demonstration of Christian Science cannot be fully understood, theoretically, therefore it is best explained by its fruits, and by the life of our Lord as depicted in the chapter "Atonement and Eucharist" in *Science and Health with Key to the Scriptures*...[73]

In not too subtle language she was reminding her church that this was the nearest thing to a personal crucifixion that could happen to her. A month later, she also referred to "this last death knell to me" in writing to McLellan in Boston.[74]

Yet during these same months, she was still working on the final revisions in *Science and Health* and carrying on much of her normal correspondence. In June, Judge Hanna, whom she had chosen to teach the Normal class that year, wrote to her asking for some time with her to prepare him to be the teacher. She turned him down, saying, "I cannot add one iota to my labors." But what followed again gives some indication of the great emphasis she gave to stating her Science as accurately as possible in *Science and Health:* "You can find it all in your textbook."[75]

Also during the month of June, she granted three individual interviews to journalists. Each interview contributed to painting a picture of a woman who was the opposite of the allegedly ailing and aged victim of her associates. She talked with each journalist in a poised manner and, on occasion, showed the ironic sense of humor with which she occasionally laced her private comments. Each one left with strong positive impressions of her, in spite of the fact that for months they had been influenced by the reporting of the *New York World* to find something vastly different.

Edwin J. Park, the *Boston Globe* reporter, wrote:

> … I do desire to say here that if the mental competency of Mrs. Eddy had not been called in question by the "next friends," and if I had met her and talked with her as I did this afternoon, the thought that she was not fully competent mentally would have been the last one that ever would have entered my mind… . The trend of her thoughts remains unbroken, and her alert mind turns instantly from one line of suggested thought to another one put forward to take its place.
>
> She referred frankly to the allegation of the next friends, and added, "I think I am *compos mentis,* but I may be mistaken." She smiled when she said this.[76]

William Curtis, writing for the Chicago *Record-Herald,* said he had "never seen a woman 86 years of age with greater physical or mental vigor." He noted her strong handshake, although at the same time he noted, "Her hand is thin and almost transparent." He continued:

> If Mrs. Eddy had not been provident, if she had not husbanded her resources, if she had grown great only in God's work, if she had only been poor, these patriots would not know her; just as they did not know her when she was struggling with adversity.[77]

Arthur Brisbane's interview, which was published in the August 1907 issue of *Cosmopolitan Magazine,* is the best known of the three. It includes his judgment that "It is quite certain that nobody could see this beautiful and venerable woman and ever again speak of her except in terms of affectionate reverence and sympathy." Like the others, he was impressed by her obvious mental and even physical capacity. By this time, it had become clear that the suit would attempt to show her mental incapacity by claiming that Christian Science itself was a form of hallucination. Brisbane wrote:

> They will not show this unless American law shall decide that fixed religious belief is a hallucination.

• • • •

> In substance, Mrs. Eddy's doctrines merely take literally this verse from the fourteenth chapter of John: "Verily, verily, I say unto you, He that believeth on me, the works that I do shall he do also; and greater works than these shall he do; because I go unto my Father."
>
> It is difficult to see why taking literally a statement which this nation as a whole endorses should be construed into a hallucination.[78]

But the most important interview from the point of view of the legal proceeding was the one she had with the court-appointed alienist, Dr. Allan McLane Hamilton (who happened to be a grandson of Alexander Hamilton). Hamilton had testified in a New York trial earlier in the decade against Christian Science; he was not predisposed to be friendly to either it or its founder. His reactions, however, were identical to those of the journalists. In a piece he wrote for the *New York Times,* he said of Mrs. Eddy's appearance and demeanor:

> Her white hair was worn in the style made familiar by her pictures. Her face was thin, as was her body.... I was immediately impressed with the extraordinary intelligence shown in her eyes. In aged persons the eyes are apt to appear dimmed, contracted, and lacking in expression. With Mrs. Eddy, however, they are large, dark, and at times almost luminous in appearance.
>
> As she talked to me, or answered my questions, the play of expression on her features evinced unusual intelligence, and was in strict keeping with what she said. Her whole bearing was dignified and reserved, in perfect accord with what one would expect in a woman of education and refinement.

> … For a woman of her age I do not hesitate to say that she is physically and mentally phenomenal.[79]

In view of the frequent private use Mrs. Eddy made of the phrase "malicious animal magnetism" and the ridicule by others who did not understand what she meant by it, it is noteworthy that Hamilton picked up on the phrase and did not think it all that unusual:

> The allegations concerning Mrs. Eddy's belief in "malicious animal magnetism" are ridiculous. I am convinced that the words are only used synonymously with "malign influence," "malignant" or "mendacious animal magnetism" and is therefore a *façon parler,* as the French say. She certainly has been subject to sufficient annoyance to entertain the fear that she is to be subject to further disturbance.[80]

When the court hearing before the judge and the three court-appointed masters finally opened on August 13, it was apparent that Senator Chandler intended to throw ridicule on Christian Science and, in so doing, to establish that Mrs. Eddy was mentally incompetent. In an actual trial, such allegations, at least today, would likely be disallowed in pretrial hearings. But this was not an actual trial, rather a hearing, and a reading of the conversations between the judge and the petitioning attorneys sounds as if all of the participants were treading on new ground.

What finally turned the case was not what happened in court, but a visit on Monday, August 19, after a weekend recess, of the three masters to Mrs. Eddy at Pleasant View. In the relatively short conversation they had with her, regarding her background, her management of her house and staff, and her decision making regarding her investments, it became clear that there were no grounds for questioning her competency. Even Senator Chandler, who may have half-believed in his case by this time, remarked as the group left Pleasant View, "She's smarter than a steel trap." Two days later, Chandler himself moved to have the suit dismissed.

General Streeter, her main attorney in the case, demurred, since the defense had not had an opportunity in court to counter the outrageous charges and lies that the Next Friends publicity had been spreading about Mrs. Eddy. The judge found no alternative but to drop the suit, however, since those bringing it had withdrawn it. There were a few more meetings with the judge during the fall months, meetings that included discussions as to who was to pay for the proceedings; charges were assessed against the next friends. The victory was clearly Mrs. Eddy's. The unwanted publicity she had gotten over this period, including the various interviews she had granted and the visit by the masters, had all gained sympathy for her and her cause.

In the outpouring of newspaper editorials after the end of the proceeding, it was clear that many newspaper editors saw the suit as an attack on a rapidly spreading religion and were incensed at this display of religious intolerance. The *Daily News* of Pasadena, California, wrote:

> To intrude into the privacy of an American home for the purpose of annoying a woman eighty-six years of age, who seeks only peace and retirement and freedom from the slavery of suffering, proves that religious bigotry and the spirit of persecution as well as cupidity are still in full vigor.
>
> Suffering men and women, to whom a belief is held out singularly in line with that held out by Christ, whereby physical and mental suffering and slavery to sin were healed by one and the same Principle, will be slow to join in the persecution of those who are attracted by this doctrine. It is a doctrine which, if true, is incomparably magnificent in its possibilities. That the Christian Science practitioner does not invariably succeed proves nothing. *Materia medica* can stand no such test. That this new-old truth does heal even in cases of so-called "incurable" diseases, we have the

> testimony of scores of men and women of the highest character and intelligence.
>
> If Christian Scientists are to be discredited in their effort to relieve suffering, physical and mental, it will have to be accomplished in some legitimate, honorable way.... These "next friends" have simply been used. The real attack has been against Christian Science.[81]

The *New York American* opined that Mrs. Eddy was "more vigorous in mind and body than a number of United States senators who are in their seventies." More seriously, it said:

> Religious tolerance has been practised in this country from its foundation – it has been a principle which has hitherto been held sacred. That the first conspicuous violation of this principle should be an attempt to drive a woman from a position she holds by the cheerful consent of thousands of followers is not very flattering to our supposed enlightenment.
>
> Now that Mrs. Eddy has demonstrated that she not only is competent, but is in astonishing physical health for a woman nearly ninety years old, it would be more in keeping with American ideas to allow her remaining years to be spent in peace.[82]

❖ ❖ ❖ ❖

Whether or not they would be spent in peace remained to be seen; but they were not to be spent at Pleasant View. The peaceful setting of her remodeled farmhouse, the modesty of which had been remarked upon by some of the reporters who came to Concord during the Next Friends Suit, was about to be exchanged for a larger house in the suburbs of Boston. The months after the Next Friends Suit was settled saw a continuation of the search for a proper home that had begun a year earlier.

Pleasant View – Retirement Postponed

Mrs. Eddy had learned through the trials of the past nine years, beginning with the Woodbury suit, that there had been no more chance of retirement than in her first decade away from Boston. As long as she lived she would give her entire thought and energy to the movement she had begun. The suit had perhaps left some question in her mind about the laws of New Hampshire (although even after returning to Massachusetts she did not rewrite her New Hampshire will). It was probably more important to her that she put an end to the inefficiency of having so many church officials and messengers making frequent trips back and forth from Boston. In particular, she was formulating plans for the last major building block in her church, the publishing of a daily newspaper.

Chapter 9

Return to Boston

Final Steps at Chestnut Hill

Mrs. Eddy lived at her house in Chestnut Hill for close to three years, from January 26, 1908, until her passing on December 3, 1910. Her final three years mark an epoch in her life just as distinct as the two periods at Pleasant View. The first of those had been filled with organizational activities, with her establishment of those various activities of The Mother Church, under the *Manual* that she wrote, which she saw as distinct and essential to carrying forward the Christian Science movement. The second period, beginning in about 1899, was marked less by innovation than by further testing of both her and Christian Science. The two most notable events in this period were, as has been seen in the previous chapter, the Woodbury trial and the Next Friends Suit.

The Next Friends Suit, advancing to the hearing stage the summer Mrs. Eddy turned eighty-six, tested her mettle as much as any previous episode in her life. Although she endured the ordeal very well, the experience undoubtedly strengthened her desire for privacy. Thus, if her first retirement in 1889 had been a retirement in name only, this time the retirement was real and permanent. The newspaper interviews were finished; she had earned her peace. Whatever her full reason for wanting to be closer to Boston again, her final three years were years of physical withdrawal from the world and of her turning over most of the duties of running the Christian Science movement to those officials who, under the *Church Manual,* would continue in those functions after her passing.

These were definitely not years of mental decline. In fact, some of the finest anecdotes about her come from the Chestnut Hill period, in which she made more time to discuss matters with her intimate household. They were years of physical challenge, however, challenge that was often connected with developments in the movement or with animosity she sensed toward her and Christian Science from outside the movement. By the third of the three years, 1910, it was clear to her household that she was gradually withdrawing.

Two major events were still to occur: her establishment of a daily newspaper, *The Christian Science Monitor,* and the final eclipse of her ambitious student in New York, Augusta Stetson. The *Monitor* came first, during four incredible autumn months of 1908. Mrs. Stetson's case occupied the last half of 1909. Besides these two matters, Mrs. Eddy gave more attention to developing a stronger sense of co-existence between Christian Science and other religions, and to preparing her directors to carry on what she felt she had done largely alone: keeping the watch. It was a retirement from the world's eye. But she could not have retired in any other sense until her life on earth had come to an end.

❖ ❖ ❖ ❖

During their search for a proper Boston home for Mrs. Eddy, her agents in Boston had looked at two or three properties in Brookline and Newton. Mrs. Eddy expressed a preference for Brookline, just a few miles west of her church. Her trustees eventually purchased a twenty-five-room house on Beacon Street in Chestnut Hill (a part of Newton). This was only slightly farther away than Brookline. The house itself was a far cry from the modest, remodeled farmhouse that she had called home since 1892. Even today, the gray stone mansion at what is now 400 Beacon Street is imposing as well as somber-looking. Mrs. Eddy had asked that her furniture be moved; she did not want unnecessary change at that stage in her life. But she had been given no idea of the size of the rooms in Chestnut Hill. Once in the house, she ordered that some of the rooms be partitioned so that her study and bedroom would be the same size as those rooms had been at Pleasant View.

The actual move took place on Sunday, January 26, 1908. She had told very few people, including her household staff, of the move. A private train had been arranged for her, and virtually no one in Concord knew that she was leaving when she drove out of her gate, presumably for her habitual daily drive. By the time the train had been switched onto different tracks in Boston so as to deliver her close to her house, newsmen had found out about the move and were waiting at the gates in Chestnut Hill. John Salchow, her grounds attendant for years, picked her up in his arms from her carriage and carried her into the house and up to her bedroom. What looked to her something like imprisonment for several months had begun!

What appeared to some of her household to be a fitting setting for a woman of her accomplishments merely appalled Mrs. Eddy. John Lathrop, a young teacher in New York who was temporarily working as part of the household, wrote somewhat naively to Professor Hering, "There is much about this location which seems particularly appropriate for our Leader's higher work, another proof that God is leading us step by step out of the wilderness into the land of Truth."[1] To the contrary, the day after the move she notified her household: "The costly silver dishes that are ordered. . . are no better for use than earthen ones are; and he or she who orders them without my knowledge and consent, shall pay for them."[2] She apparently even considered leaving Chestnut Hill for several months. In April she wrote to Mr. Beman, The Mother Church architect, that she would try one summer there. Yet in midsummer she wrote in a note to Archibald McLellan, "O for the freedom I had before I came here but you are not to be blamed for my coming. *No indeed.*"[3]

In October, she asked to have an architect come to see her, and she made a list of the rooms she wanted for a house to be built in Concord, New Hampshire; but she rescinded the request for the architect before he came. She said as late as November that she had had no idea of the dimensions or expense of the Chestnut Hill house and that when she "looked on the house I now own I was shocked, and went to my room and wept. Had I seen it before purchasing it I should not now be occupying it."[4] And she told John Salchow, "This is not my home. Pleasant View will always be my home." Salchow noted in his reminiscences that a lawyer told him some years later that, when it was being determined whether Mrs. Eddy's will would be probated in New Hampshire or Massachusetts, his [Salchow's] testimony about this statement was the determining factor in the court's decision that she had remained a legal resident of New Hampshire.[5]

All of the preceding commentary would be of only peripheral interest, except for the evidence it shows of Mrs. Eddy's disdain for material opulence. She had supervised the creation of a comfortable estate at Pleasant View, but it was always on a utilitarian scale. Chestnut Hill spoke more of the Gilded Age; it represented more materialism than she could be comfortable with. In any case, by the end of the first year, there were no more suggestions of a return to Concord.

Besides the help for the household and grounds, she had five regular metaphysical workers at Chestnut Hill. She had, on many occasions beginning at the time of the Woodbury suit, had metaphysical help in the form of "watchers" to pray during the night hours. Now, at Chestnut Hill, she had a regular night watch, and these workers were Laura Sargent, Ella Hoag, Irving Tomlinson, Adam Dickey, and William Rathvon. Hoag's husband was not a Christian Scientist, and during 1909, Mrs. Hoag felt she must return to be with her husband in Toledo. She was replaced in the house by Rathvon's wife. This was the group, along with Calvin Frye, who remained with Mrs. Eddy until her passing and whose memoirs give a many-sided picture to the final years.

During 1908, Mrs. Eddy issued several statements that indicated not only the strength and recognition Christian Science had achieved, but also her desire to avoid unnecessary controversy with others. She asked McLellan not to publish any more statistics on the decrease of membership in other churches:

> It is not complimentary to them and it may be offen-

> sive.... "As ye would that others do unto you do ye." Praise the Catholic Churches for all that is praiseworthy and speak lovingly of the Christian Psychologists on the basis of loving our enemies. *Love* is all that can overcome hate - use it wisely as the antidote for sin as well as sickness in your editorials.[6]

The former Methodist minister and then Christian Science practitioner Severin Simonsen wrote to her that Yale University would include Christian Science in a new course at its Divinity School on "Christian and Current Day Views." He said that her works, "together with those of Emerson, Huxley, Maeterlinck and Felix Adler will be studied next year." She approved of this inclusion, even though she realized that she could not expect it to be "taught" in the same sense a Christian Scientist would teach it. She instructed her secretary to "Write for me my thanks for the glorious contents...."[7]

She also had her secretary instruct Alfred Farlow to "say in all your articles where the occasion demands it, that she loves the Protestants, the Catholics and the Christian Psychologists, and would not harm any of them knowingly."[8]

At the end of the year she contributed $500 to the Newton-Wellesley Hospital, along with a cordial letter saying that she trusted "you will be successful in wiping out the debt on the Hospital entirely."[9] None of these actions indicated any change of heart regarding the usefulness or uniqueness of Christian Science. What they did represent was Mrs. Eddy's vision that her movement had reached a threshold of recognition from which, it might be hoped, it could deal more generously – and reciprocally – with religious systems that had opposed it. Her relocation near a large city that had major religious and medical institutions may have tangentially affected her thinking on these matters, but more important was her recognition that Christian Science and its students would be dealing increasingly with the entire world and all its forms of thought.

❖ ❖ ❖ ❖

The major project that Mrs. Eddy undertook, beginning in the summer of 1908, had been on her mind for many years. Exactly when she decided to have a daily newspaper is uncertain; her treatment by some of the New York press during the Next Friends Suit may have been the final sign to her that Christian Scientists could not rely on the press for fair treatment. But her motive in starting *The Christian Science Monitor* later that year went far beyond one of self-defense. It arose largely from her own expanding sense of the mission of Christian Science in the world at large. In her textbook, she had written:

> To-day the healing power of Truth is widely demonstrated as an immanent, eternal Science, instead of a phenomenal exhibition.... Now, as then, signs and wonders are wrought in the metaphysical healing of physical disease; but these signs are only to demonstrate its divine origin, — to attest the reality of the higher mission of the Christ-power to take away the sins of the world.[10]

In a conversation she had had with a young woman in Boston in the early 1880s, at least twenty-five years before this, she had agreed that Christian Science must be applied to all the social ills of society. She had also indicated her belief that Christian Science needed to become established first as a metaphysical system for the healing of individual ills and that the other areas in which its power was available would follow.

Mrs. Eddy had always tried to use the Christian Science periodicals as efficiently as possible to communicate with her movement. When she started *The Christian Science Journal* in 1883, she wrote, "An organ from the Christian Scientists has become a necessity." When she edited this passage for inclusion in her compendium of early *Journal* writings, *Miscellaneous Writings,* in 1896, she changed the word "organ" to "newspaper." She may have felt this more precisely explained what she had hoped to accomplish with the *Journal;* it may also have been an unconscious signaling of the kind of publication she still had in mind for the future.

In 1898, as we have seen, she began a weekly publication, soon named the *Christian Science Sentinel.* This included numerous news items. Erwin Canham, editor of the *Monitor* from the late 1930s until 1964, noted in his history of the first fifty years of the *Monitor,* written in 1958, that three of the fourteen columns in the first issue of the *Sentinel* were given over to news items.

There were other indications that a newspaper had been in Mrs. Eddy's thought for a good while before the Next Friends Suit. Just before the turn of the century, a group of Christian Scientists presented a plan for buying control of one of the leading Boston newspapers. Mrs. Eddy rejected that particular plan, but a few years later, in 1902, after Archibald McLellan had come to Boston to edit the religious periodicals, she wrote to Mr. and Mrs. Kimball, "Until I start a widespread press we should have in Boston a born editor." [11]

In the years since the turn of the century, Mrs. Eddy's opinions had been sought on many public issues. At the time of the Russo-Japanese War in 1904-05, she had contributed a piece for the *Boston Globe*, part of which reads:

> The Principle of all power is God, and God is Love. Whatever brings into human thought or action an element opposed to Love, is never requisite, never a necessity, and is not sanctioned by the law of God, the law of Love. [12]

In the summer of 1905, she requested the members of her church to pray for an equitable settlement. When a peace treaty was negotiated in nearby Portsmouth, New Hampshire, with the help of President Theodore Roosevelt, the *Globe* again solicited her comments. Moreover, in the course of the interviews she gave during the period of the Next Friends Suit (the summer of 1907), some of the newspaper reporters were amazed at her interest in and knowledge of world affairs.

From her childhood days in the farmhouse, when she had overheard her father conversing with visitors regarding public events, she had never been far from a concern for the social and political environment in which the individual works out his or her own life. Her mission, particularly as she defined it in the years after 1866, had kept her focused on what she had to do in life. But she was an avid and fast reader, and over the years, annotated many of the magazines that she read.

Now, as she looked over the needs of her movement, she saw the time was right for Christian Scientists to look farther afield when they used that word "healing." In the textbook, she had written, "Mortals must emerge from this notion of material life as all-in-all. They must peck open their shells with Christian Science, and look outward and upward."[13] Part of this looking outward must now encompass a world beyond that of personal concern.

Just a few months after moving to Chestnut Hill, she drafted her first letter on the subject, but did not send it. In it she said, "The time has come when we must have a daily paper entitled Christian Science Monitor. Allow no hesitation or delay on this movement.... When I proposed having the weekly Sentinel students held back at first; they may hold back this time but I in the name of God direct you to do this. Answer me immediately."[14]

Mrs. Eddy did not want to proceed with definite plans until the new Publishing House had been paid for. On July 28, she wrote to the directors, "So soon as the Pub. House debt is paid I request the C.S. Board of Directors to start a daily newspaper called *Christian Science Monitor.* This must be *done* without fail." Less than two weeks later, she wrote to the trustees of the Publishing Society to get started at once. "The Cause demands that it be issued now."[15]

The details of the *Monitor's* start are as remarkable as the building of the original Mother Church edifice. In a little more than three months, apartments had to be torn down, wooden piles driven into the tidal marshland of Back Bay to support printing presses that had not even been ordered, a building constructed to house the operation, and over one hundred employees hired. All this, plus developing an editorial concept for the paper! Mrs. Eddy did not involve herself in the details. By this time, she had experienced men in all the key positions and had worked with many of them for nearly two decades. And they were convinced from past experience that if she said it could be done, it was only up to them to do it.

On one major detail there was quibbling. Many, if not most, of those who were preparing the paper felt it better to leave out the name "Christian Science." Many of these same individuals had wanted a paper with the idealism of Christian Science, the absence of sensationalism and overreporting of crime, and an emphasis on those developments that constituted progress in society. But they felt that a paper that bannered the name of their religion would drastically curtail its circulation prospects.

William R. Rathvon, who was one of Mrs. Eddy's corresponding secretaries at Chestnut Hill, wrote later:

> The Editor, the Manager, the entire force hoped until the last moment that the repeated efforts made to have our Leader share their viewpoint would be successful, but they might as well have hoped that the sun would shine at midnight. Mrs. Eddy was the one person in all the world who knew that the words "Christian Science" at the head of that paper would not only aid its mission as a journal, but would in time add luster in the minds of men to the religion it stood for.[16]

The newspaper and its name were not a fortunate afterthought that Mrs. Eddy had. She said on several occasions, using not exactly the same words, but language similar in thought, that establishing the *Monitor* was the single most important thing she had done next to writing the textbook. The *Monitor* did not achieve immediate greatness, although she lived to see and judge its material and presentation for two years. Her enthusiasm for it demonstrated an almost prophetic foresight that this reaching out to the world through an attempt to report on the entire human condition would be a link to the rest of humanity long before the religion itself would be.

Although she hoped the newspaper would be read in homes that were not yet interested in Christian Science *per se,* she hoped and expected first of all that Christian Scientists would subscribe for and read it. The *Monitor* supplied the application to the immediate situation of Christian thinking in its broadest sense – both its morality and its message of eternal hope – that one might get from the best of sermonizing in the other churches. The Lesson-Sermon as read in Christian Science churches on Sunday laid the metaphysical base for the individual's thinking, but it could not, by the nature of its source, address contemporary issues with specificity. Thus, the *Monitor* was destined to round out the individual Christian Scientist's practice by engaging his thinking with the issues of society.

Mrs. Eddy wrote a short editorial for the first edition of the *Monitor* on November 25, 1908. In it, she gave as its purpose "to injure no man, but to bless all mankind." She also said that the paper was meant "to spread undivided the Science that operates unspent." She did not give many specific instructions regarding the paper. In the spring of 1909, she did suggest that there be less reporting of automobile accidents, giving as one reason "not to make those who have interest in the automobiles our enemies." [17] She also told McLellan, "I perceive distinctly in divine Science the harm this booming [of] Boston in our Monitor is doing the Christian Science Church, in New York and other places, but especially in New York." [18] From the start, she conceived of the paper as a medium for all Christian Scientists, not just those living in Boston.

When the paper started, she had chosen an Englishman, Frederick Dixon, to head its editorial page. He had substantial intellectual credentials, but she decided it was better to have him heading up the Committee on Publication in England, and he returned home in April 1909. (He was later called back, in 1914, to become the editor.) Until that time, the editorials had frequently mentioned some aspect of Christian Science. In his book on the *Monitor,* Erwin Canham writes that, although there is no written record to explain the change, no more of what might be called denominational editorials appeared after April 23, 1909. This almost surely coincides with the departure of Dixon from the page. Although the *Monitor* from its start has had a daily metaphysical article written from the viewpoint of Christian Science, it has, other than those first few months, tended to keep frequent overt references to Christian Science out of its news and editorials. From the change in 1909, one must assume that this is the way Mrs. Eddy wanted it to be.

An article in the *Sentinel* a few weeks after the *Monitor*'s appearing expressed Mrs. Eddy's purpose for the paper. It contained a conviction that, if maintained in practice, would bring the application of scientific Christianity to the threshold of every phase of the human condition needing healing. It was written by Helen Nixon, wife of one of Mrs. Eddy's early publishers. In it, Mrs. Nixon wrote that the newspaper lifted "one's eyes to an horizon far beyond one's own doorstep… Things we did not like to look at nor think of, problems we did not feel able to cope with, must now be faced manfully, and correct thinking concerning the world's doings cultivated and maintained."[19]

❖ ❖ ❖ ❖

Mrs. Eddy was about to face "manfully" the problem she had already, in one way or another, been coping with for twenty-five years: Augusta Stetson. Since the time Mrs. Eddy first sent Stetson to New York to help establish Christian Science there, she had been both a problem and a promise for Mrs. Eddy. Her success as a healer, combined with her ability to speak well in public and her flamboyant style, had contributed to the growth of the movement in New York. But "Gussie" Stetson was hard on the other teachers in that field; she regarded them as unfriendly competitors. Over the years, Mrs. Eddy had had complaints from others in New York about Stetson. Sitting in her study at Pleasant View, she had not been immune from attempts to influence her opinion regarding one student or another. But she had the advantage of often hearing the same story from several sources. With her insight, which she regarded as coming from her frequent communion with God in long hours of prayer, she would, in short order, sort out the false information from the true. For almost twenty years, her letters to Stetson were a combination of praise for her work in helping the movement grow and pleas for her student to grow in grace and selflessness. The pleas were often stern reprimands, and Stetson respected Mrs. Eddy enough to accept, at least superficially, her correcting.

In the period leading up to 1908, however, Stetson's personal ambitions finally got the better of her. She built a large church edifice in New York – actually the second major edifice that First Church had built – at 96th and Central Park West. In it she had twenty-five practitioners' rooms, and there she met daily with these practitioners – her pupils – and counseled them. This kind of personal control had no precedent from Mrs. Eddy and no place in the kind of prayerful individual work of a practitioner. Stetson had also introduced an emphasis on material success into Christian Science that was foreign to its metaphysics. While Mrs. Eddy looked on poverty as something to be overcome as much as any other individual ill, she did not consider an abundance of material possessions or other signs of material success to have any necessary connection with the demonstration of spiritual qualities. Just as Puritan thinking in its day had been secularized, and latter-day Puritans had sometimes looked on material success as a present sign of one's election for salvation, Stetson seems to have been influenced by the materialism of the Gilded Age and the opulence of New York City itself.

In addition to this, Stetson began implying that she had a special relationship with Mrs. Eddy, both in a business and a spiritual sense. In 1906, she had written to Mrs. Eddy, "If I thought there would come an hour when I could not hear you, mentally, or see you through the veil of flesh, as spiritual substance, idea, I could not press forward..." [20] Mrs. Eddy recognized this apparent idolization of her as akin to a belief in spiritualism, and in one of her strong letters, she wrote to Stetson, "You are never safely guided by personality, your own or anyone else's. I am not your guardian spirit here, and I shall not be hereafter." [21]

The week after the launching of *The Christian Science Monitor,* the *New York American* ran a story about a new Christian Science church to be built in New York. It was to rival The Mother Church in size and was described, whether accurately or not, as being a branch of First Church, New York. Thus began the final struggle with Stetson, which was to occupy most of 1909.

The next week, the *Sentinel* published two editorials, one making it clear that only The Mother Church had branches and that one branch did not control another, the other reaffirming Mrs. Eddy's concept that Christian Science should avoid ostentation in the way it presented itself to the public. Then Mrs. Eddy invited Stetson to come to Chestnut Hill to see her. This was their first meeting in more than two years, Stetson's first view of Chestnut Hill, and her last visit with Mrs. Eddy. Gussie played the role of the humble student in what was superficially a meeting of longtime friends. Mrs. Eddy called her back as she was leaving, and Stetson knelt at her feet. She had agreed to pull back on the plans for the new church in New York, which she said, in any case, she had not intended as a branch of her own church. The immediate issue seemed to be taken care of.

There it might have ended. But Mrs. Eddy had a dilemma. She was undoubtedly uncomfortable with the peripheral lines of thought in Stetson's teaching that diverged from pure Christian Science. Moreover, there had been speculation from time to time during the decade about who would succeed Mrs.

Eddy at her passing. Mrs. Eddy had finally laid this to rest by stating that there would be no personal successor. It was clearly her intention that the Board of Directors, acting under the authority of the *Manual,* would govern the affairs of her church. But her own discernment must have made her aware that Stetson, with a large, loyal, and wealthy following in the nation's largest city, represented a potential breakaway threat that, if followed by other ambitious people in the movement, could fracture it within months of her passing. The warning that she had been given by the aborted plans to build a major edifice in New York kept her on the alert.

Two events in the summer of 1909 brought the matter to a head. Some of the New York practitioners gave Mrs. Stetson a gift of gold along with an idolatrous letter; one of them spoke of their being "members of your body," in an obvious comparison of her to Christ Jesus. Stetson may have thought she was exercising sound judgment in sending the gold pieces on to Mrs. Eddy and telling her that they really belonged to her. But Mrs. Eddy caught the sense of idolatry and worship of human personality that had apparently escaped Stetson. She wrote to her in straight language:

> You are aware that animal magnetism is the opposite of divine Science, and that this opponent is the means whereby the conflict against Truth is engendered and developed. Beloved! You need to watch and pray that the enemy of God cannot separate you from your Leader and best earthly friend.[22]

The other event that happened almost simultaneously was the uncovering of what Stetson had actually been doing at her daily meetings with the practitioners. Virgil Strickler was First Reader of First Church, New York. Although he was not a Stetson pupil, he was allowed to attend her meetings. Strickler was so shocked by what he heard that he began keeping a diary, and finally, in July 1909, he came up to Boston to tell the directors about it. Strickler had become convinced that Stetson had become a moral idiot. He found that she was entirely normal in dealing with everyday affairs, except in the case of those persons who got in the way of her ambitions:

> I do not know by what name alienists designate the form of insanity which causes a person to desire to kill everyone against whom they have a grievance. I think it is paranoia… She works for hours every day to destroy by the use of mental weapons the persons against whom she has real or fancied grievances.[23]

The same day he had noted in his diary her comment, "I strike to kill." She appeared to be determined to do no less than destroy the other teachers in New York as well as the five directors in Boston. Strickler's revelations to the directors were at first only partial, but they set in motion a chain of events. At one point, Mrs. Eddy went through one of her painful attacks of kidney stones and had to have morphine administered. She then asked the directors to leave the matter alone, to let Stetson's own church in New York discipline her. But as it became clear how vicious Stetson's plans had been and the degree to which she had been malpracticing, the directors had no choice but to remove her name from the *Journal* as a teacher and practitioner. Later in the fall, after a three-day hearing in Boston, they also excommunicated her from The Mother Church.

It was not a joyful victory for Mrs. Eddy. Like the changes in command she had made when she removed Judge Hanna as editor of the periodicals in 1902, or ended Kimball's period of teaching the Board of Education classes after 1903, she did whatever was necessary in her eyes to forward her movement. But unlike those changes, which involved students who remained completely loyal to her direction, she was dealing here with someone who would almost surely have fought for control of the movement after her death and negated the almost twenty years of work that had gone into building the organization provided for in the *Church Manual.* Because Stetson had figured so prominently both in the start and the growth of the movement in New York, the situation was a particularly sensitive and challenging one for Mrs. Eddy to deal with. But in the end, the procedures she had built into the *Manual* handled the challenge successfully.

It is ironic that Augusta Stetson looms as large as she does in these last years of Mrs. Eddy's life, when other faithful female workers such as Annie Knott, who first studied with Mrs. Eddy in 1887, was one of the first Christian Science lecturers, was associate editor of the religious periodicals from 1904 to 1919 and then a director of The Mother Church from that year until 1934, or Julia Bartlett, who went through class with Mrs. Eddy in 1880 and continued to practice and teach until her passing in 1924, may be less generally known. Stetson remained a figure in New York until the late 1920s, maintaining that Mrs. Eddy had led her to a new phase of Christian Science in which there was only spiritual organization. But the branch church that she had controlled escaped from her clutches at the end of 1909 when Mrs. Eddy wrote to its members, urging them to unite behind the Board of Directors in Boston.

❖ ❖ ❖ ❖

The Stetson drama had been the predominant event of the latter half of 1909, just as Mrs. Eddy's establishment of the *Monitor* had been the major event of 1908. As the year 1909 came to an end, Mrs. Eddy said somewhat enigmatically to her household staff on Christmas Day, "By another Christmas there will be great changes. See that you make them for the better."[24] She had had several physical challenges since moving to Chestnut Hill, but always surprised even her own metaphysical workers with her quick rebounds. It was clear to them, at the same time, that she was looking ahead to a time when she would no longer be with them. She was eating less. She dictated fewer letters to her secretaries, with more of the church work going directly to the directors in Boston. In the spring of 1908, she had thanked Alfred Farlow for some pudding his mother had made, but added, "I did not relish it as I should because it was so fine. Tell her not to trouble herself over me. I have an experience all my own and no one else can enter into it."[25]

As the Discoverer of the Science that promised ultimate freedom from all the beliefs of the flesh, she realized and often said that she had demonstrated only a little of it herself. At one morning meeting with her household, she questioned them as to whether anyone understood all of Christian Science. One of the workers replied that only Mrs. Eddy did, to which she in turn replied that she had so far learned only the ABCs of Christian Science. Her aim was undoubtedly to impress on them the vastness of the spiritual universe they were just beginning to glimpse in their practice. As for her own stage of experience, she felt a strong need to make a continual and convincing demonstration of the presence of Life, God, even as she recognized the approach of the transitional experience that mortals call death. She had already made this demonstration to an amazing degree, when one considers her advanced age, her written works, the size of the movement she had set in motion, and the myriad kinds of misunderstanding and opposition she had encountered and overcome in the more than four decades since 1866. But she worked on until the end.

Several times during the Chestnut Hill years she made inquiries as to whether she could change the title of *Science and Health with Key to the Scriptures* by removing the word "with." She considered the entire book, not just the last three chapters, to be the key to the Scriptures. Apparently finding that this could not be done without affecting the copyright, she gave up on the attempt.

Finally, in the spring of 1910, she arrived at a compromise for translating the textbook into foreign languages: running the English text on alternate pages. It was Helmut von Moltke himself who came to Boston to suggest this course of action in March 1910. (It had also been suggested by Lewis Strang after a trip to German-speaking Europe in the autumn of 1909.) This allowed her to give the go-ahead for the first translation into German, which was completed in two years.

There were abundant signs of Mrs. Eddy's looking ahead during these three years in Chestnut Hill. Beyond the statement that she was having "an experience all my own," she addressed her groundskeeper, Adolph Stevenson, in ascetic language:

> ...no garden or flowers shall be cultivated on my place. Make no road for me to see such things on this place; the road to Heaven is not one of flowers, but it is strait and narrow, it is bearing the cross and turning away from things that lure the material senses, denying them and finding all in Spirit, in God, in good and doing good.[26]

In August 1908, she had instructed McLellan to go to Mount Auburn Cemetery in Cambridge, surely the Elysium of cemeteries in the Boston area, and buy "a beautiful burying lot for one. No one in particular. There is no death; Life is everlasting. The evidence of the material senses is not the reality of life. Keep this as private as possible."[27] He apparently did not follow through on this order, as Rathvon in his memoirs tells of picking out a lot at Mount Auburn in the days following her passing. In the same month, she commented that she was less active than she had been when she came to Chestnut Hill: "Then I went all over my house up and down stairs."[28] Later that year, she closed the Mother's Room in the original edifice of The Mother Church. (This was a room that had been furnished especially for her if she was to visit the church, and had become an object of curiosity for visitors to the building.) A few months later, when she was having a difficult physical challenge, she wrote a "To whom it may concern" note, turning over the custody of all her scrapbooks and private papers to McLellan.[29]

Even during periods when she must have considered her individual demonstration of life as her first imperative, she rose to the occasion when the occasion demanded it. She had found her personal secretary, Calvin Frye, unimaginative and probably uninspiring to work with, but like an old glove, he fitted her requirements for the many tasks he performed. One evening, just two weeks before the first edition of the *Monitor* was to come out, Adam Dickey and Irving Tomlinson found him, apparently lifeless, in his room. When Mrs. Eddy sensed some disturbance in the house and was told what had happened, she asked that he be carried to her. She had already retired for the night. Frye was brought in to her room on a small rocker. Tomlinson described in his diary how Mrs. Eddy took charge:

> With the voice of authority Mrs. Eddy commanded Mr. Frye to rouse himself, to awaken from his false dream. At the spoken word he gave evidence of life, partly opened his eyes and slightly moved his head. On further urging he muttered the words: "Leave me alone."

Tomlinson described how Mrs. Eddy then argued down all his half-conscious arguments, including that Foster-Eddy could take his place in the household. At the end of the treatment, Frye was able to get up and walk unaided to his room. Tomlinson concluded:

> [Mrs. Eddy] spoke in strong clear tones, raised herself upon her elbow and firmly grasped his hand. There was no fear, no doubt, no discouragement; only absolute confidence, perfect assurance in the victory of truth. Mrs. Eddy was in no way shocked at his appearance. She handled the case as composedly and as serenely as that of a toothache. [30]

Mrs. Eddy never gave any sign that she feared the passage of death. In the textbook she had written:

> The relinquishment of all faith in death and also of the fear of its sting would raise the standard of health and morals far beyond its present elevation, and would enable us to hold the banner of Christianity aloft with unflinching faith in God, in Life eternal. [31]

But apparently, she also never felt that her work in firmly establishing the Christian Science movement was entirely finished. In the fall of 1909, she wrote that "the world still needs me here on earth." [32] Since coming back to Boston, she had seen how far other institutions had also progressed during the two decades of her absence. Almost across the street from her house, the Jesuits were building Boston College. Boston was becoming a major medical center. The United States, by virtue of its continental land mass, natural resources, free institutions, and, at that time, an immense increase in annual immigration, was on the verge of becoming a major world power. At the same time, the modes of thought and expression that had dominated humankind since the Enlightenment were breaking up. The Einstein revolution in physics had not yet burst on human thought; his first paper on relativity had been published only in 1905. Freud and the other psychologists were exploring the depths of the human mind, and for many, their systems of thought would soon offer an alternative to a religious model. In the arts, painting was about to splinter in many directions, just as twentieth- century musical form would.

While Mrs. Eddy could not know what had not yet happened, she had sensed a breaking up of the old model of the universe and of human behavior. In fact, if the question had been put to her, she would have replied that Christian Science was the new model, the correct model for both the universe and human morality. She would not have feared the breakup of old beliefs, although she did know it would be a disconcerting period for those who did not have the Christian hope and assurance of the spiritual model. In the textbook she had written:

> Mortal error will vanish in a moral chemicalization. This mental fermentation has begun, and will continue until all errors of belief yield to understanding. Belief is changeable, but spiritual understanding is changeless. [33]

There was her constant reminder of the need to practice a full Christianity in Christian Science, that is, to cultivate the whole category of traditional Christian virtues of love, hope, patience, selflessness, and so on, as well as to rely increasingly on the reality of Spirit in daily life. She also wondered, not whether Christian Science could meet the demands of the changing times, but whether her church and Christian Scientists were mature enough in both the spirit and the letter to meet the demands of the new century. Both of these concerns are seen in some of the articles that appeared in the religious periodicals during her last years. In a short article for the *Sentinel* in August 1909, A. C. Dickey wrote about a trip across the prairie in midwinter to visit a patient. The boy driving the sleigh never took his eye from the road, knowing that one false move in the snowbound landscape might upset the sleigh. Applying this metaphor of watching to the work of a Christian Scientist, Dickey continued:

> Then the thought came to me how apt we are as Christian Scientists to feel ourselves well ensconced in the background, with no particular responsibility, – this great Christian Science movement going right along through storm and stress, and we never realizing what it means to our Leader, Mrs. Eddy, who is constantly watching the road, and who has so faithfully and silently kept the watch. [34]

She had almost daily chats with the practitioners who were helping her in her Chestnut Hill household, and in one of these morning sessions at about the same time, Rathvon recorded these admonitions: "I want a revival in your religion. Turn your thoughts away from materiality. Live each hour as though it was to be your last and watch always." [35]

Mrs. Eddy also marked with approval an article by Clarence Chadwick in a December 1908 *Sentinel*, entitled "The Need of Mental Activity." It included these statements:

> The true disciple knows only too well that there is a cross to be carried, and that this means greater mental

> activity on his part. It never means mental stagnation, apathy, or indifference. It means alertness, watchfulness, and earnest striving to express the Mind of Christ and to put off the so-called mind of mortals, which ever argues for the reality of all that is unlike God.... The human mind has a positive need of being aroused to a higher order of thinking before it can escape from the bondage of false belief, which denies the all-power and presence of Spirit. In the realm of spiritual sense and activity there is no laziness, no idleness, no dreaming, no guessing.[36]

As one final example of where Mrs. Eddy's thought was tending, she dictated a short article, a few months before her passing, entitled "Principle and Practice." It was a simple plea for growth in understanding of the Principle of Christian Science, instead of passive acceptance or mere belief in its metaphysics. She recognized that some part of what was occurring as Christian Science healing was little more than human faith on the part of the patient. It continued:

> In this very manner some students of Christian Science have accepted, through faith, a divine Principle, God, as their savior, but they have not understood this Principle sufficiently well to fulfill the Scriptural command, "Go ye into all the world, and preach the gospel." "Heal the sick."
>
> ... Christian Science is not a faith-cure, and unless human faith be distinguished from scientific healing, Christian Science will again be lost from the practice of religion as it was soon after the period of our great Master's scientific teaching and practice.[37]

One night just a few months before her passing, Irving Tomlinson was serving watch as practitioner. On coming near her room, he heard her speaking. He listened and realized she was deep in audible prayer. He was so impressed by the simplicity, unselfishness, and orderliness of her statements that he put the following entry in his diary the next morning:

> The entire petition was scientific, orderly in its procedure, choice in language. It contained no request for a special blessing for health, comfort, or prosperity for herself or her Cause, but was a beautiful declaration of Truth for a full realization of truth of being for herself and for her followers and for all mankind. The entire prayer was in accord with her characteristic phrasing and breathed the profound faith shown in her most spiritual writings. She would voice her inmost desire for a realization of God's presence and power and follow it with a declaration that that presence and power was an eternal manifestation and fully realized by His children. She would petition that no temptation could assail; and follow by the declaration that the real man was free from temptation. She affirmed that there was no lack in God's promises for His offspring and asserted that this truth was realized by all. The prayer had introduction, progress and conclusion. The language was chaste and well chosen. Spoke of God's presence hourly and momentarily and asked that we might know that there was "no rift in the rhythm of the eternal harmony." …The prayer which I heard brought to my consciousness the truth that real prayer is the very heart and soul of C.S. its founding, its growth and its fruits.[38]

In the final months of 1910, Mrs. Eddy took several other steps that, together, indicate her belief that she would not be here much longer. She wrote, in July 1910, an almost sentimental letter to Captain Eastaman, who, at one time, had worked for her as a practitioner and who had been an early member of the Board of Directors:

> My Dear Old Friend: Old things are better than new, if they preserve their luster, comliness and durability,

> as you seem to have done in relation to me. Allow me to make my courtesy, while [you?] are taking off your hat to shake each other's hands, and be honest with each other's hearts. God bless you; goodbye, Longingly yours.[39]

She also wrote to Mary Beecher Longyear, a Christian Scientist who had moved to Boston from the Middle West and stood ready to use her vast fortune to help the cause of Christian Science in any way she could, "Allow me to wish you long years life perfect and immortal. May God crown your years with blessings."[40]

While more and more of the business relating to branch churches and practitioners had been coming directly to The Mother Church, at the end of September, Mrs. Eddy directed that all church business should now go directly to Boston and none to her secretaries.

Finally, on the 28th of November, she dictated a short statement to Laura Sargent and signed it: "It took a combination of sinners that was fast to harm me."[41] A few days later, she developed the cold that kept her from her ride the last two days of her life. On December 1, as she was taking her last drive, and apparently seeing the end, she commented to Laura Sargent, "Oh, if the students had only done what I told them, I should have lived and carried the cause."[42] The concern of a mother to protect, to watch over her offspring had never stopped being her first concern. Coming in from the drive, she was faint. On being somewhat revived, she wrote with an unsteady hand on a tablet, "God is my Life." On the day of her passing, December 3, she said to Ella Rathvon, another of the mental workers and Rathvon's wife, "I have all in divine Love that is all I need."[43] The last two days she had kept largely to herself, her helpers realizing that she was working out another step in her experience, alone with God, who would never fail her. Late on Saturday evening, December 3, she slipped away so quietly that those who were with her were not sure when she had gone.

Return to Boston

Mrs. Eddy had been deeply concerned that she had had to use painkillers a few times in her last decade. The peaceful manner of her passing, however, was such that some of the workers at Chestnut Hill felt they had been given a new insight into life. Four days later, Rathvon noted in his diary, "From the very first there has not been the slightest sense of death present with me or, so far as I can see, with the rest of the household either." [44] Years later he amplified his feelings about that hour:

> Every member of her devoted household was deeply conscious that a tremendous change had just taken place, a change that would stir the world to its depths and place upon us, one and all, the necessity of undivided allegiance and reliance upon God now that our beloved mentor and guide had been promoted. All went about their usual tasks soberly and seriously but not despondently or dejectedly. [45]

The position that Mrs. Eddy and her flourishing movement had achieved during the first decade of this century was shown by the amount of press coverage given to her at the time of her passing and the tone of the obituaries that newspapers across the country carried. Many of them still showed an ignorance of Christian Science, but there was overwhelming recognition for the example given by Christian Scientists in their local communities and for the selflessness of Mrs. Eddy's life. As for the manner of her passing, *Goodwin's Weekly* in Salt Lake City commented:

> She lived here on earth twenty years beyond man's allotted time, then, unafraid, and with faculties undimmed, without a sigh, sank peacefully into her final sleep. The impression she leaves is perhaps the most profound that any mortal, putting on immortality, has left in this age. [46]

Because her death had occurred late on a Saturday evening, the Sunday papers did not have the story. It was announced first by Judge Smith, who was then the First Reader at The

Mother Church, as he closed the Sunday morning service. He read from a statement Mrs. Eddy had made in 1891 after she had retired to New Hampshire. In it she referred to the fact that her students must not expect to find her in "my accustomed place with you" any longer. Then she had added, "You can well afford to give me up, since you have in my last revised edition of *Science and Health* your teacher and guide." Smith continued, "Although these lines were written years ago, they are true to-day, and will continue to be true. But it has now become my duty to announce that Mrs. Eddy passed from our sight last night at 10:45 o'clock, at her home in Chestnut Hill."[47]

What her life had meant would continue to be debated. But in reading to her followers her statement from 1891, Smith had turned their thought, as she most certainly would have done, from her personality to the book that was the centerpiece of her life as a Christian Scientist – the book of which she remained both author and student.

Epilogue

The world's great leaders, somewhat like large ships plying the deep waters, leave a wake behind them. As the wake broadens, it also becomes weaker, mixing with the other currents around it. In the case of political figures, the effects may be felt for generations – or, with a change in circumstances, they may be short-lived. Napoleon's plan for French hegemony in Europe ended with his defeat at Waterloo. On the other hand, the Napoleonic Code and other changes he introduced into French domestic society set the tone for the France of the next two centuries.

To the extent that Mary Baker Eddy introduced a radically new element into Christianity – the absolute supremacy of Spirit, one of her definitions of God, and its corollary of the impotence of matter – she broke with the mainstream of the major branches of Christianity. Few sentences in the Christian Science textbook sum up the major thrust of her work more than these: "For right reasoning there should be but one fact before the thought, namely, spiritual existence."[1] And, "The central fact of the Bible is the superiority of spiritual over physical power."[2] In referring to the spiritual sense of being as the birth of a "new-old" idea, she was identifying what to her was the most important element of Christianity as one that had been present from the beginning, but had lain dormant in the Bible until her discovery.

In her emphasis on the majesty of God and the need to turn to God for her daily guidance, she remained true to her family heritage of Calvinism. In her emphasis on the individual's responsibility to work out his or her own salvation, she clearly was identifying Christian Science with Protestantism. But that salvation for her included a growing sense of dominion over the material senses. Physical healing was one evidence in human experience of that dominion.

Perhaps her narrative speaks for itself. In connecting the

events and laying out a chronology of her life, however, there seemed to be no appropriate place to pause and sum up. In most individuals' later years, when they are in retirement, they may look back and try to assess what they have accomplished. This was not the case with Mrs. Eddy. Her years of discovery, of honing both her teaching method and her written exposition of Christian Science, were followed by the twenty years in Pleasant View and Chestnut Hill during which she worked out the details of her church's organization. The movement she had begun entered into a phase of phenomenal growth during the last decade of her life, giving her new challenges, some pleasant and some, such as the Next Friends Suit and dealing with Augusta Stetson, decidedly unpleasant. She did take time in informal sessions with the members of her household, especially in the three years at Chestnut Hill, to talk a little about her earlier days. But this was usually with the purpose of giving them some particular advice or lesson. She never looked back to make an overall assessment, and had she been pressed, she most likely would have responded that that assessment was being made daily in the growth of Christian Science.

If one does pause and look back on Mrs. Eddy's accomplishments, at least two elements call for brief consideration. The first is the degree to which Mrs. Eddy's leadership - and, in particular, her total commitment to what she identified as her mission in life – accounts for the success of Christian Science within her own lifetime. The second element is more problematic, in that it has a more speculative conclusion. How Mrs. Eddy comes to be regarded sometime even farther into the future than the point at which we stand today will inevitably be linked with how Christian Science itself is regarded. Nevertheless, the criteria for judging the success of this religion a century later is more complex than one might suspect. Like the ship that has left its wake behind, that wake has widened through its interaction with other forms of thought and practice. In a relative sense, it can be said that it has also weakened, as the entire ocean of thought has been overwhelmed by other ships ploughing their way through the seas of a post-Newtonian physical world and an ever more eclectic religious world.

❖ ❖ ❖ ❖

Mrs. Eddy's sense of mission and her own spirituality certainly explain much of the reason for the success of Christian Science during her lifetime. After the appropriate and often sincere remarks were made about her at the time of her passing, it was frequently said that, without her presence, Christian Science would quickly fade. This was clearly an incorrect prophecy on the part of those who made it. Judged by numbers alone, Christian Science enjoyed phenomenal growth for at least a generation after 1910. Judged by its impact on the other branches of Christianity and on the other healing professions, one's conclusion would have to be more subjective. Whatever the conclusion, the mark left by Mrs. Eddy certainly widened and continued to deepen for some decades.

Yet the groundwork for much of that widening had already been laid by Mrs. Eddy. Although she appeared to the public at large as living in retirement for the last two decades of her life, the narrative shows how she continued to think about ways to protect her teaching and promote it through the various organs she established within The Mother Church and the Publishing Society. Her leadership during these decades was not through a personal presence or through preaching or even teaching, as it had been in the 1880s. But through the authority she had gained among her students, she could command their attention and, in most cases, their ready acquiescence with the steps she took toward organizing the Christian Science movement.

Her unflagging commitment – no vacations, no weekend days off, nights often spent praying about problems she saw in the movement – for a period lasting more than four decades has probably been matched by only a handful of other individuals. Most of them were likely either as devoted to a religious goal as she was or engaged in scientific research that was for them equally engrossing. Because of the singular nature of her accomplishments, one might be correct in assuming that she would not have expected the lives of other Christian Scientists to be quite as disciplined or identified with a single purpose as her own. Or can one really make that assumption? She certainly recognized that many, if not most, Christian Scientists, would have secular occupations. The need to earn a living, to care for a family, to carry out some part of the common civic responsibility were all parts of normal life. For it was largely in the arena where human contacts occur that the Christian qualities could be exemplified, where Christian Science would prove its utility.

As part of her Calvinist heritage, Mrs. Eddy had a strong sense of purpose. It was inconceivable to her that a person who seriously undertook the study of Christian Science would not soon learn that he needed to apply it to every aspect of living. The details of her manner of living during the last two decades of a very long life, however, are of less importance than the example she gave of total commitment to an idea and letting that idea carry one as far as it could.

Some of Mrs. Eddy's letters to close students show her concern that they not dilute their commitment to the practice of Christian Science. James Neal, a banker from Nebraska who became a very successful healer at a young age, wrote to her that he was taking piano lessons. She objected that this would interfere with his growth as a practitioner. She would not have given such advice generally, but in the years when the numbers of good healers were limited she would naturally have been concerned that any outside interest might serve as a distraction.

Four centuries before the time of Jesus, Plato had written, "The life that is unexamined is not worth living." The conditions under which people in the industrial democracies live are so different today than they were even at the end of Mrs. Eddy's lifetime that it is as difficult for us to fully understand the culture of that day as it would be for them to understand ours. The general level of wealth, the abundance of leisure-time activities, the availability of travel and the opportunity to personally experience other cultures around the world, the pace of change, the challenge of change in an individual's own career – these are only some of the elements that affect one's outlook differently today.

One factor has not changed, however: the need for commitment, the need that mature people feel for serious purpose in their lives. And from that viewpoint alone, the variety of options available today makes commitment seem more difficult. But, looking at the life of Mary Baker Eddy from the standpoint of seeking guidance in how to live, it is clear that a consideration of her life would recommend seriousness of purpose to one's endeavors. She wrote in her textbook, "The devotion of thought to an honest achievement makes the achievement possible."[3]

❖ ❖ ❖ ❖

Centuries from now, Mrs. Eddy's significance will stand in direct relation to the position of Christian Science as a system of religious thought and healing practice. In the case of a religion, one must first of all consider how to measure that influence. Is it felt in numbers of members or churches? Is it felt in the general changing or leavening of thought in other religions? And in the case of Christian Science, this question would also apply to changes of thought in medical theory and practice.

Mrs. Eddy's thoughts about the future of Christian Science seem somewhat ambivalent, even allowing for the inevitable contextual differences surrounding some of her statements. Looking at the textbook, which contains her most definitive statements, she wrote, "Until the author of this book learned the vastness of Christian Science, the fixedness of mortal illusions, and the human hatred of Truth, she cherished sanguine hopes that Christian Science would meet with immediate and universal acceptance."[4] This generally sober viewpoint is reinforced by a few of the statements she made to her household in the days just before her death. She was concerned until the end about the future of what she had founded. Thinking of Christian Science as her child, as she did, it was perhaps natural for the mother never to feel that the need for nurturing had come to an end.

She was always glad to hear of substantial healings and the impetus they gave to Christian Science. She was heartened by the numbers of people who came to hear Christian Science lectures in the first decade of this century. Edward Kimball, who was probably the most popular lecturer of the day, wrote to her about one town in Indiana where a good portion of the town's elite had turned out to hear him. She wrote with satisfaction about the numbers of new members joining The Mother Church each year. She certainly did not look on her discovery as something for an intellectual or spiritual elite. But knowing the effort it took to be a consistent Christian Scientist, it does not seem likely that she would have expected her church to grow to the proportions Mark Twain had perhaps somewhat sarcastically prophesied ("the dominant religion in America in fifty years").

What, then, of a statement she made that "in the twentieth century every Christian church in our land, and a few in far-off lands, will approximate the understanding of Christian Science sufficiently to heal the sick in his name"?[5] Here the leavening effect must be considered. There are indeed more churches practicing some kind of healing worship today. Most of it is in an attempt to apply Jesus' command to heal the sick and has no conscious connection with the existence of the Christian Science movement. But the fact that Christian Science healing, or at least the claim to it, is a well-known phenomenon, was one major reason for other churches originally giving Jesus' command more attention. There are also some instances of Protestant ministers using the Christian Science textbook, or even the weekly Bible lessons, as the basis for some of their sermons.

In measuring the success, or effect, of Christian Science in the fields of both religion and medicine today, one also has to take into account a century of development in those fields. In religion alone, the field has vastly changed. In the last forty years, the Dead Sea scrolls and the Nag Hammadi texts have opened up new fields of discovery about the time of Jesus and about the Bible texts. Some serious Bible scholars, who are in no way connected with any attempt to discredit the Christian message, now feel certain that some of the foundational events of orthodox Christian dogma, such as the virgin birth and the physical resurrection of Jesus, were not an original part of the Christian message. The Protestant churches, at least in the United States, have moved away from much of their denominational divisiveness. The mainline Protestant churches are being challenged by a surge in fundamentalism. But Protestant fundamentalism has also changed in some of its emphases. Churchgoing today, if one can make a generalization, is less concerned with doctrinal matters and more with giving people a basis for sorting out their complicated lives. None of these changes makes the practice of Christian Science any less viable, but the terrain on which the Christian Science church operates has undergone eruptions akin to a strong earthquake. And that terrain continues to shake.

Some of the change in the other churches can be viewed as an accommodation to the principles of psychology. The "Christian psychology" that concerned Mrs. Eddy briefly in the first decade of this century has been followed by a century of development and widespread public interest in the mind sciences. In the last three decades, a new interest in Oriental religions, particularly Buddhism, has appeared in the Western world. Christianity is increasingly called on to emphasize its universal aspects without weakening its grounding in the historical life experience – and uniqueness – of Christ Jesus.

Christian Scientists are as aware of these changes around them as are most other people. But they have not been as involved in the ongoing evolution of Protestant Christian thought as others, because Christian Science has its own defining statements in *Science and Health.* In the end, even though Christian Science gives a wholeness and meaning to their existence that others find in their particular religious experience, Christian Scientists probably think of themselves as practicing a science as much as a religion. If it is a science, that is, a statement of fixed rules that are applicable everywhere – if spiritual existence is the only question to be considered – then one's main assignment is to get on with practicing it.

Meanwhile, there are all those other ships out on the ocean, each leaving its wake. There are the groups trying to practice Zen Buddhism. There are numerous self-help groups, some with a spiritual orientation, that believe one can make more progress alone or in a small group than in an organized church. The phenomenal growth of Alcoholics Anonymous and its large accomplishments in reforming the lives of alcoholics must be mentioned; AA is not a religion, but in many persons' lives, its organization and meetings serve as a quasi-religion. The success of AA has also spawned the creation of other twelve-step programs. While they may not have the staying power of a major church, they provide some shape and continuity to an individual's attempt to find some structure in his day-to-day existence.

On the medical side, even though there have been gigantic leaps in medical technology, there are also many groups besides Christian Scientists practicing alternative methods of healing – mind/body feedback, meditation, acupuncture, herbal medicine, and homeopathy. Many of these practitioners also offer classes or some method by which individuals find encouragement to continue with what they may have only read about in a book. While psychology as a whole operates on a different premise from revealed religion, one finds in some of the mental methods a reliance, if not on God in the Judeo-Christian sense, on an ultimate basis of being that can be described as a universal, loving intelligence. One finds this, for instance, in two popular books by the New Haven surgeon, Bernie Siegel, *Peace, Love, and Healing,* and *Love, Medicine, and Miracles.*

Measured against this veritable garden of choices, what can one say of Mrs. Eddy's discovery a century later? As for the world of Christian Science itself, in terms of numbers, it has been declining somewhat since the middle of this century. Even while this decline may be continuing, however, Christian Science is spreading to new parts of the globe. Nor is there any evidence of diminution in the ability of Christian Scientists to heal through the healing method taught in Christian Science.

At the same time, we come to the end of a century of materialism, in which much of the rich Western world has become mired in the trivia of materialism – an overconcern with sexual allure and fulfillment, fashion in the home and on one's body, and food and drink. Yet there is without doubt a rediscovery of spirituality. The word does not denote the same experience to everyone who uses it, but there is a greater awareness that life is not defined entirely by the material senses. The opportunities for personal growth – as well as physical healing – that are opened up by spiritual awareness are hopeful signs for the future. In this environment, one may expect some renewed interest in finding out what Mrs. Eddy had to say about spirituality. Since she gave expression to her revelation in an environment in which much less was known about the physical universe and its evolution, today's "discoverers" of Christian Science may need to make a greater mental leap, as it were, onto the spiritual platform from which she envisioned the universe.

Beyond today's interest in spirituality, Christian Science remains grounded in the Bible. To the extent that the Bible means less in human society, the Bible stories will resonate less. To the extent that the factual history of Christ Jesus is questioned by modern research, Christianity as a religion based on a series of historical events could be weakened. But to the extent that the Christian "story" remains as basic historic fact, the spirituality that Mrs. Eddy presented is unique among modern systems of mental healing practice. It is unique in two senses: first, in the link Mrs. Eddy made between the story of Jesus and his works and her healing method; second, in her insistence that the practice of Christian Science as a healing agent cannot be unconnected from the regeneration of human character – from the new birth – that is the basis of Christian experience.

That the basis for this kind of practice remains, in spite of the volcanic eruptions of human thought in this century, one needs to credit Mrs. Eddy for the lifelong nurturing she gave to the statement of Christian Science in the textbook and to her establishment of a church organization to help protect her discovery.

Whether the swells that Christian Science causes on the ocean of thought will still be discernible, or will merge with the current of other searches for spirituality and healing, or will perhaps become even wider, remains for future generations to determine. But one might consider whether Mrs. Eddy did not, in fact, leave more than one wake behind her. The first was the influence of her life and work. The second, the Christian Science textbook itself, could also be considered a ship, whose sails she set, that is still sailing the seas. The textbook is newly discovered by each generation and causes a reaction in that generation comparable to the wake already described. It is always a new book to the individual who has just found it. In that sense, it causes a continuing wake of its own that will not diminish in its significance as long as its message continues to resonate in human hearts.

Footnotes

Writings of Mary Baker Eddy (identified in footnotes only by title):

Science and Health with Key to the Scriptures

(final edition, unless otherwise noted)

Retrospection and Introspection

Unity of Good

Rudimental Divine Science

Pulpit and Press

Miscellaneous Writings

Message to The Mother Church for 1902

The First Church of Christ, Scientist, and Miscellany

Manual of The Mother Church

Footnotes preceded by the letters A, F, H, L, or V refer to documents or letters in the Church History Department of The First Church of Christ, Scientist. Other documents in that department that have no preceding letter are identified by the letters CH.

Footnotes preceded by "Longyear" refer to documents or letters belonging to the Longyear Historical Society and Museum.

Preface

1. *Retrospection*, pp. 21-2.

Prologue

1. Monetary equivalents over several generations are problematic. The same problem arises with other figures used in the text. The $300 annual fee in 1870 represented about one-third of a workingman's annual wages.
2. Samuel Putnam Bancroft, *Mrs. Eddy As I Knew Her in 1870,* Brookline, Mass., 1923, p. 8.
3. Georgine Milmine, *The Life of Mary Baker G. Eddy,* London, 1909, p. 156.
4. Bancroft, *op.cit.* This and the surrounding quotes are from pages 6 to 52.
5. *Rudimental Divine Science,* p. 15.

Chapter 1

1. Adam H. Dickey, *Memoirs of Mary Baker Eddy*, Brookline, Mass., 1927, p. 132.
2. *Retrospection,* p. 2.
3. Horace Bushnell, "The Age of Homespun," in *Work and Play,* New York, 1884, p. 387.
4. *Retrospection,* p. 5.
5. *Ibid.* p. 5.
6. *New Hampshire Patriot and State Gazette,* Dec. 6, 1849.
7. Alexis de Tocqueville, *Democracy in America,* Oxford Univ. Press (1947 edition), p. 202.
8. *Retrospection,* p. 13.
9. *Ibid.,* p. 14.
10. *Ibid.,* p. 14. .
11. Hugh A. Studdert-Kennedy, *Mrs. Eddy: Her Life, Her Work, and Her Place in History,* The Farallon Press, San Francisco, 1947, p. 15.
12. Elisabeth Griffith, *In Her Own Right,* Oxford University Press, New York, 1984, p. 19.
13. *Ibid,* p. 21.
14. Longyear, May 1, 1836.
15. Longyear, Sept. 7, 1835.

16. Longyear, Jul. 18, 1837.
17. Longyear, Aug. 6, 1837.
18. Longyear, Oct. 15, 1837.
19. Longyear, Oct. 13, 1837.
20. Longyear, Mar. 27, 1837.
21. Longyear, Jan. 29, 1840.
22. Longyear, Jan. 16, 1840.
23. *Retrospection,* p. 10.
24. *The History of Cass and Bates Counties, Missouri,* National Historical Company, St. Joseph, Missouri, 1883, p. 477.
25. *Retrospection,* p. 10.
26. *Ibid.,* p. 10.
27. *Ibid.,* p. 6.
28. Longyear,
29. L2678, undated
30. Sibyl Wilbur, *The Life of Mary Baker Eddy,* The Christian Science Publishing Society, 1907, p. 33.

Entr'acte 1

1. Sydney Ahlstrom, *A Religious History of the American People,* Yale University Press, New Haven, 1972, p. 130.
2. *Ibid.,* p. 348.
3. Cohen, Charles L., *God's Caress,* Oxford University Press, New York, 1988, p. 5.
4. *Ibid.,* p. 4.
5. Ahlstrom, *op. cit.,* p. 350

Chapter 2

1. Longyear, Feb 6, 1844.
2. Longyear, May. 6, 1844.
3. CH,Reminiscences of Elizabeth Earl Jones, p. 48.
4. Ibid., p. 50.
5. Ibid., pp. 40-45.
6. Ibid., p. 28.
7. *New Hampshire Patriot,* Feb. 7, 1850.
8. Longyear, F00035, Nov. 22,1848.
9. L11150, Mar. 5, 1848.
10. CH, letter from Townsend Abell.
11. Longyear, F00031, Nov. 22,1849
12. *Retrospection,* p. 20.
13. L08903, Mar. 1853.
14. L08900, Apr. 29, 1853.
15. L08899, May 2, 1853.
16. CH, Patterson to Mary Baker Glover.
17. *Retrospection,* p. 20.
18. Longyear, Apr. 27, 1856.
19. CH, Elizabeth Patterson to George Baker.
20. *Science and Health,,* p. 156.
21. S.C.F. Hahnemann, *Organon,* published in 1810.
22. *Encyclopedia Britannica,* 1910 edition, vol. 13, p. 646.
23. CH, letter from Patterson in prison.
24. *Science and Health,* p. 152.
25. *The Quimby Manuscripts,* edited by Horatio W. Dresser, Thomas Y. Crowell Company, New York, 1921, p. 146.
26. V03342, Aug., 1862.

Chapter 3

1. Wilbur, *op. cit.,* pp. 80-82
2. *Portland Courier,* Nov. 1862.
3. *Portland Courier,* Nov. 7, 1862.
4. CH, Unidentified newspaper clipping.
5. *Science and Health,* pp. 184-85.
6. *Quimby Manuscripts,* p. 154, April 24, 1864
7. *Ibid.,* p. 153, Mar. 31, 1864.
8. *Ibid.,* p. 152, Apr. 5, 1864.
9. *Ibid.,* pp. 154-56, Apr. 24, 1864.
10. *Ibid.,* p. 156, May 24, 1864.
11. *Ibid,* p. 169.
12. A10242, Aug. 3, 1907.

Chapter 4

Footnotes

1. *Retrospection,* p. 24.
2. CH, letter of Julius Dresser, Mar. 2, 1866.
3. *Lynn Reporter,* Feb. 14, 1866.
4. CH, Court records of Essex County, Massachusetts.
5. Julius Silberger, Jr., *Mary Baker Eddy: An Interpretive Biography of the Founder of Christian Science,* Little, Brown and Company, Boston, 1980, p. 99.
6. *Retrospection,* p. 24.
7. *Science and Health,* p. 119.
8. L11152, Feb. 28, 1867.
9. L11153, Apr. 28, 1867.
10. CH. This account is included in the third edition of *Science and Health.*
11. F00041, Aug. 13, 1867.
12. *Science and Health,* p. 109.
13. Kenneth Hufford, *Stoughton Years,* Longyear Foundation, Brookline, Mass., 1963, p. 20.
14. *Ibid.* pp. 29-30.
15. CH, Letter of Florence Scott Lothrop, Apr. 24, 1909.
16. L08306, Oct. 20, 1868.
17. L08866, June 7, 1869.
18. L07798, June 10, 1869.
19. L07799, July 28, 1869.
20. The only formal instruction in Christian Science, other than what children receive in the Christian Science Sunday School, is a two-week course given by an authorized teacher of Christian Science. These courses had their origin in the two classes Mrs. Eddy taught in 1870.
21. As mentioned in Footnote 1 to the Prologue, monetary equivalents over several generations have some ambiguity about them. In 1870, a decent working wage was in the area of $1,000 annually. Or, any monetary value from that time could be multiplied today by at least one factor (ten times).
22. *Retrospection,* p. 50.
23. Longyear, Spofford letter of June 27, 1921.
24. *Lynn Semi-Weekly Reporter,* Aug. 13, 1870.
25. All quotations here are from *The Science of Man.*

Chapter 5

1. *The Christian Science Journal,* Vol. 5, June 1887, p. 115.
2. Wilbur, *op. cit.,* p. 178.
3. F00362, undated.
4. V03416, Mar. 12, 1871.
5. L09012, Aug. 16, 1871.
6. L03923, Dec. 20, 1871.
7. *Lynn Transcript,* Feb. 3, 1872.
8. *Ibid.* Jan. 27, 1872.
9. *Ibid.,* Feb. 3, 1872.
10. *Ibid.,* Feb. 24, 1872.
11. This contretemps, carried on with Wright in the local newspaper, is illustrative of one of the roles that a public press played before the era of the telephone. While some of this disagreement might have appeared in a later day in a newspaper, it is essentially a private dispute that would have been handled differently had there been other means of communication. Mrs. Eddy, on occasion, used the vehicle of the press to warn her own students about defectors from what she considered the correct representation of Christian Science.
12. To place the other major name in the field of the mental sciences, Sigmund Freud did not publish his first paper until 1893. His first major work, *The Interpretation of Dreams,* appeared in 1900.
13. L03929, July 11, 1871.
14. V03039, 1872.
15. L05663, Feb. 6, 1872.
16. L08302, Apr. 18, 1872.

17. L05664, May 27, 1872.
18. Bancroft, *op. cit.,* pp. 16-17; V03043, Nov. 28, 1872.
19. L07802, Dec. 13, 1872.
20. A10402, 1902.
21. Bancroft, *op. cit.,* p. 127.
22. *Ibid.* p. 25; V03053, Dec. 17, 1874.
23. V03041, Jan. 1875.
24. V03057, Jan. 27, 1875.
25. CH; Jan. 17, 1876.
26. L13465, Mar. 4, 1876.
27. L07649, Feb. 24, 1876.
28. L07652, May 1, 1876.
29. L09897, Jul. 14, 1876.
30. L07809, Oct. 1, 1876.
31. L2044, Nov. 27, 1876.
32. L14315, Dec. 8, 1876.
33. L07811, Dec. 30, 1876.
34. Bancroft, *op. cit.*, p. 54.
35. L007812, Jan. 3, 1877.
36. L007814, undated.
37. L02048, Oct. 19, 1877.
38. L07816, undated.
39. CH, May 30, 1877.
40. L13376, Oct. 8, 1878.
41. L02051, Mar. 19, 1879.
42. Related to the author by Robert Peel in 1991.
43. Reminiscences of Irving Tomlinson, Apr. 1, 1902.
44. *Science and Health,*, 1st edition, pp. 166-67.
45. L02463, Jan. 24, 1879.
46. L12621, Oct. 24, 1879.
47. L12622, May 26, 1880.
48. L08657, Jul. 29, 1880.
49. L02473, Aug, 1879.
50. L07686, Oct. 29, 1880.
51. CH, minutes of Christian Scientist Association, Oct. 26, 1881.
52. CH, Ibid., Nov. 16, 1881.

Chapter 6

1. L02054, 1881.
2. L13364, Feb. 17, 1882.
3. L02499, Feb. 28, 1882.
4. L07689, Jan. 20, 1882.
5. L04088, Mar. 15, 1882.
6. L12626, Apr. 10, 1882.
7. V03042, Spring 1882.
8. L13467, June 3, 1882.
9. F00390, June 13, 1882.
10. L02059, June 22, 1882.
11. L04089, July 16, 1882.
12. L07691, July 19, 1882.
13. L10643, July 28, 1882.
14. Van Wyck Brooks, *New England Indian Summer,* E. P. Dutton & Co, New York, 1940, p. 330.
15. *Ibid.,* p 140.
16. Brett Howard, *Boston: A Social History,* Hawthorne Press, 1963, p. 66.
17. *Ibid,* p. 68.
18. Lilian Whiting, *Boston Days,* Little Brown & Co., Boston, 1902, p. 331.
19. L04885, Oct. 25, 1882.
20. L07822, Oct. 11, 1883.
21. L02062, Aug. 11, 1883.
22. This information regarding Julius Dresser was related to the author by Dresser's granddaughter, Dorothea Reeves, in an interview at her house in Marshfield, Massachusetts, in 1988.
23. *Boston Post,* Feb. 8, 1883.
24. *Ibid.,* Feb. 19, 1883.
25. *Ibid.,* Feb. 24, 1883.
26. *Ibid.,* Mar. 9, 1883.
27. V00805, Feb. 12, 1884.
28. V00826, Aug. 29, 1884.
29. *The Christian Science Journal,* Vol. 1, No. 1, Apr. 1883, p. 3.
30. *Ibid.,* p.3.
31. *Ibid,* Vol. 1, No. 6, Feb. 1884, p. 6.
32. V00820, undated.
33. L03612, Dec. 5, 1884.
34. V00859, Dec. 16, 1884.
35. V00827, Sept. 1, 1884.
36. L09936, May 5, 1888.
37. L12898, July 28, 1886.

38. CH, Chevaillier reminiscences.
39. L02519, Dec. 11, 1883.
40. L02520, Dec. 12, 1883.
41. *Miscellaneous Writings,* pp. 97-98.
42. Acts 5:38,39.
43. L04105, Jul. 5, 1886.
44. L02159, Jul. 30, 1885.
45. L02164, undated.
46. L02159, July 30, 1885.
47. L04552, Mar. 22, 1886.
48. V0884, May 25, 1885.
49. L10069, Sept. 24, 1885.
50. V00916, Dec. 30, 1885.
51. V00913, Dec. 8, 1885.
52. Wilbur, *op. cit.,* p. 297.
53. CH, Jul. 1, 1886.
54. CH, Nov. 26, 1886.
55. *Unity of Good,* p 6.
56. The first book, published in 1897, was entitled *Miscellaneous Writings;* a posthumously published volume, *The First Church of Christ, Scientist, and Miscellany,* was published in 1913.
57. *Chicago Times,* June 15, 1888.
58. L02085, Oct. 31, 1887.
59. L02089, Mar. 1, 1888.

Chapter 7

1. L12782, Mar. 8, 1889.
2. L11039, Mar. 22, 1889.
3. V03289, May 3, 1889.
4. V03103, May 12, 1889.
5. V03060, May 23, 1889.
6. L01778, May 26, 1889.
7. N00027, May 29, 1889.
8. L09472, Oct. 1889.
9. *Retrospection,* p. 49.
10. L07700, Nov. 23, 1889.
11. *The Christian Science Journal,* Vol. 7, Feb. 1890, p. 566.
12. L13959, Nov. 2, 1889 (to Bates); L03471, Dec. 21, 1889 (to Eastaman).
13. L04675, Mar. 26, 1889.
14. L04339, Jan. 1890.
15. L11026, Mar. 2, 1890.
16. L08931, Apr. 6, 1890.
17. L08498, Apr. 23, 1890.
18. L13562, May 5, 1890.
19. L08024, Mar. 25, 1890.
20. L02585, Feb. 10, 1895 (to Knapp); L10555, Jan. 9, 1893 (to Linscott).
21. L01780, Oct. 31, 1890
22. L04134, Apr. 10, 1890.
23. L07623, May 13, 1890.
24. L02217, May 16, 1890.
25. L02218, May 28, 1890.
26. L14090, Jun. 28, 1890.
27. L04504, Oct. 2, 1890.
28. L04505, Nov. 21, 1890.
29. L04137, Nov. 12, 1890.
30. L02256, Sept. 22, 1890.
31. L02652, Mar. 24, 1896.
32. CH, undated.
33. L03475, Feb. 15, 1891.
34. L08558, Jun. 12, 1891.
35. L04144, Jul. 20, 1891.
36. L08571, Jul. 1, 1891.
37. L04345, Jul. 1891.
38. L03994, Nov. 27, 1891.
39. L05583, Dec. 29, 1891.
40. L01062, Apr. 10, 1892.
41. L04152, Sept. 2, 1892.
42. L11056, Oct. 29, 1892.
43. CH, James Gilman, diary, p. 71.
44. Ibid., p. 93.
45. Ibid., p. 73.
46. Ibid., Aug. 3, 1893.
47. Ibid. p. 91.
48. Ibid., p. 159.
49. L08052, Mar. 29, 1893.
50. V03411, Sept. 21, 1893.
51. Gilman, op. cit., p. 162.
52. L09475, Sept. 27, 1893.
53. L04690, Jul. 2, 1893.
54. L07434, Oct. 1893.
55. L00053, Sept. 29, 1893.
56. L00038, Jan. 23, 1893.
57. F00100, Apr. 9, 1894.
58. L01897, May 3, 1894.
59. L01903, May 16, 1894.

60. L07734, May 22, 1894.
61. L03440, May 28, 1894.
62. L00066, July 1894.
63. V03019, Aug. 25, 1894.
64. L10741, 1893.
65. L07876, Mar. 10, 1893.
66. L04000, Mar. 31, 1893.
67. L08502, Apr. 20, 1893.
68. L05037, Dec. 18, 1894.
69. L02748, Dec. 19, 1894.
70. L02702, Jan. 9, 1895.
71. William Dana Orcutt, *Mary Baker Eddy and Her Books,* The Christian Science Publishing Society, 1950; p. 47.
72. L05739, Jul. 19, 1893.
73. L02695A, Nov. 2, 1893.
74. L08708, Nov. 7, 1894.
75. L01926, Nov. 26, 1894.
76. V01327, Dec. 7, 1894.
77. L15114, undated.
78. L02751, Jan. 10, 1895.
79. L02664, Apr. 27, 1895.
80. F00107, May 6, 1895.
81. CH, Jun. 27, 1897.
82. L11056, Oct. 29, 1892.
83. *Miscellaneous Writings,* p. 148.
84. L07903, Mar. 28, 1893.
85. L05874, Jun. 19, 1893.
86. L05976, Apr. 15, 1895.
87. L03451, Apr. 18, 1895.
88. L02368, Dec. 9,1895.
89. L05130, Jan. 17, 1896.
90. L02776, Feb. 4, 1896.
91. L08321, Dec. 1, 1897.
92. F00140, Jan. 31, 1898.
93. L08542, Nov. 19, 1897.
94. L00206, Dec. 19, 1898.
95. L05996, Jan. 8, 1897.
96. *Miscellaneous Writings,* pp. xi-xii.
97. Charles Totten, *Our Race: Its Origin and Destiny,* p. 38.
98. F00115, Jan. 29, 1896.
99. F00116, Feb. 8, 1896.
100. L05759, Oct. 1897.
101. V03361, May 11, 1898.
102. V01300, Apr. 2, 1894.
103. L04373, Jul. 7, 1897.
104. V01549, Oct. 26, 1897.
105. H00042, 1898.
106. H00038, Apr. 7, 1898.
107. L03644, Oct. 1, 1898.
108. L03445, Aug. 15, 1894.
109. L05226, Jun. 22, 1898.
110. L08849, Sept. 19, 1895.
111. L02789, Jul. 15, 1896.
112. *Miscellany,* p. 248.
113. L13163, Nov. 17, 1898.
114. *We Knew Mary Baker Eddy,* p. 108 (1979 edition)
115. L08850, Nov. 25, 1898.
116. L02127, Apr. 27, 1898.
117. L08031, Feb. 9, 1897.
118. L12999, Apr. 9, 1897.

Entr'acte 3

1. *Miscellaneous Writings,* p. 58.
2. *Science and Health,* p. 114.
3. *Ibid.,* p. 573.
4. *Message to The Mother Church for 1902,* p. 10.
5. Larry Dossey, *Healing Words,* HarperSanFrancisco, 1992, p. 157.
6. *Christian Science Sentinel,* Vol. IX, No. 48, July 27, 1907, p. 906.
7. I Peter 5:8.
8. *Science and Health,* pp. 570-71.
9. *Manual,* p. 40.
10. *Science and Health,* p. 442.
11. *Christian Science Sentinel,* Vol. X, No. 20, Jan. 18, 1908, p. 383.

Chapter 8

1. *Science and Health,* p. 48.
2. CH, Reminiscences of Antoinette Mosher.
3. L02652, Mar. 24, 1896.
4. *Miscellany,* pp. 125-26.
5. CH, Jan. 6, 1901.
6. L09319, Apr. 17, 1901.
7. L05364, May 3, 1901.

Footnotes

8. L07567, May 30, 1901.
9. *We Knew Mary Baker Eddy,* p. 185 (1979 edition).
10. L05362, Mar. 31, 1901.
11. L03462, Nov. 24, 1899.
12. L00322, Dec. 8, 1902.
13. A10926, undated.
14. A10407, undated.
15. *New York Journal,* May 31, 1901.
16. L05319, Feb. 12, 1900.
17. L05322, Apr. 3, 1900.
18. L05324, Aug. 22, 1900.
19. L05325, Jan. 25, 1901.
20. L07503, Jan. 31, 1901.
21. CH, Reminiscences of Irving Tomlinson, p. 690.
22. L10617, Nov. 23, 1901.
23. L07588, Dec. 17, 1901.
24. CH, Jan. 19, 1900.
25. L07488, Jan. 12, 1900.
26. L07590, Jun. 3, 1902.
27. L02937, Dec. 6, 1902.
28. L07594, Jul. 3, 1902.
29. L00323, Feb. 5, 1903.
30. CH, Apr. 13, 1904.
31. Ibid., Jul. 7, 1903.
32. L02613, Apr. 27, 1904.
33. *Christian Science Sentinel,* Vol. 7, No. 44, Jul. 1, 1905, p. 709.
34. L09705, Jan. 21, 1902.
35. L01648, Dec. 30, 1902.
36. CH, Reminiscences of William McCrackan.
37. L11093, Jan. 7, 1903.
38. Frances Thurber Seal, *Christian Science in Germany,* Philadelphia, 1931.
39. L09568, undated.
40. CH, Mar. 21, 1903.
41. L14587, Dec. 31, 1902.
42. *Boston Post,* Aug. 13, 1900.
43. L02412, Apr. 23, 1900.
44. L07595, Jul. 15, 1902.
45. *Science and Health,* p. 464. The added sentences read: "If from an injury or from any cause, a Christian Scientist were seized with pain so violent that he could not treat himself mentally, — and the Scientists had failed to relieve him, — the sufferer could call a surgeon, who would give him a hypodermic injection, then, when the belief of pain was lulled, he could handle his own case mentally."
46. *Ibid,* p. 572
47. L04755, Oct. 5, 1905.
48. L12328, Feb 5, 1906.
49. L05838, Mar. 9, 1903.
50. *Miscellany,* p. 170.
51. *We Knew Mary Baker Eddy,* p. 115 (1979 edition).
52. L01257, Sept. 3, 1901.
53. L00285, Sept. 5, 1901.
54. L00315, Sept. 3, 1902.
55. The Christian Science movement at this time must have appeared much larger than these membership figures suggest. One reason for this is that many Christian Scientists became members of a branch church without joining The Mother Church at the same time. Another is that, except for the fact that church membership denoted a commitment to the religion, there was no external compulsion to become a church member.
56. *Miscellany,* p. 5.
57. *Ibid.* p. 6.
58. *Ibid.,* p. 71.
59. *Ibid.,* p.79.
60. *Ibid.,* p. 80.
61. *Ibid.,* p. 85.
62. *Ibid.,* pp. 89-90.
63. *Science and Health,* p. 96.
64. CH, Oct. 27, 1906
65. Michael Meehan, *Mrs. Eddy and the Late Suit in Equity,* Concord, N.H., 1908, p. 285.
66. CH, Reminiscences of Irving Tomlinson, pp. 471-474.
67. L02139, Dec. 25, 1906.
68. *New York World,* Mar. 2, 1907

(letter dated Nov. 22, 1906).
69. L11851, Nov. 30, 1906.
70. Meehan, *op. cit.*, p. 33.
71. L11237, Mar. 24, 1907.
72. *We Knew Mary Baker Eddy*, p. 181 (1979 edition).
73. L00533, Apr. 2, 1907.
74. L03156, May 25, 1907.
75. F00571, Jun. 12, 1907.
76. *Boston Globe*, Jun. 16, 1907.
77. Chicago *Record-Herald*, Jul. 19, 1907.
78. *Cosmopolitan Magazine*, Aug. 1907.
79. *New York Times*, Aug. 25, 1907.
80. Meehan, *op. cit.*, p. 238.
81. *Ibid.*, pp. 282-83.
82. *Ibid.*, p. 315.

Chapter 9

1. L12397, Feb. 9, 1908.
2. L06499, Jan. 27, 1908.
3. L03183, Jul. 2, 1908.
4. L07169, Nov. 1908.
5. CH, Reminiscences of John Salchow, pp.94-95.
6. L03172, Apr. 13, 1908.
7. L09779, May 7, 1908.
8. L09208, Jun. 4, 1908.
9. L15512, Dec. 31, 1908.
10. *Science and Health*, p. 150.
11. L07593, Jun. 22, 1902.
12. *Miscellany*, p. 278.
13. *Science and Health*, p. 552.
14. L07146, May 3, 1908.
15. L00596, Jul. 28, 1908; L07268, Aug. 8, 1908.
16. CH, Reminiscences of William Rathvon, p. 30 of Addenda.
17. L03213, Jan. 22, 1909.
18. L03224, Apr. 5, 1909.
19. *Christian Science Sentinel*, Vol. XI, Dec. 26, 1908, p. 324.
20. CH, Aug. 2, 1906.
21. L02568, Aug. 9, 1906.
22. H00130, Jul. 11, 1909.
23. CH, Virgil Strickler diary.
24. CH, Reminiscences of William Rathvon.
25. L01759, Mar. 25, 1908.
26. L08961, May 17, 1908.
27. L06475, Aug. 18,1908.
28. L08968, Aug. 28, 1908.
29. L05867, Mar. 17, 1909.
30. CH, Reminiscences of Irving Tomlinson, pp. 30-31.
31. *Science and Health*, p. 426.
32. L04725, Sep. 8, 1909.
33. *Science and Health*, p. 96.
34. *Christian Science Sentinel*, Vol. XI, No. 49, Aug. 7, 1909, pp. 966-967.
35. CH, William Rathvon diary, Oct. 13, 1909.
36. *Christian Science Sentinel*, Vol. XI, No. 15, Dec. 12, 1908, pp. 283-84.
37. *Christian Science Sentinel*, Vol. XX, No. 1, Sep. 1, 1917, p. 10.
38. CH, Tomlinson diary.
39. F00405, Jul. 9, 1910.
40. L05406, Sep. 15, 1910.
41. V03121.
42. CH, Reminiscences of Adelaide Still.
43. L13841.
44. CH, William Rathvon diary.
45. Ibid., August 1934.
46. *Editorial Comments on the Life and Work of Mary Baker Eddy*, The Christian Science Publishing Society, Boston, 1911, p. 99 (1993 edition).
47. *The Christian Science Monitor*, Dec. 5, 1910.

Epilogue

1. *Science and Health*, p. 492.
2. *Ibid.*, p. 131.
3. *Ibid.*, p. 199.
4. *Ibid.*, p. 330.
5. *Pulpit and Press*, p. 22.